STRENGTH FOR THE STRUGGLE:

INSIGHTS FROM THE CIVIL RIGHTS MOVEMENT AND URBAN MINISTRY

STRENGTH FOR THE STRUGGLE:

INSIGHTS FROM THE CIVIL RIGHTS MOVEMENT AND URBAN MINISTRY

Joseph W. Ellwanger

MavenMark Books
Milwaukee, Wisconsin

Published by
MavenMark Books
an imprint of HenschelHAUS Publishing, Inc.
www.henschelhausbooks.com

All HenschelHAUS titles, imprints, and distributed lines are available at special quantity discounts for educational, institutional, fund-raising, or sales promotion.

Book Design and Typography by Express Creative
www.express-creative.com

Publisher's Cataloging-In-Publication Data
(Prepared by The Donohue Group, Inc.)

Ellwanger, Joseph W.
Strength for the struggle : insights from the civil rights movement and urban ministry / Joseph W. Ellwanger.

pages : illustrations ; cm

Includes index.
Issued also as an ebook.
ISBN: 978-1-59598-296-4
E-ISBN: 978-1-59598-297-1

1. Civil rights--Religious aspects--Christianity. 2. Race relations--Religious aspects--Christianity. 3. Civil rights movements--United States. 4. City churches--United States. 5. Ellwanger, Joseph W. 6. Church work--United States. I. Title.

BR526 .E44 2014
261.7/0973

Printed in the United States of America.

Cover photo: Rev. Joseph W. Ellwanger faces Dallas County deputy sheriffs at the county courthouse in Selma, Alabama, on March 6, l965. He was at the head of a column of 72 "Concerned White Citizens of Alabama," who had gathered from over a dozen cities and towns in Alabama. They were stating publicly that there were white Southerners who stood in solidarity with the Southern Christian Leadership Conference demonstrations that had been waged almost daily since January 1, 1965, calling for a strong federal voting rights act.

DEDICATION

The account of my experience and the stories of the people with whom I have walked over the years, as together we discovered strength for the struggle, is dedicated to Joyce, my wife and companion on my journey for almost 50 years, and to our three children: Jonathan, Joel, and Judy. All of them have been at the heart of the story of this journey.

From the moment of our meeting in Chicago in 1961, where I was attending a Lutheran Human Relations Association Board meeting, while in the midst of my third year as pastor at St. Paul, Birmingham, and Joyce was serving as a parish worker at the racially-integrated First Immanuel Lutheran Church in Chicago, our hearts, our sense of vocation, our worldview, our openness to transformation via the Church, were amazingly and mysteriously tuned to the same melody and to the same beat. That closeness of heart and soul did not evaporate over the years; it grew closer and nurtured our relationship and our life together.

That closeness was sealed and strengthened again and again. It was sealed when she moved into the parsonage in the heart of the black community of southwest Birmingham in 1964. It was sealed when she insisted on participating in the march in Selma the day before Bloody Sunday in March, 1965, four months pregnant with our first child. It was sealed when she experienced in Milwaukee on three occasions physical confrontation and theft and on another three occasions break-ins and theft from our home, without wavering in her commitment to urban ministry. It was sealed when she crossed the line at Fort Benning, in Columbus, Georgia, and spent six months in federal prison in Danbury, Connecticut, as a witness to our government and to our nation that torture tactics taught there at the School of the Americas by U.S. army officers to Latin American soldiers to use against their own people, was contrary to our nation's commitment to human rights and to the UN-sanctioned Geneva Accords.

It has been sealed again and again and again in her witness to the Gospel and to the love of Christ on the grassroots level in Sunday school/Bible class teaching, her hospital and home visits, and her prayer vigils at the sites of homicides in Milwaukee. The heart of her witness at my side over the years has been consistent, resilient, resolute. Her heartbeat is part of every chapter of this book.

I dedicate this volume to our three children: Jonathan, Joel, and Judy. Their growth, their flowering, their fruit-bearing, then and now, have been part of the joy of the transforming journey recorded in this book. They have been a source of "strength for the struggle." I am deeply grateful that each of them has learned what it means to live life "for the other" and what it means to embrace the diversity of the human family.

Table of Contents

FOREWORD

“Artless1” A friend said that the word made my endorsement sound like faint praise. No, I meant it to be strong praise.

Look it up. Artless is “natural.” “Without artifice.” “Unpretentious.” “Free from guile.”

Joseph Ellwanger, in the vision of those who have observed and cheered him through the years, has not cluttered his prose or his life with artifice. You will look in vain for efforts to dandify his story or clot it with jargon. The theme is too urgent to be weighted down or slowed down. Pastor Ellwanger is in a hurry to get his point across. Seldom will one find a more straightforward and natural telling of the story of a contemporary pastor, his parishioners, and the people they serve.

Both in his accounts of deep-South Birmingham in the years of most intense racial struggles and in his account of Milwaukee’s “up-North” times, he simply recounts “how we did it,” the “we” being the contemporary people of God in two specific places, as they fed and were fed, suffered and triumphed, and fended off opposition in church, state, marketplace, and neighborhood.

The book can be read as a call to action, a booster of morale, a “how to” guide in perplexing times. For all that, I prefer to think of it as a simple story faithful to the main Gospel approach to making a point, setting examples, and leading people.

It’s not all sweetness. I found it hard not to sulk or rage as I read of the barriers people put up against the Gospel’s working. But as this pastor shows: still, in spite of it all, it works.

If Ellwanger were given to bragging, he’d have a lot about which to brag. But doing so would slow him down, and we would lose the plot, the artless story which we will long remember.

—Martin E. Marty,
Emeritus Professor, the University of Chicago, and a Lutheran pastor

PREFACE

The year was 1961. The spirit of the time among African Americans in the U.S. South was one of high expectations. For whites, it was a time of fear and hate-filled attacks on blacks and especially on blacks and whites who were pressing for change in the South's segregated way of living.

I was a 28-year-old white pastor at a coming-alive African American congregation in southwest Birmingham, Alabama: St Paul Lutheran.

I received an invitation directed to the youth of St. Paul from an intern pastor, James Fackler, serving a white congregation, University Lutheran Church, Tuscaloosa, Alabama, 60 miles southwest of Birmingham. Tuscaloosa was the site of the University of Alabama and headquarters of an active clavern of the Ku Klux Klan.

The invitation was an open welcome to any high school youth at St. Paul to join the youth of University Lutheran for a Sunday night fellowship. There would be informal worship, sharing of stories, and, of course, some refreshments. It sounds like an ordinary church youth gathering with an ordinary agenda.

However, in 1961, in Alabama, this was no ordinary event. This Sunday evening fellowship would bring black and white youth together for an evening of socializing and swapping of personal stories. This never happened in Alabama in 1961. Black and white youth could pass each other on the street and possibly shop at the same department store. But never would they have the normal experience of youth attending the same school, hanging out at the local fast food place or restaurant, attending high school football or basketball games together, or sharing together in a Bible study or worship. The proposed bi-racial youth event called for some counter-cultural courage and some risk-taking on the part of the intern pastor and youth at the white Tuscaloosa congregation, as well as for any youth at our Birmingham parish who would accept the invitation.

When I announced the invitation to the St. Paul youth, there were two fifteen-year-old girls, Carolyn Freeman and Betty Wells, who responded affirmatively and eagerly. I was somewhat surprised that Betty Wells was able to get permission from her overly-protective parents to participate in this unusual, out-of-the-box youth event. It undoubtedly helped that this was a church event with two pastors slated to be present.

The sharing of the youth that Sunday night was Spirit-driven. Youth from both sides of the racial divide were open and frank with each other about what life was like on their side of the divide.

As we were driving back to Birmingham after the event, it became clear that Betty and Carolyn had been energized by the rare experience of black and white youth talking, singing, praying, eating together, as though the cultural wall of segregation did not exist. They discovered how similar their lives were on so many levels and how different they were on other levels. Signifying their hopes for the future, both Carolyn and Betty expressed the desire to do something like this again—soon.

The bubble of the beautiful Sunday evening fellowship burst suddenly the following Wednesday morning, when I picked up the Birmingham paper from my front porch. There on the front page in bold headlines and in great detail, was the story of the KKK's capture and beating of our Sunday night host pastor, James Fackler, and his harrowing experience of being forced to walk back to Tuscaloosa on the railroad tracks in the wee hours of the morning.

The newspaper article went on to describe a cross that had been burned on the lawn of the church and the message that had been sent to the pastor of the congregation, warning him that there would be grave consequences for the congregation if there was ever another racially-mixed youth meeting there again.

I was still in shock and disbelief and poring over the newspaper coverage, when the phone rang. A rough voice on the other end asked: "Is this the reverend?"

Not catching the identity of the caller, I responded simply, "Yes, it is."

The voice on the other end came back quickly, "Well, you and the two girls are next." Click.

I was stunned. Obviously it was not an idle threat. I knew that I needed to inform Carolyn and Betty and their parents of this ominous cloud over our heads.

I will never forget my conversation with Carolyn. After I told her of the threat, I asked her whether she was afraid. With only a brief moment for reflection, Carolyn responded, "No. I am not so much afraid as I am ashamed."

A bit mystified by her answer, I asked Carolyn what she meant—that she was ashamed. Her unforgettable response was immediate and profound: "I'm ashamed that others have suffered so much for the freedom of our people, and all people, and I have suffered so little."

In one short sentence Carolyn had said so much—about herself, about her faith, about her hopes, and about the spirit of the times. The importance of her witness to the white youth in Tuscaloosa and the prophetic experience of white and black Christian youth coming together as sisters and brothers, trumped her fears of the KKK and what could happen to her physically. Her vision of freedom and a desegregated society, and her yearning for such a world, was rooted in something much deeper than a Sunday evening lark. And she recognized that her small contribution to the struggle for freedom was minuscule compared with the contributions of those who had gone before her and those who surrounded her. Permeating her words and her passionate tone of voice was the belief that freedom was something possible, something she had a responsibility to work for and even to sacrifice for.

An amazing witness of a 15-year-old girl—never to be forgotten.

People sometimes ask me where I got the strength for 43 years of urban ministry and justice work and the energy for continuing that journey more than ten years into my retirement from parish ministry. I seldom have the time to tell this story, but it is one of many stories that was part of my journey in the past and that still feeds my spirit and stokes my passion for trying to live out the Gospel in a radical way and to continue in the struggle for God's justice and peace.

This story of Carolyn's vision and courage, and others like it, have humbled me and kept me for a long time from writing a book such as this. At the same time, they have finally brought me full circle, to feel compelled, now, to write down their story that is so intertwined with mine.

I had the special experience of growing up in a storefront church four blocks from the Mississippi River in St. Louis and then in the segregated Black Belt city of Selma, Alabama. My pastoral experience was forged on the anvil of urban ministry in two enriching congregations: St. Paul Lutheran, an African American congregation in southwest Birmingham, Alabama (1958-67), and Cross Lutheran, a racially diverse, predominately African American congregation on the near north side of Milwaukee, Wisconsin (1967-2001). In my retirement from parish ministry, I have been active at Hephatha Lutheran Church, just ten blocks north of Cross Church, with a similar membership and ministry, and I worked as an organizer from 2002 to 2012, with a congregation-based organizing network in Wisconsin, to bring about a greater degree of justice in Milwaukee and throughout the state.

Over my 50-plus years of life and ministry in the Church and among the people of God, I could use many words to describe the journey. But I think that "struggle" is a word that is especially descriptive of that journey. There have been the normal struggles of life, the struggles with illness, with relationships, with personalities, with financial sufficiency. There have been theological struggles: what does God's Word really have to say about non-violent resistance, and public demonstrations calling for justice, and the rights of gay and lesbian persons in the church and in society, and the way to witness to the Gospel across denominational and faith lines? There have been the struggles to discern God's will in such matters as how to prioritize aspects of life and ministry, how to rebuild a sanctuary after a devastating fire, how to determine which issues in church and society to address and which to let go. All of these struggles have been caught up in the one major struggle, the struggle against the forces of evil and the struggle to faithfully and authentically live out the Gospel of Jesus Christ and to be a part of the coming of God's kingdom of justice and peace and freedom and reconciliation for all people.

For the first 30 years of ministry, I never thought of writing a book about this journey, a journey that was full of struggle on the one hand, and was fulfilling on the other. The experience was too intriguing, too urgent, too demanding, to think of writing about it.

Furthermore, I have always sensed, with Carolyn Freeman, that others have done so much and suffered so much to proclaim and to live the Gospel, to bring about a greater degree of justice, and to build the beloved community. Who am I to write a book about my attempts at trying to carry out the mission of the church and my experience of the struggle "to do justice, to love mercy, and to walk humbly with God"?

True enough, the journey was at some of the most important, critical years in the history of the Church and of our nation. But my story was such a tiny part of the big story, and there were others whose leadership was so great and whose witness was so awesome.

Now in the past 15 years, I have been nudged by pastors, coaxed by lay people, and agitated by my colleagues who have been engaged with me in congregation-based organizing, to write a book. In fact, after presenting a call-to-action, in which I included a couple of stories from the 1960s, to a hundred persons gathered for training in justice organizing, I actually had people lining up for my autograph! As if these stories, and my testimony, had special meaning for them, as they left the training for the realities of the struggle for justice!

I have come to a much clearer awareness that the learnings from the 1960s and from the Carolyn Freemans of that era, as well as the learnings from the people of God in a black poverty pocket in Milwaukee, struggling to live out the Gospel in a relevant, authentic manner, are learnings for the people of God anywhere—city or suburb, small town or rural, black or white, Hispanic or Asian, gay or straight, young or old. The congregation in Birmingham may "only" have been 300 in number, and the congregation in Milwaukee may "only" have been 600 in number, but looking back, I see that their risk-taking, courageous witness to the Gospel that gave such strength to me for the struggle, has the potential to give others, strength for the struggle as well.

It is my prayer that the learnings and the stories that I share in this volume will nurture and energize the intellect and the soul at such a depth, that the reader might experience the exhilarating air that Carolyn and Betty experienced one Sunday night in Tuscaloosa, Alabama, in 1961. And I pray that bishops, pastors, lay leaders, peacemakers, justice workers, students of history, persons caught in the poverty pockets of our nation, ordinary people everywhere struggling to make this world a better place for all, will gain insights and seeds of courage for their own journeys.

Above all, I pray that the reader will experience in the stories from the Civil Rights Movement and from the Gospel communities in Birmingham and Milwaukee, real strength for the real struggle, a strength that will trump all the fear and cynicism and apathy that the forces of evil and darkness can muster.

Joseph Ellwanger
Milwaukee, Wisconsin

CHAPTER 1

ACCOMPANIMENT AS LIFESTYLE

As they talked and discussed their things with each other, Jesus himself came up and walked along with them,
–Luke 24:15

What appeared at first to be simply a servant event in El Salvador in 1987, turned out to be, for me and for my colleagues in urban ministry in Milwaukee, a powerful parable and image for doing ministry anywhere.

I pastored in Milwaukee from 1967 to 2001 at Cross Lutheran Church. The congregation had declared itself a "sanctuary congregation" in 1983, and had offered refuge to an undocumented Guatemalan refugee. "Jorge" (his assumed name) was in danger of being sent back to Guatemala, where his life was in danger due to his union activism. Because of our advocacy on behalf of Central American refugees, we received an invitation to send someone to "accompany" the first wave of Salvadoran refugees who had decided to return to El Salvador after seven years in a refugee camp in Honduras.

People of faith from the United States were asked to participate in this "accompaniment ministry" to help provide protection for the refugees, as they returned to their village of Guarjila. The Salvadoran government was still at war with the guerrillas in the hills and opposed the return of refugees and threatened to block their passage into the country.

The government wanted Guarjila, and the surrounding countryside, to remain depopulated by civilians, so the army could more easily attack the guerrillas.

At Cross Church, we were amazed the refugees were so courageous that they would risk being attacked by their own military in an effort to return home. They said they had two reasons for attempting to make this risky journey back to their homes. First, they wanted their children to grow up knowing their own village, their own garden, their own countryside. And second, they hoped to be a creative, neutral buffer between the army and the guerrillas that would somehow convince both sides to declare a truce and negotiate peace.

I was personally moved by the story of these brave refugees. In addition, I had met the Lutheran Bishop of El Salvador, Bishop Medardo Gomez, when he had to leave his country because of threats to his life and had spoken to an interfaith audience in Milwaukee. I was deeply moved by the brave stand of Bishop Gomez and the relatively small Lutheran Synod in El Salvador, on behalf of the peasants and the poor. The Salvadoran Lutheran Church had founded the Faith and Hope Refugee Camp outside of San Salvador, to offer hospitality and the basics of life to families and individuals who had felt the violence and the pressures of the guerrilla war in the countryside. The very existence of this refugee camp put Bishop Gomez and the Lutheran Church at odds with some of the Salvadoran Army leaders, who charged them with "harboring guerrillas."

The vibrant, courageous witness to the Gospel by Bishop Gomez and a few hundred Lutheran Christians in El Salvador, as well as the bold plan of the Salvadoran refugees in Honduras to return to their village in El Salvador, stirred up profound awe within me. I felt compelled to accept the invitation to join in "accompaniment ministry." It was an experience of a lifetime, which had many more results than anyone could have predicted.

Was this the right time for the refugees to return to El Salvador? Should the Lutheran Church offer logistical support to the refugees whose return was openly opposed by the Salvadoran government and army? Should U.S. Christians be involved in this controversial "accompaniment ministry?" If I had waited for clear intellectual answers to all these questions, I would never have gone to El Salvador.

Lessons from El Salvador

The first lesson I learned from this "accompaniment ministry" was that such ministry is never without risks. It is definitely controversial. But when brothers and sisters, out of their faith in God, are putting their lives on the line for an effort that gives promise of healing and of peacemaking, the tug of the Spirit says, "Go." So I went.

As soon as I arrived in El Salvador, I was hooked up with Reverend Margaret Suiter, an Anglo Lutheran pastor who was working with Bishop Gomez and the Salvadoran Lutheran Church in various capacities. At the time of our accompaniment journey, she was in charge of getting Lutheran World Relief supplies to the refugees returning to Guarjila. She was driving an old pickup truck loaded with three or four hundred-pound bags of rice and a similar quantity of bags of beans and of shelled corn, from which the women would daily bake tortillas after grinding the corn by hand. The truck also contained an assortment of lumber for repairing homes abandoned seven years before.

I hadn't been there long before I learned of Margaret Suiter's tug of the Spirit that had brought her to El Salvador for an extended accompaniment ministry with the Salvadorian Lutheran Synod and with the people of El Salvador caught in the crossfire of a long civil war. She had been diagnosed with terminal breast cancer three years before, and had been given, at the time, five years to live. This is how she had chosen to live out the years she would be given.

Margaret Suiter was driving the pickup. A twenty-something Salvadoran woman was in the cab with her, and a thirtyish Salvadoran man was riding with me on top of the precious, life-sustaining commodities loaded on the bed of the truck.

The one-hour trip over the concrete highway checkered with potholes, took us straight north from San Salvador through one military checkpoint and past many soldiers with M-16s, to the older city of Chaletenango, whose very modest buildings and homes were largely unpainted stucco with a few buildings displaying a variety of faded colors. There we picked up an older Catholic nun, who had lived and worked in Chaletenango for years. Margaret said we needed her to help us get past the military check point at the turnoff road to Guarjila.

In less than a half hour, we were at the checkpoint, where we turned onto a narrow, one-lane, rutted road, about five miles from Guarjila. Sure enough, there was a young, perhaps 16-year-old, soldier, with the famous M-16 and a walkie-talkie. He was by himself, but he was talking tough.

"You can't go any further," the young guard said. "My commander gave me strict orders not to let anyone pass except soldiers."

The sister in the cab recognized the guard as a young man whom she had taught in school, so she had a lot of credibility going for her. Still it took a great deal of courage for her to bluff an immediate response: "I talked to your commander before we left Chaletenango, and he gave me his permission to go to Guarjila."

This was a bold response. She was counting on his walkie-talkie not working so that he couldn't check with his commander. She told us later that she hadn't talked with his commander. This was sheer bluff.

We felt the tension back in the truck bed, as the guard turned away from the truck and acted as though he were checking on his walkie-talkie with his commanding officer. After a few tense moments, he turned around and waved us on.

If Margaret Suiter was looking for an exciting, breathtaking, meaningful way to spend her last months on earth, she couldn't have chosen anything to eclipse this accompaniment ministry.

We weren't certain whether the refugees would be in Guarjila or not. We were exceedingly relieved and grateful to find that they had just arrived ahead of us. Each family was searching for its old house. Some were delighted to find that their house was still there in relatively good shape except for an overgrowth of vines and seven years of accumulated leaves and debris. Other homes that had been poorly built had collapsed roofs and, in some instances, collapsed walls.

A few families managed to clear away collected debris so they could stay that first night in their own homes. The rest of the families, along with the half dozen U.S. accompaniment folks, slept on the concrete floor of the school, wherever we could find space to roll out our sleeping bags. It was a hard concrete floor. And the temperature got down into the 50s during the night. But the sense of celebrating a safe journey back home in the midst of a war zone was such an over-riding, energizing sensation that no one felt the hardness of the floor or the chill of the night air through the wide-open windows. It was as if everyone were singing; "We are safe! We are with family! We are in community! We are home!" After seven years of waiting in the rigors of a refugee camp, their daily hope was now fulfilled.

The next morning broke with the crowing of a rooster, and everyone was out and about at the break of dawn. I wasn't sure what accompaniment would mean on this first full day in Guarjila. So I walked down the one road that goes through the center of the village, and I saw what the day meant for the families experiencing the euphoria of being finally at home. Young women were walking to a nearby stream with five-gallon plastic buckets, and other young women were walking back from the stream, with the plastic buckets filled with water on their heads. Men and boys were gathering firewood. Women were busily engaged in the ancient process of mashing the corn by hand, stone pressed against stone, to produce the flour to bake the day's tortillas for their families.

Watching a mother take a roll of dough and slap it into a nearly-perfect circle of dough about 12 inches across and a quarter-inch thick within a minute, was an awesome experience of a skill handed down mother to daughter, generation to generation. Then to be invited to share with the family a little later, the warm, tasty tortilla with beans, was a breakfast not to be forgotten.

The leaders of the community were quick to prioritize tasks that needed to be done for the community. The first major task was to check out the fresh water supply that had been piped into the village from a well about a mile away, up until the time the villagers had been pressured by the Salvadoran army to take refuge in Honduras seven years earlier. A half dozen men from the village asked for three of us Anglos from the U.S. to accompany them as they followed the pipeline through some open fields, to examine it for any needed repairs. They wanted some U.S. presence for their protection just in case they met up with Salvadoran soldiers.

I volunteered for the accompaniment job. After all, that's why I was there. The Anglo accompaniment people were asked not to wear anything on our heads so that soldiers looking through field glasses could see we were not Salvadoran. Fortunately we had no encounters with the military, but two things were clear from this two-hour expedition. First, the ex-refugees were alert to possible dangers and took necessary precautions to sustain their bold move to reclaim their village and to call guerrillas and Salvadoran officials to the first steps of a peace process. And secondly, they knew the importance of a consistent supply of fresh, clean water for the future of their community.

After returning safely from the pipeline project, two of us accompaniment folks began to offer our services to families who were obviously busy cleaning up their deserted homes and overgrown yards. We came to a house where we met a woman with two small children. We greeted her with our limited Spanish, "*Buenas tardes!*" With some sign language, we offered to help with cleaning.

The woman responded to us in a very friendly way and immediately asked us to be seated on a low stone wall separating her kitchen and her backyard. Between her broken English and our skimpy understanding of Spanish, we got her message. She was so grateful for our accompanying them back home that she was inviting us to a meal she wanted to prepare for us.

She pointed to some dried fish that were hanging from her overhang roof, two small fish she had brought back from the refugee camp.

We tried to convince her to save the fish for herself and her children, but she insisted on frying the fish as we watched. Reluctantly we saw that we would not deter her, so we insisted that she and her children share in the meal with us. The profound gratitude and the sharing of the best that she had, her two dried fish, along with beans and rice, and a warm tortilla, was one of the rich, unforgettable gifts we received on this memorable accompaniment journey.

This appeared to be an insignificant event in Salvadoran history. The return of the people of Guarjila after seven years in a refugee camp did not make the newscasts in the United States or in El Salvador. However, the long-range results were significant. The bold move of the villagers pushed the government and the guerrillas to begin thinking about peace talks. The newly formed Greater Milwaukee Synod of the Evangelical Lutheran Church in America declared a companion synod relationship with the Lutheran Church of El Salvador, after my report to Cross Church and the Synod upon my return. And Cross Church called Reverend Margaret Suiter as "Accompaniment Minister in El Salvador."

As I shared a report of the accompaniment mission in El Salvador with my colleagues in urban ministry in Milwaukee, it dawned on us that accompaniment ministry is an accurate and helpful way of looking at ministry on the urban scene in the United States and ministry anywhere.

What is Accompaniment Ministry?

"Accompaniment" is a good way of describing the methodology that Jesus asked his disciples to use as he sent them out in teams of two (Luke 10:1-24). They were to go from village to village, announcing peace and the nearness of the kingdom. They were to live with the people, accepting whatever was offered in the way of shelter and food. If the people welcomed them and their message of healing and peace and the rule of God, they were to stay and nurture that emerging faith and vision. If the villagers rejected their message, they were to move on.

This accompaniment model is quite different from the method of John the Baptizer, who preached on the banks of the Jordan River and expected people to come out and hear his message. It's quite different from the policy of a congregation that expects people from the neighborhood to come to the worship on Sunday morning.

Accompaniment ministry means first of all, going to where the people are and offering to walk with them. In the Western, individualistic world, this means finding groups of people who are together, or who might consider coming together because they have similar interests or needs. As we look around our neighborhoods, we can see such groups of people whom we might accompany: senior citizens, youth, children, single-parent families, persons in recovery, ex-offenders, persons living with AIDS, low-income folks, professionals, job seekers, and the like.

Accompanying these different kinds of "communities" will look different from place to place and from congregation to congregation. But doing accompaniment ministry means being ready to respond when a community asks us to walk with it.

Secondly, accompaniment ministry calls for an attitude of love, respect, openness, and humaneness toward those with whom we walk. These attitudes are the opposite of arrogance and pity and paternalism.

When we accompany people in the name of Christ, we walk alongside them. We listen to them. We learn from them.

True, we come with a message of God's love and peace and forgiveness and healing through Christ. But that message is not laid upon people from above. It is expressed and communicated by the way we walk with them and listen to them and demonstrate that we genuinely care about them. Apart from that attitude of openness and appreciation for the other person's gifts and great worth, our message of God's love and peace would be incredibly difficult for the other person to believe. We may walk with people for months or years before we have the opportunity to verbalize the reasons for the hope that is within us. Accompanying people prepares the way for that message and actually communicates the message nonverbally.

Thirdly, a ministry of accompaniment calls for relationships that grow over a period of time precisely because of the hopes and fears, and the experiences of success and struggle and failure, that have been shared.

Congregations have a much deeper sense of community as people walk with one another, listen to one another, and take risks together for the sake of the Gospel. We may share pews with people Sunday after Sunday, but it is in walking with people inside and outside the sanctuary that we develop and deepen community and communicate the Gospel. When accompaniment is taking place outside of the Sunday worship, then the worship becomes more significant and more authentic, more deeply rooted in the whole warp and woof of life. When accompaniment is not taking place outside of worship, the worship can easily become sterile and certainly less fruitful in our personal lives and in the congregational life.

Above all, it must be stated that accompaniment ministry is enriching for all who are involved. It is not spiritually draining or burdensome to walk with refugees returning home after seven years of painful exile, or to accompany persons in prison or returning from incarceration, or to journey with someone who has experienced the sudden loss of a loved one. It may at times be physically draining and demanding. But it is always spiritually enriching.

Accompaniment ministry nurtures and enriches in ways that we often do not realize until years later. We are granted unique experiences of the grace and the presence of God. It's what Jesus is talking about in Matthew 25. He says that when we offer a drink to the thirsty, food to the hungry, clothes to the naked, and when we take in a stranger or visit the sick or the prisoner, we are actually meeting him and experiencing his presence.

In accompaniment ministry, we are amazed and enriched by the depth of the struggle, the profound sense of gratitude, and the authentic faith and hope of persons with whom we walk. We are led to see ourselves, others, the world, God, the mission of the Church, our own purpose in life, in ways that we would never have discerned had we not been accompanying others.

The ministry of accompaniment is at the heart of the Gospel and at the center of the struggle for justice and peace and the beloved community—that community lifted up so often by Martin Luther King—that draws together people from all walks of life, from all religions, from all races and income levels, and from all political and philosophical persuasions.

CHAPTER 2

GOD'S PREFERENTIAL OPTION FOR THE POOR

The Spirit of the Lord is upon me
Because he has anointed me
To preach good news to the poor,
He has sent me to proclaim freedom for the prisoners
And recovery of sight for the blind,
To release the oppressed,
To proclaim the year of the Lord's favor.
–Luke 4:18-19 / Isaiah 61:1-2

I remember accompanying my father on a pastoral visit in St. Louis. I was about eight years old. The year was 1941, a time when most of the country was still in the backwash of the Great Depression. My dad was pastor of A.G. Brauer Memorial Mission and teacher at the one-room school on the second floor of the storefront Lutheran congregation, Fourth and Choteau, four blocks from the Mississippi River.

We entered a three-story brick building from the sidewalk through a short tunnel that led into an open courtyard with wooden stairs to porches at the second- and third-floor levels, enabling tenants to access their apartment from this inner rectangular courtyard. It was dark and dingy, away from the sunlight in the street. An aroma of dank, putrid garbage filled the air. Clothes were hung to dry over the railings around the courtyard. I stayed close to my dad as we climbed the stairs and arrived at the door of the family we were visiting. We offered a bag of food to a grateful woman, and my dad had a conversation and prayer with her and her children.

I don't remember the name of the family we visited or any of the conversation. However, I do remember the sights and the smells of poverty. And I had a little deeper appreciation of the lives of some of the children who were in my Sunday school class Sunday after Sunday at the Brauer "Mission," as it was commonly called.

Fast-forward almost 20 years, to Birmingham, Alabama, 1958. I had just been ordained on my mom's birthday, July 13, 1958. At the young age of 25, I was staring at my first parish, St Paul Lutheran Church in Southwest Birmingham in the African American community of Titusville, about 20 blocks from downtown Birmingham.

Along the east side of the church building was Second Street South, a gravel street, with dirt paths for sidewalks. On the east side of the street lived one of the families of the congregation. Ada Scruggs, along with her husband, Shields, and her five children, lived in one of three side-by-side houses that are described in the South as "shotgun" houses.

I've heard two reasons why they're called "shotgun" houses. Some say it's because if the front door and the back door are open, you can take a shotgun and shoot through the house without damaging it, since the doors at front and back, as well as the two doors inside the house between the three rooms, are lined up in a row. A second explanation for the term "shotgun house" is that it's long and narrow, like a shotgun.

A shotgun home is built on "stilts," with brick pylons at the four corners and two or three pylons spaced between the corner pylons on both sides of the house, to keep the middle of the house from sagging. Besides the pylons, there is nothing else for a foundation. The air blows freely through the open space between the ground and the floor of the house, which makes for a cooling effect in the summer and a freezing effect in the winter. Of the three 12-by-12 rooms, one behind the other, the first room usually doubles as a living room by day and a bedroom by night. The middle room is a bedroom and the rear room is the kitchen/dining room. It would be cramped quarters for a family of two or three. It was more than cramped for the Scruggses, a family of seven. The "shotgun houses" built in the 1920s and 1930s out of pine lumber cost, at the time, about $500 dollars to build. They were prevalent throughout the South, especially in African

American communities, but also in some white communities, particularly in mill villages built by corporations for their workers.

To put bread on the table and to pay the bills, Ada Scruggs worked part-time as a custodian at St. Paul Church, and she did laundry and ironing for families. Her husband worked low-paying jobs when he could find and maintain them.

To my knowledge, the Scruggses never received welfare payments. Mrs. Scruggs was hardworking and as dependable as sunrise in the morning, both on her jobs and in her weekly worship. The Scruggses probably did not consider themselves poor, but they were clearly at the bottom of the economic ladder.

Fast forward to 2006, Milwaukee, Wisconsin. My wife, Joyce, or I, typically would pick up one or two persons who were staying at the Salvation Army Emergency Lodge, and take them to Sunday worship. These were persons who had hit on hard times and who were "on their way up." They were no longer on the streets or sleeping in their cars. They were in alcohol or other drug addiction treatment, or they were looking for a job, or they had gotten a job and were trying to get enough money salted away for two months' rent, enough to get themselves started in their own living unit.

The family living in the tenement house in St. Louis in the 1940s, the Scruggs family in Birmingham, Alabama, in the 1960s, and the folks at the Salvation Army Emergency Lodge in Milwaukee in 2006, were real people who were living in poverty.

Who Are the Poor?

Poor people are folks with many faces—white, black, brown, young, adults, middle-aged, senior citizens, people with alcohol and other drug addictions, ex-offenders, city people, rural folks, renters, home owners, trailer park dwellers, people with mental disabilities, people with physical disabilities, people from "solid" families, folks from dysfunctional families, nursing home residents, recent immigrants, eighth-generation Americans, Native Americans on reservations and in cities, working people, people looking for work, retired folks. The number and variety of persons living in poverty is staggering.

To many people, the poor are invisible. They may encounter a panhandler or see street persons warming themselves over a grate. But for many, the sight of such a person is infrequent. And to be sure, they are not walking with these poor persons, mutually sharing the nitty-gritty of life. They are not living next door to them. They are not seeing them on a regular basis in Kiwanis Club or in their congregation or in their Bible Class.

To many people, the poor are either lazy or ignorant people who have brought their poverty down on themselves. They are not worthy of associating with, on an equal basis. And any assistance that might be offered, according to the thinking of these people, would only enable the poor to continue in their poverty.

The poor are often seen as moochers who suck up more and more of our tax money. Consequently, the smart thing to do, according to this viewpoint is to cut services going toward the poor, such as services for the elderly, for persons with mental illness, for uninsured people with alcohol and other addictions, for at-risk children, and the like.

However, the Bible has a very different take on the poor. Both the Old Testament and the New Testament talk about the poor as part of the human community, worthy of our remembrance and our assistance. Again and again in the Hebrew Scriptures, God's people are urged to care for "the widows, the orphans, and the foreigners" in their midst (Exodus 22:21-22). Jesus says in Matthew 25, that when we feed the hungry, clothe the naked, welcome the stranger, visit the prisoner, care for the sick, share water with the thirsty, we are not only fulfilling his will, we are encountering him.

It was not simply that Jesus talked a lot about the responsibility of his followers to care for the poor. Jesus modeled in his public ministry what it means to walk with the poor and the outcasts. His enemies constantly found fault with him because he ate with "tax collectors and sinners." "Sinners" was the buzz word for such people as former offenders, prostitutes, and beggars.

Roman Catholic Bishops from Latin America, meeting in Medellin, Colombia, in 1968, coined a phrase that drives home the Scriptural view of the poor. They talked about "God's preferential option for the poor." Call it "divine bias," if you will. It is written throughout the Bible. God identifies with the poor and the oppressed.

God identified with the Israelite slaves in Egypt and freed them from slavery in an epic story of miracles and amazing commitment to an oppressed community.

The Old Testament prophets were constantly calling the children of Israel to center their lives in God and to live justly with the poor and the oppressed.

Jesus, Son of God, was born in a stable, accumulated no earthly wealth, ate with tax collectors and sinners, and died the death of a criminal.

Scripture testifies to "God's preferential option for the poor"

A Lutheran pastor serving in a suburban community once confided to me that there were members of her congregation who complained to her that she spoke of the poor too much in her sermons. The pastor didn't attempt to explain the underlying cause of her parishioners' complaint. However, it's likely that the parishioners were not ready to struggle with the realities of the poor and their responsibility, as people of faith, to the poor. That is a common attitude of congregations, but it is seldom stated so openly.

It is also possible that some people of faith in suburban and urban areas are frustrated because they are willing to struggle with their responsibility toward the poor, but don't know where to start or what to do.

Our eyes glaze over when the media plays up the sensational fire, murder, jury trial, or latest sex scandal, and then, on occasion, talks about such things as "the growing gap between the haves and the have nots," the emergence of a "permanent underclass," and the system that pays some CEOs and athletes millions of dollars per year and pays laborers working at the minimum wage of $5 or $6 per hour, a little more than $10,000 per year. Whatever injustices exist in all of these realities, what can one person of faith, or one congregation, do about it?

It is precisely that question that has pushed people of faith to confront poverty and to walk with the poor, to find small things and huge things that can be done to perform works of mercy and to advocate for changes in the systems that perpetuate poverty.

In his "ordination" at the synagogue in Nazareth, recorded in Luke 4:14-21, Jesus quoted Isaiah, as he laid out his mission statement: "The Spirit of the Lord is on me, because he has anointed me to preach good news to the poor. He has sent me to proclaim freedom for the prisoners and recovery of sight for the blind, to release the oppressed, to proclaim the year of the Lord's favor."

At first, the people at the Nazareth synagogue were delighted that a "hometown boy" had grown up to be such a spiritually-minded, articulate messenger for the Lord. But the acclaim turned into downright venom a few minutes later, when Jesus interpreted his mission to the poor to include gentiles as well as Jews. Jesus barely escaped with his life as he experienced the first assassination attempt after the start of his public ministry. And it happened when he held up a Gentile widow and a Gentile army officer as recipients of God's grace and as persons of faith. Apparently it was all right for Jesus to talk about bringing good news to the poor in general terms. But it was not all right to get specific about who the poor includes and to hold up the poor as persons to be considered as equals and as people from whom we can learn.

Walking with the Poor

Soon after I arrived in 1967 as a pastor of Cross Church in the heart of the African American community of Milwaukee, just ten blocks north of Wisconsin Avenue and Marquette University, our congregation was asked by the local chapter of the Black Panthers to allow them to serve breakfast in our fellowship hall to children on their way to school.

The Church Council of Cross Church took the request seriously and studied the matter for several weeks before making a decision. We discovered that the Black Panthers planned to teach the children who came for breakfast something of their philosophy, which at that time included violence as an acceptable method of achieving one's goals. So we decided to turn down the Black Panthers' request.

However, our consciences began to bother us. If children were going to school hungry, they really did need breakfast for nutritional reasons, and for the sake of achieving academically. So we did some homework. We checked at our local elementary school, Siefert School, to find out how many children were coming to school without breakfast, and discovered that over half of the 400 students were in that category.

We also discovered that every Milwaukee public school boasted an award-winning lunch program, but not a single school offered a breakfast program that was available to every school in the country through federal funding.

We decided that the Black Panthers were God's channel of communication to us, to put us in touch with real needs of poor children who were living all around us. We determined that we would do something about it, so we called a meeting of concerned persons from the community and from congregations in the area. The result was the formation of an organization called Citizens for Central City School Breakfast Programs (CCCSBP), that methodically worked at getting breakfast programs into the schools where the majority of students were eligible for free and reduced price lunches. For many years, the only Milwaukee schools that offered breakfast programs were several community schools and the three public schools where the CCCSBP had been successful in getting the School Board to establish "experimental" programs.

Finally, after nearly 20 years of faithful advocacy, a new Director of Food Services, Mary Kelly, was instrumental in establishing breakfast programs in every public school in Milwaukee.

In another positive result of following the nudging of the Spirit, to walk with the hungry children of the community, the ecumenical groups of folks who formed the CCCSBP, morphed into the Hunger Task Force of Milwaukee in the 1970s. The Hunger Task Force became an agency that, in turn, advocated for positive hunger-related policies to serve the needs of the poor, and coordinated some 70 food pantries in the Milwaukee area. It also helped launch MICAH (Milwaukee Inner-City Congregations Allied for Hope), a congregation-based justice organizing group, in the late 1980s, that was formed to work at removing the causes of hunger and homelessness and poverty.

The Cross Church Council could simply have said no to the Black Panthers' request in the late 1960s, without responding to the call to walk with the children going to school hungry. If that had happened, Cross Church would have missed out on a long-lasting relationship with the nearby school. They would have failed to develop appreciation for the realities of children in poverty. And the actual development of school breakfast programs for hundreds of children would likely not have happened.

Dietrich Bonhoeffer, in his *Letters and Papers from Prison*, states unequivocally that persons of faith and congregations who don't walk with the poor, miss invaluable gifts of discernment and perspective and spiritual enrichment: "There remains an experience of incomparable value, to see the great events of world history from below, from the perspective of the outcasts, the suspects, the maltreated, the powerless, the oppressed, the reviled—in short, from the perspective of those who suffer… to look with new eyes on matters great and small."

Bread of Healing

One day in the mid-1970s, Annie Porter, a member of the congregation, along with her husband and two younger sons, came to me with an urgent plea: " I see so many people in our neighborhood scuffling for rent money and food. I think we should open a food pantry at Cross." Mrs. Porter had a heart for everyone in need. When her youngest son was in high school, she started taking in foster children. So it was not surprising that she suggested a food pantry at Cross.

I was very open to the idea of a food pantry, but I was quick to remind Mrs. Porter that maintaining a food pantry would first of all require some regular volunteers. Secondly, it would require some significant effort to maintain a steady stream of food sources to stock the food pantry. Mrs. Porter said she was aware of the challenges involved, but she was ready to serve as one of the volunteers and she believed that somehow God would provide the food. She was true to her word. She not only served regularly as a volunteer. She soon became coordinator of the food pantry and remained in that capacity until her death about 12 years later.

Offering food to people in the neighborhood was a way of walking with the poor. The Cross Social Ministry Committee easily approved the launching of a food pantry and quickly discovered the challenges involved in operating a food pantry in a way that maintains the dignity of those who come asking for food and in a manner that empowers people to move beyond dependency to a mode of self-sufficiency and productivity.

Over years of experience, we found that 70 percent of those asking for food were families with children, mainly female-headed households. The other 30 percent were largely men, with a few women, who were separated from family and who were at various stages of homelessness or trying to make it with friends or relatives. Probably 30 percent were people who had hit a difficult snag in their life and came only once or twice a year to the pantry to help them over the hump. At least 70 percent of the chronic pantry visitors had a serious alcohol or other drug addiction issue. About 10 percent of the pantry frequenters were seriously looking for work and were good job candidates because they were not struggling with some kind of illness, disability, or serious crisis in their lives. Another 20 percent were working, but found their subsistence wages too little to cover the basic expenses of rent, utilities, transportation, food, and medical costs.

Meeting these people who were struggling with life's issues was a healthy experience for our congregation. Of course, not everyone in the congregation was engaged with the food pantry and the approximately 60 people who came each week. And different members of the congregation had different perspectives on the people who came asking for food. But there was no denying the reality and seriousness of poverty in the neighborhood that in the 1970s and 1980s was 70 percent under the poverty line and 75 percent renters with absentee landlords. The weekly food pantry saved us from living in a bubble apart from the poverty. It helped nurture us to believe deeply the Gospel truth, that all people are created in the image of God and are of great worth, and nudged us to encounter Christ in our neighbor who was in need.

After several years of distributing food as fairly as possible to those who came asking, we realized that we really had a responsibility to do more than hand out bags of rice, canned goods, bread, with fruit and produce when possible. We determined that we needed to offer people an experience of warm affirmation and genuine community, along with some spiritual food. After all, Jesus said that "humans do not live by bread alone."

The Social Ministry Chairperson, Nellie Davis, offered to prepare and serve a hot meal every week. We accepted Nellie's generous offer, thinking that we would have to find a replacement for her within a few months. As it turned out, Nellie prepared tasty home-cooked meals, everything from okra to water cornbread and sugared sweet potatoes to salmon croquettes and fried green tomatoes for several years, until her health forced her to give up her labor of love.

At the same time that we started serving the meal, we also instituted a Bible study/ prayer time, immediately following the meal and before we distributed the food. The meal and the Bible study were not required in order for a person to receive food. However, the majority of the people came for the meal and the Bible study, and a sense of community was nurtured each week, around Nellie's down-home cooking and around the bread of the Word that was shared by all.

We decided to change the name of the weekly event from "Cross Food Pantry" to "Cross Bread of Healing." We really wanted volunteers, food recipients, and the congregation, to see this moment in the week's schedule as a time to share physical food, to feed one another with spiritual bread, and to look for healing of body, mind, spirit, and community.

We purposely set up the tables in one huge square, large enough to seat 50 to 60 people around the outside of the tables, so that each person could see everyone else, and so that there was a sense of community as we sat in a circle.

I made it a point to join the meal and to lead the Bible study at least three Wednesdays per month. I wanted to walk with the people. I wanted to model Bible study that builds community. And I needed to be fed by the witness of these sisters and brothers from all sorts of life situations. After a brief study of a Bible text, usually the Gospel lesson from the previous Sunday's lessons, I would pose a question to which I asked everyone to respond. We would literally go around the table, from one person to the next, with responses to such questions as: What leads you to believe that Christ forgives you? What is a good way to show childern that we love them? What special gift do you have to give to others? What brings you joy? What have you experienced this week, for which you are especially grateful? What gives you hope?

Asking each person to respond one by one is an important way to develop community among people who feel bruised and disconnected from God, from family, and from community. It is a way of making it clear that each person has a gift to give the community. Our amazing experience was that 95 percent of the people would respond to the question asked, and some of the answers were profound. Almost always there was someone who was ready to lead the group in a closing, spontaneous prayer, binding our conversation together with cords of plainspoken hopes and fears.

Quite often the prayer would begin with the classic African American prayer: "God, I thank you that you woke me up this morning, clothed in my right mind." Hearing that prayer from someone who came asking for food was an enriching reminder for all of us, and especially for us volunteers, that we are all blessed, if we simply give thought to the fact that we have been given another day of life, and that we can communicate meaningfully with everyone we meet, because we are "clothed in our right mind."

Dignity was granted to each person, and authentic community was built as vulnerable people shared the highs and the lows of their precarious journey. We sometimes stopped the flow of conversation and offered up prayer when people shared a tragedy, such as the death of a loved one, the disappearance of a relative or friend, or the discovery of a terminal illness. On the other hand, the methodical, round-the-circle sharing was punctuated with spontaneous applause when personal triumphs and experiences of divine grace were shared. Landing a job seemed to warrant the most sustained applause, thus urging the rare person in the group to follow through on his or her special opportunity, and urging everyone else in the group not to give up on the seemingly impossible mission of finding a job. Other moments of grace that affirmed individuals and nurtured community were the announcements of the birth of a child, or the accomplishments of a son or daughter, or the healing of a broken relationship.

Beyond Bread

After a few months of the new Bread of Healing approach—breaking bread together, sharing God's Word with one another, and celebrating community—we knew we were on the right track. However, we knew there were still some missing pieces in our ministry, if we really intended to empower people to live out their God-given potential and bring profound healing to their lives. We knew we couldn't have everything as part of the Bread of Healing, but our Social Ministry Committee wrestled with what was needed and what was possible. They decided that there were three more elements that could be added: job preparation and placement services, AODA (alcohol and other drug addiction) counseling and support groups, and some primary care medical services.

We managed to initiate all of these elements into the three-hour, every-Wednesday Bread of Healing ministry. Project RETURN, the ministry we had established in 1980 to assist ex-offenders as they are released from jail or prison, was glad to extend their services to the 50 to 60 persons who came to Bread of Healing every week. Every week, after the meal and Bible study, we asked people who were ready for a job and looking for a job, to see the staff person from Project RETURN about preparing a job resume and then getting referrals for job applications.

We had no idea how this job preparation/placement component of the Bread of Healing ministry would work out. We knew that the majority of those asking for food were struggling with substance abuse problems and were not job-ready. We also knew that about 20 percent of the attendees were people with mental health issues or with other major crises in their lives, and thus not ready for work. We were happily surprised at the end of the first 12 months of offering job placement services that a total of 23 persons had actually found jobs. That was almost two persons per month. For hard-nosed statisticians, 23 persons out of the total 1,500 persons served throughout the year would probably be rated a failure. For us merchants of hope, the transformation of 23 persons from dependent, almost despondent, needy persons into self-supporting productive neighbors was an occasion for celebration.

At almost the same time that we initiated the job placement services as a part of the Bread of Healing weekly event, we started medical clinic services.

The clinic was made possible because of the parish nurse program that was evolving in Milwaukee. The Aurora Health Care system had come to recognize that parish nurses, stationed on the front lines of congregations, especially congregations relating to low-income persons and families, could divert many persons from the expensive emergency room services by simply catching a worsening high blood pressure or diabetes condition, for example, before it reached a critical stage. So Cross's Bread of Healing Empowerment Program was blessed to have the services of Rick Cesar, parish nurse at Cross Church, who helped us launch the Bread of Healing Clinic.

Precisely because so many people who came to the Bread of Healing program for food were uninsured people with physical and mental health problems, the Bread of Healing clinic every week had no dearth of persons checking in with Rick Cesar to have their blood pressure or sugar level checked, to receive free sample medicine when it was available, and in the process, to experience healing of body, mind, and spirit. We soon added such services as HIV-AIDS screening and even needle exchange for intravenous drug users.

In collaboration with Project RETURN, Cross Bread of Healing also initiated two AODA support groups, one for men and one for women. The women's group was smaller, with five to ten participants. The support groups gave people the opportunity to talk about their substance abuse issue that was causing them stress, under the guidance of a trained facilitator (RADC-1, Registered Alcohol and Drug Counselor Level One) and in an atmosphere of openness and trust. A goal of the support groups was to motivate and to assist persons who needed AODA treatment to be able to access it.

Once or twice a month, one of the participants in AODA support groups actually took that difficult, courageous step of entering AODA treatment. It was difficult and courageous because most of the support group participants were long time (15-20 years) alcohol/crack abusers, who often were still in denial ("I can stop using whenever I want to") or had given up all hope that they would ever be able to move into lasting recovery. It was always a cause for celebration when persons announced at the Bread of Healing meal that they had completed treatment or were 90 days or one year or two years clean and in recovery.

There may be some who would imagine that participating in the Bread of Healing weekly event and experiencing the brokenness and the profound physical and spiritual needs of people, week after week, would be a draining, de-energizing, even a hardening experience. In many respects, it is not easy to be a volunteer in such a weekly parade of hurt and need, especially when tempers flare, or when people are high on drugs or when interpersonal feuds explode or when people are convinced that the food was not fairly distributed to them. It may be that one's emotional or spiritual make-up is such that it would be difficult to volunteer at the Bread of Healing (or for that matter, to be a recipient).

However, if a volunteer, pastor included, can walk with the people who come to a Bread of Healing program with a genuine sense of mutual humanness, if a volunteer truly believes that all people are redeemable, if a volunteer can see and celebrate the growth and the healing that is taking place in people, then it is possible to encounter Christ in each person, to see all of life from a fresh perspective, and to be fed by the very people who are being fed.

It is clear that walking with the poor in a real, intentional, and long-term manner, nurtures pastors, lay leaders, and congregations to experience the Gospel and life itself in new ways. Living the grace of God and experiencing the power of Christ's forgiveness and the power of being forgiving people, is different from intellectualizing the grace of God, the forgiveness of Christ, and the forgiving spirit that loves the seemingly unlovable.

The Poor at Your Doorstep

It may appear to many that only urban congregations have the poor at their doorstep, and therefore suburban and rural congregations do not have that opportunity to walk with the poor. Nothing could be further from the truth.

Almost every rural/small town community has the "shacks" at the edge of town, the trailer parks with low-income persons, the children and youth at local schools who are derided in stinging fashion because of the soiled and ragged clothes they wear.

Suburban communities are inhabited by the invisible poor. Most suburban neighborhoods include nursing homes and widows and widowers living on low, fixed incomes. In addition, most suburban areas hire low-income people as housekeepers, lawn and garden caretakers, security persons, and clerks and custodians in stores and office buildings. Usually the low-income people who work in the suburbs are unable to live there. All the more reason why people of faith need to make visible these low-income people, who are not only in the midst of them, but on whom the livelihood of the area literally depends. It will take more creativity and more ingenuity to find ways of walking with the poor in suburban areas, but even there it is possible.

I do want to suggest ways in which congregations and individuals may walk with the poor, whether in urban, rural, small town, or suburb. Food pantries are usually the first, and often the last, attempts on the part of people of faith to respond to the presence and the needs of the poor in their midst. Food pantries are viable ways of recognizing the low-income and no-income persons in the community. However, it is essential that two pitfalls are avoided.

Food pantries, in the process of record-keeping and in an attempt to be fair in the distribution of the food, must constantly work at avoiding the dehumanizing procedure of grilling people in a tough-sergeant tone of voice. In fact, communities of faith need to work creatively at surrounding the food pantry experience with a culture of hospitality and overt ways of communicating God's love and the value and potential of all human beings at all stages of their lives, especially when they are at the humbling, devastating moment in their lives when they need to ask for food. The overarching image of a faith-sponsored food ministry must be a "walking with" people, not a condescending, self- righteous "hand down" to people. Without forcing the Bible on anyone, opportunities should be available for people to be fed with spiritual food, as well as physical food. Even as Jesus fed the multitude with bread and fish, he also fed them with the bread of the Spirit.

A second pitfall to be avoided is operating a food ministry and doing nothing more to address the needs of the poor. If we are genuinely walking with the poor, listening to them, talking with them as real people, we are discovering the underlying issues that are driving this request for food. If, for instance, the underlying issue is alcohol and other drug addiction, then we ought to help the persons connect with appropriate counseling and treatment. If treatment is not available for the individual because of lack of treatment for the uninsured or because of lack of treatment infrastructure in the area, then congregations need to come together to work on systemic change. That is what congregation—based organizing is about. If a compelling reason behind people asking for food is the high cost of housing and utilities, then congregations need to work at securing affordable housing in the area. This effort to provide affordable housing would be especially important for congregations to take on, in communities that keep low-income and even middle-income families out of the community with restrictions against lower-priced houses, rentals, and subsidized housing.

Congregational Partnerships

A method of walking with the poor that has many possibilities is the development of partner congregation relationships between urban/suburban/rural congregations.

Unfortunately, partner relationships between urban and suburban congregations have often remained on a financial level almost entirely. There are people-to-people relationships of all types that offer some amazing opportunities to walk with the poor. At Hephatha Lutheran, Milwaukee, every Sunday, there are six to 30 persons from a partner congregation present in worship, and with children, youth, and adults often participating in the Sunday School/Bible classes following the worship, as well. Then following the education classes, they serve and eat a meal (provided by the partner congregation) along with members of Hephatha. Members of partner congregations walk with members of Hephatha in such activities as the Hephatha social justice committee and the Hephatha youth work program. Several partner congregation members hold a joint membership in the two congregations. One of the partner congregations has joined the congregation-based justice organization that Hephatha is part of, as an authentic way of walking with the people in the poverty pockets in Milwaukee.

Urban/suburban congregational partnerships that are seriously looking for mutual interaction, service, and enrichment can become very creative and effective in achieving those goals, and in shaping congregational culture, in combating racism, in doing justice, and in building the "beloved community."

Some additional concrete ways for congregations and individual members to walk with the poor will be discussed in more depth in other chapters, but are listed here so that congregations and members seriously looking for ways to match the gifts of the Spirit given to every congregation and every believer, with the massive challenges of walking with the poor, may consider the variety of opportunities that are available:

- Prison and jail ministry
- Circles of re-entry: walking with persons as they are released from incarceration
- Restorative justice initiatives
- Support groups for persons struggling with mental illness, with substance abuse addictions, with grief, with losses of all sorts, with parenting, with conflict, with family and marital tensions
- Refugee resettlement
- Immigration services
- Transitional living services
- Homeless shelters
- Affordable housing efforts
- Adoption and foster care
- Literacy programs
- Mentoring children and teenagers
- Youth-serving programs
- Shelters and services for abused persons and for abusers
- Empowerment programs for persons with disabilities
- Neighborhood organizations that empower residents to bring about change
- Congregation-based organizations that work on justice issues, building community, and empowering people to overcome a victim mentality and to work for change

This long list of concrete ways of walking with the poor is not meant to overwhelm congregations and persons of faith or to lay guilt trips on congregations and members. Rather, it is intended to stimulate creative planning and action. There is no congregation or individual who can do it all.

Sources of Energy

Congregations that deeply believe that God has a preferential option for the poor and that Christ calls us to walk with those at the edges, will develop a culture in their liturgy, in their Bible study, in their committee structure, and in prioritizing the mission of their congregation, that encourages, affirms, and empowers people to walk with the poor. Which ministries are chosen and entered into will hinge on the prayerful discernment of a "human concerns/ social action/outreach" committee and on the felt concerns, passion, and gifts of individual members.

Walking with the poor, and all the ministries that clergy and people can be engaged in, does not minimize or replace the worship and Bible study. The worship and Bible study nurture the walk with the poor, and, in turn, the walk with the poor informs and enriches the worship, the sermon, the prayers, and the Bible study. In fact, those at the edges, hopefully, will be invited and encouraged to be part of worship and Bible study, and everyone is enriched, not just those who are closely involved with the walk with the poor.

As pastor of two congregations that were in the midst of the poor, and who tried to walk with the poor, I became personally involved in many of the ministries that emerged out of our congregational discernment. I definitely encouraged member involvement and tried to equip members who were catching the call of the Gospel, and to empower people to avoid the pitfalls of condescension and cynicism. I felt that I needed to be seriously engaged in the various ministries, both to learn and to be enriched, and to model the attitudes and patterns of "walking with." Especially since many persons of faith have grown up in congregations where worship and Sunday school were the be-all and end-all of congregational experience, it is important for members to see their pastor and a cadre of members modeling new life in Christ that clearly includes walking with the poor.

As I look back on the experience of walking with the poor and with people "at the edges," I see three distinct blessings that came to me and to our congregation.

First, the presence and witness of others in worship and Bible study, when the circle includes people at various stages on the continuum of income and needs levels, on the same journey of faith and hope in Christ and in the same struggle for justice and peace, is especially strengthening. (Of course, if those who gather seem not to be on the same journey, or if there are a significant number of nit-pickers who have lost sight of the vision of the Gospel and of justice and peace, the gathering can be de-energizing.) But for Christians, honestly sharing their struggles and their "aha" moments, worship and Bible study are also an encounter with Christ, whose Word and presence in Communion is the good news of forgiveness and empowerment and exhilarating challenge.

Second, walking alongside of those at the edges, not in a condescending posture of aloofness, but in an attitude of mutual worth, means that I am open to receiving from the very person with whom I am walking. I think of an ex-offender who stood up to speak to a group of people and began with a phrase that is familiar in African American Christian circles, "Giving honor to God, without whom I would not be here today." He could have started with stories of harsh treatment while incarcerated, or with stories of being turned down by potential employers because of his ex-offender status. Instead, he expressed a deep faith, in the midst of some tough times and unrealized goals, that there is a God who is looking out for him and has brought him to this point in his life for a purpose. What a powerful, energizing witness for me, whose experience at the hands of fellow human beings has not been nearly as harsh, but whose struggle for the goals of justice and peace has been thwarted again and again by well-intentioned people. And that witness by an ex-offender is just one of hundreds I have received from those at the edges, helping to save me from burnout.

A third source of energy for those walking with the poor is the active memory and awareness of victories won. How easy it is not even to see the victories, much less remember them, savor them, and be fed by them. But when we do remember the Spirit-led victories in the midst of the disappointments and challenges, it truly is strength for the struggle.

I vividly recall an experience while pastoring at Cross Church. It was about 1971, four years after arriving as pastor. I had led the gas meter reader to the hard-to-find room on the lower lever of the church where the gas meter was located, and I was leading him back though the sanctuary along a side aisle. He looked wistfully around at the stained glass windows and the beautifully-carved wooden altar and blurted out, "You know, I used to belong to this church—back when it was a success." It was clear that this man was a burned-out meter reader and a burned-out former member of Cross Church. I'm sure there were several reasons why he felt that Cross Church in 1971 was a failure. It no longer had 2,500 members. It no longer had an elementary school. It was situated in a neighborhood with deteriorating housing and with many poor families.

If the meter reader had asked me, I could have told him about the successes, the victories that were happening at that very moment that he saw failure. I could have told him about the Cross Youth Choir that was singing twice a month in the Sunday worship, empowering the youth and lifting our spirits. I could have told him of the dozens of persons whose lives had been enriched by Cross's witness to the Gospel and who had joined Cross Church during the previous years. I could have told him about the Citizens for Central City School Breakfast Programs that had formed to start breakfast programs in poverty-ridden schools, through the initiative of people at Cross Church. I could have told him about the Cross Youth Center that employed youth and tutored children, especially during summer months. I could have told him about the yearly youth confirmation class of eight to 12 youth, affirming their Baptism and participating in the life of the congregation. But he didn't ask. And he didn't see the victories. And so he was burned out and missed the very energy that he could have received from those around him, if he had intentionally chosen to walk with them to give to them and to receive from them, instead of seeing them as failures from whom he should distance himself.

By the grace of God, we saw the victories. We saw the work of the Holy Spirit. We were nurtured by the powerful victories, not in spite of our walk with the poor, but precisely because we were trying honestly to walk with them. And we were pulled out of the dangerous burnout zone that easily gives in to defeatism, cynicism, and spriitual death.

I have not said anything about the poor of the world. We dare not forget the poor of Haiti and Mexico and Sudan and Bangladesh. Even urban congregations in the U.S. surrounded by poverty and strapped with financial challenges dare not overlook their responsibility toward the marginalized of the world. However, it is walking with the poor in our midst that will save us from hypocrisy, will enrich our spiritual lives, and will open our eyes, our hearts, and our pocketbooks toward the poor of the world.

It was Jesus who said at the beginning of his public ministry that he came to bring good news to the poor. Then he honored them by walking with them, identifying with them, eating with them, empowering them, and calling them to follow him. When we begin to do the same, we discover in a rich and transforming way what the Gospel is all about, and we are strengthened for the struggle.

CHAPTER 3

NURTURING AND GROWING THE CONGREGATION

I am not ashamed of the Gospel, because it is the power of God for the salvation of everyone who believes.
–Romans 1:16

Jesus answered: "It is written: Man does not live on bread alone, but on every word that comes from the mouth of God."
–Matthew 4:4

The urban centers of the United States are filled with churches that once were thriving Lutheran, Catholic, Methodist, Episcopal, United Church of Christ, Presbyterian congregations, and now they are weak, struggling congregations, or the congregations have folded or moved out of the area, and the buildings have been sold. Now there may be a thriving African American, Hispanic, or non-denominational congregation holding forth in the building. Or in some instances, the formerly European background congregation has become an African American or Hispanic congregation of the same denomination, sometimes in survival mode and sometimes thriving. Sometimes with a handful of "old guard" white members and sometimes with a significant number of "new" Euro-background members, who have come to be part of a "new thing."

The huge question is: "What contributes to a wilting congregation in a racially changing or changed neighborhood? And what contributes to a thriving congregation in the same set of circumstances?

If there were a simple textbook answer to those questions, it would have been written long ago. The truth is that pastors and congregations are still learning answers to those questions. And pastors and congregations and neighborhoods are all so very different.

A Thriving Congregation

Having spent nine years pastoring an urban congregation in Birmingham, Alabama (1958-67), and 34 years pastoring an urban congregation in Milwaukee (1967-2001), I have gleaned a few insights, which are scattered throughout this book.

One fundamental insight into what contributes to a thriving congregation anywhere, including a challenging urban neighborhood, is that the ministry must be Gospel-centered and must be geared to meet the spiritual hunger and needs of people.

After nine years of fulfilling, enriching ministry in the African American community of southwestern Birmingham, Alabama, I received a call to serve Cross Lutheran, Milwaukee. Cross Church in 1967 was a congregation at a crossroads. It had made a decision in the late 1950s that many congregations in a similar situation had been unwilling to make. Surrounded by a racially changing neighborhood and experiencing a rapidly declining membership (losing about 100 members per year), Cross Church had decided to receive African American children in their parish school, and African Americans as members of the congregation. They called me as pastor because they had heard that St. Paul Church, in an African American community, under my pastoral leadership, had grown from 30 to 300. They were hoping that under my leadership, Cross Church could stem the tide of membership losses and rebuild some of its strength, perhaps reaching its peak membership of 2,500 baptized members in 1955.

I struggled with the call from Cross Church. I loved the people of St. Paul. I felt a special tug to serve in the South. But in the end, my wife, our two very small children, and I, left Birmingham in August, 1967. I had a profound lump in my throat as I headed toward Milwaukee and Cross Church.

But I felt a real call to test the waters in a congregation that had made a small beginning toward a racially integrated congregation. I was convinced, and I am still convinced, that if the people of God cannot learn to live and work together across racial lines in a community gathered around the Gospel, then how can we expect secular society to overcome racism and the residue of 250 years of slavery and 100 years of racial segregation, to form a truly integrated community?

So Cross Church and I had similar dreams. We both wanted to see a strong congregation in the central city. We both had a vision of a racially integrated congregation.

However, there was a subtle, but real, difference between the vision of the "old guard" of Cross Church and my vision. The second- and third-generation members of Cross Church envisioned African Americans becoming members, swelling the ranks, rebuilding the numbers, without any change in the culture and the worship life of the congregation. I had no preconceived notion about changes that had to take place or that would take place. But I had a deep sense that the Holy Spirit was doing a new thing and that if people from two different cultures, and especially people from the historically privileged and historically oppressed groups, are to learn to live together, worship together, and do a new thing together, there are going to be some changes, and we need to be open to those changes.

Open to Changes

And changes did come. As pastor, I did not initiate the changes. I did sow seeds of openness to new directions and to the Spirit's leading. Two major changes took place rather quickly after my arrival as pastor. The Youth Choir and the congregation began singing some hymns that were not in the regular Lutheran hymnal. For old-time members of Cross, the new hymns were a Sunday morning jolt. For newer members, the new hymns were acknowledging and receiving some of their gifts. As pastor, I could have put my foot down on the new hymns. But using the Gospel as the criterion, I encouraged the congregation to be open to trying new hymns and to judge their value in our worship on the basis of whether they helped us communicate and celebrate the Gospel. If so, they would help us grow spiritually. So the new hymns were something to welcome, not to rule out.

A second change occurred when some newer members of Cross started to meet with the People's Committee for Model Cities (PCMC). The PCMC was a grassroots gathering of people, black and white. They could be described as radical because they were demanding that people in the community should elect their own representatives to the board of the

Model Cities program, rather than permit Mayor Henry Maier to appoint the members of the board. The Model Cities program was the anti-poverty program under President Lyndon Johnson designed to empower communities to create economic development plans that would forge grassroots solutions to urban problems, and would employ people in the process.

The Model Cities program, precisely because it was a program designed to alleviate causes of poverty, was a program that people motivated by the Gospel and walking with the poor, had every reason to be involved with. And pushing for community control of the programs fit with the empowerment of people concept. So I had no difficulty supporting members of Cross who got involved with the PCMC, and I felt the pull of the Spirit to get involved myself.

The People's Committee for Model Cities gained momentum and held rallies to inform the community and to enlist people in the cause. One of the rallies was held at Cross Church, with the result that old guard members of Cross read in the morning paper about the strong rally supporting the community's call for democratic elections, and opposing the mayor's plan, a meeting held at Cross Church! Some of the old-time members, almost all of them living outside of the Cross neighborhood and the central city, were up in arms over this change at Cross Church. "That Model Cities business is all political," they charged, "and we're the Church. We're supposed to be about spiritual things."

They were wrong in claiming that trying to alleviate poverty is "all political." It has everything to do with demonstrating God's love, with doing justice, and with empowering the poor. But they would have been correct in criticizing us if we had gotten so wrapped up in the efforts in the public arena that we had abandoned, or even minimized, the building of the community of believers and the spiritual feeding and nurturing of God's people at Cross Church.

I said it loud and clear by my words and actions, that we dare not be embarrassed by the Gospel, or be timid about building and growing the community of believers, or about nurturing children, youth, and adults spiritually. Without a strong spiritual, Gospel-centered community of people, there is no base from which to work for justice and peace and for the common good. And it would be difficult to keep the vision sharp and to maintain strength for the long haul. Furthermore, it is of the essence of the Gospel, the Good News of God's love and forgiveness in Jesus Christ, that calls for a personal response of faith and personal transformation of one's thoughts and values and attitudes and priorities and inner being. The Gospel is the power of God that saves and transforms. Everyone who believes it is nurtured by it and is guided by it.

So, I differed from most old guard members of Cross in seeing the necessity for change in the culture and the worship life of the congregation and in its involvement in the pubic arena. However, on one thing we were in agreement: We should work to build a strong, vibrant, growing congregation, and to do that, we would need to be regularly engaged with Word and sacrament and to offer opportunities for people to be fed on that powerful Gospel that saves and heals and transforms.

Nurturing and Growing the Congregation

With commitment to that vision of community-building and spiritual feeding of youth and adults, there are four areas of congregational life that we found at Cross Church required consistent, creative focus on the part of pastor and people, if we were to be true to that vision: 1. Weekly relevant, empowering Sunday worship. 2. Regular, accessible, Bible-based membership classes. 3. A strong Sunday School program. 4. Relevant and diverse adult Sunday Bible classes.

1. Weekly Relevant, Empowering Sunday Worship

The weekly Sunday worship was extremely important because that is the venue in which the largest number of members gathered regularly and because that is where many visitors came to experience personal cleansing, healing, nurturing, and transformation, and often to "size up" the health and the culture of the congregation.

A worship committee, made up as much as possible of the age/racial/gender diversity of the congregation, worked hard to shape the liturgy and creatively forge the worship to be a Gospel-centered, nurturing, relevant, celebration of God's love and call to discipleship. As important as the pastor's guidance and direction is in shaping the Sunday liturgy, it is very helpful to receive input from members, especially when there are two or more distinct cultures that are coming together in a congregation. If a goal of the congregation is Spirit-forged interracial unity, then the liturgy needs to reflect the gifts of the racial groups involved.

From the very beginning, we decided that the historic basic components of the liturgy must be there week in and week out: The lessons from Scripture, the sermon, the prayers, and Holy Communion.

The inclusion of Holy Communion as a basic dynamic in the weekly liturgy may seem questionable in the minds of some. After all, it is absent from the Sunday morning liturgies of many Protestant congregations. It does add 10 to 15 minutes to the service. And there is always the danger of ritualism. However, we included it from the beginning, and it was never seriously questioned over the years, because the weekly sharing of Christ's meal was seen as such a powerful communicator of the unconditional healing love and forgiveness of Christ and such a strong, nurturing experience and celebration of the inclusive community that transcends race and class and is rooted in Christ.

Beyond the basic components of the liturgy, there is room for various options that can help express cultural diversity, incorporate specific needs of the congregational community and the neighborhood, and can focus on specific moral and justice issues to which the people of God are called to give a clear witness in their daily lives.

The weekly liturgy that includes a variety of hymn sources will nurture children who grow up in the congregation to expect and to appreciate various types of hymnody, and the musical diversity will give visitors something to identify with, regardless of their cultural background. There is a line of thought that strongly urges worship planners to use only one kind of music in a given service and not to diversify music sources. Not throwing artistic tastes totally to the winds, the real concern in a worship service is to choose hymns that contribute to the central theme of the day or to the particular place in the liturgy. When the music and the lyrics of hymns come from a variety of ethnic sources, the diversity can testify to the diversity of God's creation and of the gifts of the Spirit.

In an effort to celebrate and to nurture community within the congregation, or to bring the neighborhood into the congregation or to focus on a specific issue, we often included in the liturgy a five-minute segment we often called a "contemporary witness." Or a "recognition moment." The segment often came after the second lesson, but sometimes was part of the sermon or after the sermon. If it was African American History Month, it might have been someone from the congregation, or from the community, whose gifts we wanted to lift up and for which we gave God the praise. Or if it was college students' recognition Sunday, we asked all the college students to take different parts in the service, and one college student would give a testimony to his or her faith. If it was "Recovery Sunday," we would ask a member or a non-member to share their journey of coming into recovery and remaining in recovery. If it was "Prison Ministry Sunday," we would ask an ex-offender or someone working in a prison ministry to witness to the work of the Spirit in their lives.

With the moments of testimony and recognition woven into the liturgy, the worship was not a liturgy read and sung from books composed of hymns and readings from the past. Worship became a "here-and-now" expression of the Spirit and a work of the people.

Other ways in which the liturgy was shaped to express and to nurture the "unity in diversity" of the congregation and to encourage liturgy as the work of the people, included use of lay members of all varieties in reading the lessons, leading at prayer time, distributing Communion, and giving testimonies. In addition, the sharing of the peace and weekly children's sermons connected with the theme of the day nudged worshipers away from the book to interaction with sisters and brothers gathered in worship with them.

Inviting people forward for anointing and laying on of hands with prayer for healing right before or during Communion, nurtured people to see the Good News of God's love as healing grace and helped to develop the congregation as a caring, healing community that recognizes the hurts of people and boldly lives out the belief that God is a God who cares and heals.

At Cross Church, we knew that our worship was far from perfect. But we also knew that a liturgy totally from a book was not perfect either. So we continually evaluated and shaped the liturgy, communicating to one another the importance of our coming together, the centrality of the Gospel, and the urgency of nurturing one another via Word and sacrament. Worship was not a ritual to be endured. It was the nurturing, empowering, healing experience that we all needed for our sanity and to grow us into the individual disciples and witnessing community that God intends for us all to be.

2. Regular, Accessible, Bible-based Membership Classes

Every pastor and every congregation proclaiming and living the Gospel can expect the Gospel to touch people's minds and spirits to the point of bringing them to faith in Christ and of wanting to be part of the new community, exemplified by the congregation.

Over the years, I developed a rhythm in the congregational life and in my ministry that planned and announced a new "Pastor's Class" for persons seeking congregational membership, but also for persons seeking to strengthen their spiritual lives, looking for an opportunity for Bible study, or simply looking for guidance and strength in the midst of the mysteries and challenges of life. So every January, May, and September, I announced the 15-session weekly class, sent out invitations to visitors at worship, and to contacts from our various ministries (prison ministry, Bread of Healing, The Adult Center, Youth ministry, support groups), and placed flyers in the bulletins preceding the start of each class, asking members to suggest names of relatives and friends and urging members and worshipers to attend, for their own spiritual nurture and as a way to witness to their faith. I made visits and phone calls, as did Evangelism Committee persons, inviting people to take this spiritual step for nurture and growth.

As the start of each new Pastor's Class approached, I usually knew of three or four persons who were definitely committed to attending. However, there were occasions when I wasn't absolutely sure anyone would show up for the class. The amazing truth is that there never was a time in the 35 years of my pastorate that people did not show up for the class. And almost always, people appeared at the class for whom I had no expectation of attendance. Simply announcing the class and holding up the value of studying the Bible, of searching for deeper meaning and for spiritual strength, with others who were seeking and searching, touched a few persons who were at that point in their lives that they felt a real need to step out of the regular routine, or out of the chaos, of their journey for a fresh look at God's Word for their lives.

There were people ready to join Cross Church who had been confirmed as youths, or had been baptized/confirmed as adults, and had been away from a congregation for years. They had a basic knowledge about the teachings of the Bible and of the Christian faith. I could have received them as members of the congregation without asking them to attend the Pastor's Class. However, I urged them to attend the Pastor's Class for two basic reasons. First, they were at a very different point in their spiritual journeys than when they were baptized/confirmed, and it would be valuable for them to bring their current questions and struggles to the light and the power of God's Word. Furthermore, I assured them that 15 weeks of interaction and authentic sharing with eight to ten others, would forge a set of relationships and a sense of community that they could take with them as they joined a large congregation, thus avoiding the phenomenon of feeling lost in a sea of strange faces.

Members of Cross experienced a regular rhythm of a Pastor's Class and the joyful experience of receiving six to 12 adults/families as members, three times a year. The lesson learned from this experience was that the Gospel proclaimed and then lived out in various outreach ministries bears fruit. As we walked with each other and with people at the edges, we could expect to build and grow the community, both in a deeper experience of oneness in the Body of Christ and in terms of new persons constantly enlivening the community with new gifts.

I might add that the regular rhythm of three Pastor's Classes per year was anything but a drain. It was an important source of spiritual food for my own soul. Although we followed an outline for each class, the approach was not to "indoctrinate" or to talk about the distinctive characteristics or history of the Lutheran Church, or to acquaint people with the structure of the congregation. The methodology of the teaching was to give class participants an opportunity to wrestle with Scripture and there to encounter the Gospel and God's Word for their lives. Calling forth people's response to the Word gave them the opportunity to testify to their doubts, their questions, and their convictions. Their testimonies were often very powerful, strengthening not only the other participants, but also the teacher.

There are many memorable experiences of the Spirit's transformation and power in the classes. I remember a class in which two gay men who were partners, one a college professor with a Ph.D. and his partner, with a degree in accounting, were seated next to a wiry, old African American grandmother who was semi-literate and very self-conscious and timid about saying anything. I thought that such an obvious spread in academic ability and social standing might place a damper on the participation of all three of them. It was truly the work of the Spirit that motivated the two men to assist the woman in finding her place in the Bible, as we studied various passages, and to show obvious respect and encouragement toward her, with the end result that the timidity gave way to honest sharing, and all three developed a genuine bond that carried over into their life in the congregation.

Kelly Schmidt, a twenty-something white woman with multiple sclerosis, and wheelchair-bound, started worshiping at Cross Church and found the affirmation and community she was looking for. Filled with a very real faith in Christ, she came to a series of Pastor's Class sessions, was received as a member of Cross, and then made it clear to me that she wanted to attend the next Pastor's Class that was starting up the following week. I welcomed her, but thought she was running on spiritual adrenalin that wouldn't last very long. As it turned out, she completed that series of Pastor's Class sessions and the next series after that. She found the small-group experience in which other class members warmly accepted her and engaged in conversation with her to be an experience of the "beloved community." Even though it was sometimes difficult for the rest of us to understand her, she found the conversation centered in the Word to be stimulating and strengthening. Her presence in the Pastor's Class sessions and in the congregation gave all of us a deeper sense of the challenges faced by persons with disabilities. But more importantly, Kelly helped us to see the gifts and the winsome witness that such persons can bring to a congregation. She reminded us of the importance of personal nurture and of the congregational focus on Word and sacrament.

Another unforgettable Pastor's Class experience started with a phone call one day from Linda Fayne Pegues, who called "out of the blue" for the time of worship and Sunday school. Urban pastors don't get that kind of call very often, so I asked whether I could visit her. She agreed to meet with me, and I asked her rather early in the conversation, "What prompted you to call Cross Church about the time of service and Sunday school?"

Her answer was very revealing: "Well, I have a son who is four years old, and I see the need for giving him spiritual direction in his life. I don't think I can do that by myself very well, so I contacted the only church I have had any real contact with, and that is Cross Church. When I was a child, our family lived right behind Cross Church. My brothers and sisters and I attended Sunday School and summer programs, and most of us were baptized there as children. I had a good experience there, and I would like for my son to have a similar experience of getting to know the Bible and God."

Not only did Linda Pegues attend Cross with her son, Anthony, but she continued coming and quickly joined a Pastor's Class, and then re-joined Cross Church.

That was only the beginning of the story. She told her siblings about her experience of community at Cross Church and the opportunity for Bible study in the Pastor's Classes. The result was that the next seven or eight Pastor's Classes had two or three brothers, nieces, nephews, in-laws, or friends of Linda Pegues.

And that is not the end of the story. Linda and her sisters and in-laws one by one offered their gifts as teachers in the Sunday School, and they formed the foundation and the framework for the Sunday School program at Cross Church for some 15 years. If the Holy Spirit has her way, members of the Fayne "clan" may form the structure of the Cross Sunday School program for years to come. What a blessing for any congregation! And nothing short of a miracle for an urban congregation, where adult leadership, continuity, and stability are precious gifts of the Spirit. It is not insignificant that all of the Fayne "clan" have cut their spiritual eye teeth on the joy and the enriching power of Bible Study in the Pastor's Class sessions.

3. A Strong Sunday School Program

If nurturing and growing the congregation is taken seriously as an integral part of the congregation's mission, then Bible study will be encouraged at all age levels and at various times during the week. Adult Bible classes and Sunday School classes for children are traditional venues for spiritual nurture that should be eliminated only when it is absolutely clear that there aren't any teachers available. A congregation without a Sunday School for children is a signal to families with children that the congregation either does not value spiritual nurture for children, or it does not have sufficient adults ready to lead the classes.

Besides the challenge of recruiting an adequate, committed staff for a strong Sunday School/Bible Class program, there is the added difficulty of getting teachers and students to the church on time. If the Sunday School sessions are held before the time of the main service, many of the children attending an urban Sunday School have to get themselves there on their own steam, and consequently are often late, sometimes very late on a cloudy, dark Sunday morning. These are the very children that a congregation exists to reach, so they cannot be discounted.

In the '70s at Cross Church, we realized that we needed to do something about the late students and teachers. For about a year, we held Sunday School and Bible Classes immediately following the sermon and then returned 45 minutes later for Communion and the benediction. It was a great way for worshipers of all ages to break into small groups after the Word of God was read and proclaimed and to ask the relevant question: " What does this Word of God mean for our life together as a community of believers, and for my own personal life?" We knew that this break for Bible study between the sermon and Communion would be a jolt for the adults who were not accustomed to Bible class participation. We hoped that people would try it and discover the power of Bible Study for personal spiritual growth and for relationship building.

We learned, however, that we were attracting only a few new Bible Class students and we were effectively discouraging people from staying for Communion, an important element in personal and congregational life.

It was at that point that we decided to schedule Sunday School/Bible Class following worship, and Cross Church has followed that pattern ever since. Many congregations around the country, especially urban congregations, have likewise found this pattern to be a solution that saves Sunday School from extinction and maintains it at a time when "children-on-their-own" are more likely to attend.

The Place of Children

There are various schools of thought about the issue of children attending adult-focused worship. There are congregations that have Sunday School simultaneously at the time of worship, with the expectation that children will attend Sunday School, while the parents attend worship. Or another version of this pattern is for children to attend worship for the first 10-15 minutes, and then to be dismissed to go to Sunday School classes. This does work for some congregations.

Our learning at Cross Church, and the learning of many urban pastors, is that children with or without positive role models and nurturing parents at home need regular opportunities to build a strong sense of community and extended family. The weekly worship is the family gathering, where children and adults not only see and experience a sense of family, but that is where it is nourished.

Of course, if children and youth are recognized as important and valuable in the life of a congregation, and are invited to participate in the weekly worship, then the worship must be designed in such a way that children and youth see and hear that they really are an important part of the congregational family gathered in worship. The children's sermon, the choirs, the music, the ushering, the Communion, the prayers, the leading in worship must make visible to every worshiper that this is not only a "child-friendly" congregation. It is a congregation that considers children and youth as valued essential members of the Body of Christ, whose gifts are encouraged and received.

My wife and I, after my retirement from parish ministry, became members of Hephatha Church, an urban congregation near Cross Church. We noticed that Pastor Mary Martha Kannass, as she looks over a chancel filled with 40 to 50 children, begins every children's sermon with an opening observation like: "We are truly grateful that you are here this morning, aren't we, Church?" And the congregation responds with "Amen" and with "That's right." Likely as not, she will move immediately into another observation like: "If you weren't here, we'd know something important was missing. Wouldn't we, Church?" Then before the "Amen's" have died down, she's likely to add a third observation, like: "You know, you help us to grow. Isn't that right, Church?" Children, youth, and adults at Hephatha Church are clearly growing into a positive awareness of the extended family that they are part of, not *in spite* of their worship, but *because* of their worship.

One of the affirming moments in my ministry at Cross Church, came when I was teaching a junior high Vacation Bible School class. I told them that for our art project, we were going to make a banner for the worship space that would tell members and visitors who we were and what we wanted to be known for. I asked them to each write down a phrase that described their experience of the congregation. Then we voted. The winning theme for the banner that hung in the sanctuary for months was: "We Are Family in Christ." That sense, on the part of children, of being included and being an important part of Cross Church, was what we worked at. It was reassuring to have the children themselves affirm it, that they really felt loved and part of the "Family in Christ" at Cross.

4. Relevant and Diverse Adult Sunday Bible Class

As important as Sunday School and worship is for children and youth, adult Bible classes are equally as important for nurturing and growing a congregation.

Bible class in connection with food ministries, adult/senior centers, and recovery groups can be spiritually enriching for the participants and can be outreach points of contact for pastors and congregations. Likewise, the Sunday morning adult Bible Class can be an important community-building, gap-bridging, outreach opportunity for congregation and pastor. It can even become a sounding board and incubator for ministry initiatives.

The Sunday morning adult Bible Class at Cross Church was an important encounter with God's Word that brought representatives of most of the significant groups of folks at Cross together to communicate with each other around the Word: "Seasoned" members, newer members, gay and straight, African American and Euro-American, inmates from nearby minimum security prisons, persons in recovery, ex-offenders, parish council members, and quite often, visitors at worship. What a treasury of gifts and perspectives to bring together around the lessons for the day or around a given issue or topic.

Precisely because we had so many people around the table who were struggling with real issues, there was a lot of vulnerability, honesty, and down-to-earth sharing in which stereotypes were shattered, tears were shed, relationships were built, and testimonies to the transforming power of the Spirit were freely expressed. The Sunday morning adult Bible Class made it abundantly clear that even though we were a congregation publicly known for its engagement in the social justice arena, we were also a congregation deeply interested in the spiritual nurture of people and in the theological underpinnings of the justice issues we stood for. It was not accidental that nearly every Pastor's Class included one or two persons who had recently attended a Sunday morning Bible Class, including men and women from the minimum security prisons.

Nurturing and growing a congregation is definitely the work of the Spirit, and happens in the suburbs, in rural areas, and in the heart of the cities. Wherever there is a Gospel-centered ministry, there is a tone and a culture, reflected by pastor and people who expect spiritual growth and systematically create spaces for that nurturing and growth to take place.

CHAPTER 4

A NEW SONG

Sing to the Lord a new song, for He has done marvelous things.
–Psalms 98:1

It was a year into my pastorate at Cross Church. The year was 1968. The congregation was more than 90 percent white. The Couples Club was hosting a special program, to which they had invited members and friends.

An African American couple, Bruce and Gloria Wright, were in attendance. They had belonged briefly to Cross Church in the mid-60s and lived a block from the church. In fact, Gloria had been instrumental in forming and leading a Girl Scout troop at Cross, which had attracted a dozen or more girls from the neighborhood. But when the Wrights moved to Waterford, a suburban community at the southwest edge of Milwaukee, they had transferred their membership to a congregation near them.

Gloria Wright made it a point to meet me at the dinner event and was quick to ask me: "What would you say if I offered to organize a youth choir at Cross?" Having heard of Gloria's excellent work with the Girl Scout troop, I knew she was very capable of working with the youth. Gloria's question prompted a quick reply, "That would be great. A pastor and a congregation couldn't ask for a better offer," I said.

However, Gloria had a second question that followed quickly on the heels of her first question: "I need to know something before I actually pull a choir together. Will the choir be permitted to sing a variety of songs? Or would we have to stick with the strictly Lutheran songs?"

Without realizing what changes would take place in the Sunday worship at Cross as a result of my answer, I replied: "Whatever communicates the Gospel and helps us worship God would be great." The rest of the story of the Cross Youth Choir and music in our congregational worship is history that is still unfolding.

Gloria Wright made good on her offer to start a youth choir. By her own admission, Gloria was not a musician. She was not even a great singer. But she was an outstanding recruiter and organizer. She loved youth. She had a deep appreciation for the Lord and the Church. She had relationships with many youth and families at Cross Church and in the Cross community. She was a tireless worker. And she had a vision of what the youth choir could become and what it could do for the youth and for the congregation.

After gathering youth together for practice during October and November of 1969, Gloria scheduled the Cross Youth Choir to sing for the first time in December that year. The choir was well received by the congregation and began singing at two Sunday services per month.

The Youth Choir was accompanied at first by guitar, because there was no piano in the sanctuary. The Youth Choir, almost totally African American, sang at the front of the sanctuary, so that it could be heard, while the adult choir, almost all white, continued to sing in the balcony, accompanied by organ, as it had done for the entire history of the congregation.

Most of the congregation was thrilled by the singing of the Youth Choir. They enjoyed the vibrance of the youthful singing. They were heartened by black and white youth taking leadership in the congregation and in the worship. They were struck by the sound of a new song.

A Variety of Songs

"Could the congregation sing some of the Youth Choir songs in our worship?" I was asked by a number of members. Struck by the energy that the "new song" was creating among youth and adults, I agreed, and suggested that we form a worship committee that would shape some liturgies and incorporate some of the songs like *Sons of God, Hear His Holy Word, He is King of Kings, Come and See,* and *Amen.*

The Worship Committee, in creating the new liturgies, followed the pattern of the traditional liturgy. For instance, the committee replaced "Glory be to Thee, O Christ," chanted traditionally before and after the reading of the Gospel, with two different stanzas of *I'm So Glad Jesus Lifted Me.* In one of the liturgies, *Woke up this Morning with My Mind Stayed on Jesus,* was sung in place of the *Glory Be to God on High.*

The prayer of the day, the First Lesson, the Second Lesson, the Gospel, the Creed (written in a contemporary form), the offering, the prayers of the people, and Holy Communion were all included in the new "Community Liturgies," interwoven with the sound of a new song. We published our own mimeographed *Urban Hymnal Supplement*, with the "Community Liturgies" in front and new songs on pages after the liturgies. Periodically, we added new liturgies and new songs.

We continued to use the regular liturgy from the old Lutheran hymnal, once or twice a month, but we would sprinkle some of the newer songs into the worship every Sunday. We wanted visitors at Sunday worship, and there were visitors every Sunday, to hear the new song. We knew that the "new songs" would have a familiar ring for visitors from the neighborhood, almost all of them first-generation African American migrants from Mississippi, Arkansas, or Louisiana, and we knew the visitors would find the chanted liturgy and the European background hymns providing a strange sound.

Even though newer members, visitors, and youth found the "new song" to be a vibrant channel for the Gospel and for their praises, many of the older members had difficulty with the changes.

Some of the older members said that if the liturgy and the hymns did not come from their Lutheran hymnal, they weren't Lutheran.

Others objected to the use of the guitar and the piano that had been placed in the corner of the sanctuary to the right of the chancel. These instruments, they said, were not intended for worship. They insisted that the organ was the only acceptable musical instrument for worship.

An organist came to me after the service one Sunday and announced his resignation. "I can't take these changes," he said. "These songs we're singing aren't good music. They aren't Lutheran. I wasn't trained to play this kind of music." No word about whether the hymns communicated the Gospel, or whether we were praising God, or about the mission of the Church. It simply wasn't Lutheran. It wasn't "good music," and wasn't "what I was trained to do."

I don't know of any of the older members who left Cross church especially because of the new song, but there were many who left "because of all the changes," and the new song was one of those changes.

After a few years of using our loose-leaf mimeographed hymnal supplements, it was clear that we needed to re-publish the supplement, mainly because of torn pages and disappeared booklets. We wanted to publish the supplement with a more permanent binding and with music.

We also wanted to share our supplement with the larger church, since a growing number of congregations, Lutherans of all varieties, as well as other mainline churches, especially urban congregations, were expressing an interest in a more diverse selection of hymns and liturgies.

We approached Concordia Publishing House, Augsburg Publishing House, and Fortress Books, in the mid-1970s, to see whether they would edit and publish a version of our booklet. All three Lutheran publishing houses turned us down, on the grounds that it didn't meet Lutheran standards, and above all, that there wouldn't be a market for it.

After the turndown by the publishing firms, we decided to publish it ourselves. We started a yearlong process of securing copyright permission and of getting the words and the music laid out on an 8½ by 5½ format, each original page printed by hand, music and text, by a dedicated, gifted calligrapher, who did it for very little financial compensation, simply because of her love of the Church and her appreciation for the new song.

Four other urban Lutheran congregations in Milwaukee joined us in the publication of the *Urban Hymnal Supplement*: Hephatha (American Lutheran Church), Gospel (Lutheran Church—Missouri Synod), Our Savior (American Lutheran Church), and Incarnation (Lutheran Church in America). Since the 1980s, all the Lutheran publishing houses have produced hymnal supplements that include most of the hymns found in our *Urban Hymnal Supplement*. Some of the supplemental hymnals include alternate liturgies.

In the 1990s, two very important hymnals were published, both reflecting the African American (with some African) experience: from the Roman Catholic tradition, *Lead Me, Guide Me*, and from the Lutheran tradition, *This Far by Faith*. Both books are widely used.

A new Lutheran hymnal was published in 2008, with nine liturgies and 654 hymns. There is wider variety of hymns, including several hymns in a variety of foreign languages. However, there are only 20 hymns of African American or African origin. There are some new hymns, some with justice and urban themes, and quite singable. The new hymnal is more diverse and includes about 15 more African American/gospel type hymns than its predecessor. But the hymnal *This Far By Faith* will doubtless continue to be the hymnal of choice for urban Lutheran congregations with significant African American membership. It has a greater selection of hymns and liturgies with which urban and African American folks can identify.

As I look back on my own transformation in regard to hymns and liturgies, I confess that I grew up using the old Lutheran hymnal with one standard liturgy that we used Sunday after Sunday and with a limited number of hymns, many of them German hymns translated into English. I enjoyed singing the standard liturgy and the hymns. I didn't know there was anything else. However, I do remember going with my dad at the age of nine or ten when he had a service at Resurrection Church, an African American Lutheran congregation in St. Louis, Missouri. Resurrection Church was worshiping in a storefront just two blocks from the Mississippi River. I recall hearing them sing the spiritual *Swing Low, Sweet Chariot.* I sensed immediately, even at the age of ten, that this was more than simply unfamiliar music, with a different set of lyrics. It was a different kind of music, with lyrics from a different origin.

It was several years later, when I was in college and at home in Selma, that I accompanied my dad to a Christmas service at Gethsemane Lutheran Church, an African American congregation in very rural Hamburg, Alabama. I noticed that as the congregation sang the familiar Christmas hymn, "Joy to the World," they added some extra notes that were not in the hymn as I had learned it growing up. At the time, I thought they had learned it "wrong." Later, I realized that they simply were making the hymn their own. Contrary to most Euro-background Christians, who think there is a "right" way to sing a hymn, and a "wrong" way, African American Christians have many ways to sing the spirituals and the Gospel songs. It is the mark of a Spirit-filled African American singer, whether in the choir or in the congregation, to add notes, repeat words, lengthen the timing on an important word—not to show off, but to make it clear that the singer is not just singing words from a page, but is expressing a real faith from the depths of an expressive heart.

In my 35 years at Cross Church, I was often deeply moved by Marilyn Miller, and by others in the congregation, who would, on special days or with certain songs add a descant or repeat words and phrases while the congregation was holding a note.

The African American practice of making a hymn or a song "one's own," is one of the key features of singing a new song in our congregation. Not that we would encourage worshipers to totally do their own thing as they sing each hymn. However, congregational singing is intended to give worshipers an opportunity to express their faith, to offer genuine, heartfelt praise to God, and to edify their sisters and their brothers. The hymns and liturgies offered in a hymnal and chosen for a worship should not be selected on the basis of a particular ethnic musical standard, but with the recognition that every ethnic group has its own style of lyrics and music that have emerged over the years out of their own cultural and historical experience. Christian worship in an urban setting should reflect the cultures represented in the area.

A very basic question that should be asked by pastors and musicians and by worship committees is: What hymns and liturgies will speak to the people from this neighborhood and congregation in such a way that people will be drawn to hear more of the Gospel, and in such a way that people can identify with the music and the words? It will never happen that all the people will identify with all the hymns and with every part of the liturgy. But hopefully, there will be one song and one part of the liturgy with which most of the worshipers will be able to identify. And pastor and musicians and worship committee should be struggling to find those hymns and those liturgies that speak to different segments of the congregation and community.

Diversity in One Body

Assuming that every congregation and neighborhood has more than one ethnic income-level/generational/cultural group, it will be necessary for a worship to include a variety of hymns and liturgical forms.

It may seem that the easiest way to accommodate a congregation and community that includes African American/Latino/Anglo/Asian/Native

American/young/old, may be to decide to have different services for each group that is represented. That is a way to attempt to "please everybody."

However, there are two theological Gospel-centered principles that pull in the opposite direction and encourage congregations to "swim upstream" and work hard to plan services that purposely nudge people our of their comfort zones, services that attempt to address the cultural needs of all the groups who are represented in the congregation, or that the congregation is seeking to reach and to include in the "beloved community."

The first strong pull in the direction of a liturgy with a diversity of hymns and music is the basic principle of accompaniment. If the Gospel calls us to walk with our sisters and brothers, then the worship time is one of the most important times to walk with one another, listen to each other's shouts of praise and cries for mercy, in their own indigenous, cultural expressions. It is important to offer and to receive each other's gifts. That is a vital way of learning and growing from the other person's witness, as well as demonstrating to the other person whom we are accompanying that we care enough about them that we will walk with them at this intimate, profound part of their journey. Not to walk with them in this part of their journey runs the risk of undermining whatever witness to God's love that we are bringing to them.

The second pull toward a service that seeks to combine our various cultures, is the thrust of the Gospel that reconciles us to God and to our sisters and brothers in Christ, unifying us, forging us into the one Body of Christ. We preach and teach that we are no longer Jew nor Greek, slave nor free, male nor female, for we are all one in Christ! If there is any place that a congregation should strive to live out that barrier-shattering, unifying oneness in Christ, it should be in our worship.

The question is often asked: "Shouldn't older Anglos have some of their hymns and liturgical chants included in the worship, as well as hymns and music of the other ethnic and generational groups?" The answer is, "Yes." But "How often?" and "To what extent?" are the questions that the pastor and worship committee have to struggle with.

Certainly, every racial/ethnic group in the congregation and in the surrounding community should sense that they are included in the format of the worship. Obviously, that is easier said than done. The pastor, musician, and worship committee should not be overly concerned about criticism if they are struggling to be culturally diverse. They will not please all the people all the time. The worship planners should be especially concerned about the reaction of visitors who worship with the congregation and who will likely never verbalize their reaction to the liturgy.

It is true that even more important than the liturgy and the music, is the hospitality that members of the congregation show toward visitors. However, the hymns and the liturgy can be experienced as hospitable or inhospitable, also.

I had the privilege of preaching once in an Episcopal church, where I was welcomed by the people and sensed an eagerness on the part of the people to reach out to the neighborhood. However, I have grave doubts that an unchurched or "semi-churched" person would have felt welcomed by the hymns and the liturgy. Even though I've been around in various church cultures, I read music fairly well, and I enjoy singing, I still had great difficulty singing the liturgy, as did many of the members.

I always praise God for a warm and welcoming congregation. I give God double praise when I experience a welcoming congregation and a welcoming liturgy with hymns that heal my soul, call me to radical discipleship, and speak to the depths of my being.

This issue of singing a new song may seem to some people an issue of little consequence. Actually, it has to do with how well we communicate the Gospel, especially to those at the edges of the Church and at the edges of society, as well as to those who have grown up with no experience of congregational worship.

In the midst of the Reformation in the 1500s, Martin Luther was convinced that the liturgy and the hymns must be in the language of the people, so that people might hear the Word of God, and specifically the Gospel, and experience the spiritual life and saving grace that God wants for all the people. For Luther, that did not simply mean translating Scripture and liturgy from Latin to German or whatever the language of the people was. It also meant translating the music of the hymns and the liturgy into the music of the people. That is why Luther wrote many new hymns and used contemporary music. That is why he developed a liturgy to replace the ancient chants.

Precisely because culture, including music, is constantly changing, it is important for the Church to constantly incorporate the new songs into its liturgies, so that its powerful message of a God who loves us and gave His Son for us, and a Christ who calls us to a radical discipleship of loving our enemy and walking with the poor and loving justice and loving kindness, is a message that is heard clearly through the language and the music of our day, not muffled by a language and a music from another era and that is difficult to grasp. That is why Gloria Wright asked me some 40 years ago: "Can we sing a variety of songs if I help recruit a youth choir at Cross?"

CHAPTER 5

REACHING AND EMPOWERING YOUTH

I tell you the truth; anyone who will not receive the Kingdom of God like a little child will never enter it.

–Luke 18:17

In the spring of 1966, when I was still Pastor of St. Paul Church in Birmingham, Alabama, I received a blistering phone call from an irate congregational member of First Lutheran, the oldest white Lutheran congregation in Birmingham. "Why did you send two of your youth to our church today, to try to integrate our service?" the voice asked. "Are you just trying to start trouble?"

"Well, you may not believe this," I answered, "but I did not send Ernest Wrenn and James Nelson to your service today. In fact, I didn't even know they went until they came back with their Bible Class teacher, and told me that they had been turned away. I can assure you that they did not try to attend your service just to stir up trouble. They went because they have a dream that their own fellow Lutheran Christians would welcome them as you welcome any white visitors who come to your church door. They were hoping that you would demonstrate to your congregation and to the city of Birmingham that God looks at the human family and welcomes all people, regardless of the color of their skin."

James Nelson and Ernest Wrenn, along with their Bible Class teacher, Mary Lynn Buss, a recent college graduate and a Prince of Peace Volunteer at

The Cross Youth Choir, 27 singers strong, singing at the service of "Inauguration of Sanctuary," September 15, 1983, when Cross Church received a Guatemalan refugee into sanctuary. The centerpiece of youth programming at Cross Church for over 40 years, the Youth Choir has empowered hundreds of youth to discover and develop their gifts and to become leaders in the congregation and in the community.

St. Paul Church that year, were led by the Spirit to discover some radical things about the Gospel, that God's love calls us to live in community without racial barriers, that it calls us to take risks, that it calls us to make a public witness to bring about change.

Young people especially are open to the Spirit's work of planting new visions, of producing deep commitment, and of leading to bold action. That is part of what Jesus meant when he said that we have to become like children and youth if we are really going to catch on to what God's Kingdom of justice and love and peace and forgiveness is all about.

So it is crucial that pastors and congregations reach to our youth and empower youth, for the sake of the youths' salvation and enlightenment, for the sake of the future Church, and very importantly, for the sake of enriching the contemporary Church. That means that we do youth ministry as much to be taught as to teach. Doing youth ministry with an expectation of being nurtured and enriched, we will be amazed at how our vision is enlarged, our commitment deepened, and our joy increased. Certainly we found that to be true at St. Paul, Birmingham, and at Cross, Milwaukee.

Summer Programs for Youth

At Cross Church, summer after summer, we found that funding through federal grants, partner congregations and foundations and some registration fees from those able to pay, enabled our congregation to hire high school youth and a small cadre of dedicated teachers and college students to offer a meaningful program of activities for elementary and middle school children.

The eight-week summer programs gave summer employment to high school youth, most of them from Cross Church. The youth learned the disciplines of holding down a job. They were mentored by a teacher or a college student. They discovered what it means to be on the responsibility end of caring for younger children. They developed a sense of community as they took children on field trips in the neighborhood. They refreshed their own appreciation for academics, as they articulated the importance of getting a good educational foundation to the children they tutored. And they did all of this learning and working and growing under the aegis of Cross Church, in the Cross Church building, under the direction of many supervisors who were Cross Church members, and with a closing program in the sanctuary on a weekday and sometimes in the Sunday morning worship.

The children engaged in this eight-week summer program obviously gained much. They focused on reading, math, and science according to their own needs. They got to know their neighborhood. They enjoyed God's beautiful creation in trips to parks in the city and throughout the area. They enjoyed balanced nutritious meals, plus snacks. Many of them came to vacation Bible school that was tucked into the eight weeks or added at the end of the eight weeks.

The impact of the positive, multi-faceted summer program for youth and employing youth every summer for more than 30 years is difficult to calculate. The impact on the youth, on their families, and on Cross Church was significant.

Gloria Wright, second from the right, founded the Cross Youth Choir in 1969. Here she facilitates a meeting of choir leaders in the early 1970s to plan one of the bi-annual, two-week summer concert tours that took the singers to every part of the country, as well as Canada and Mexico. Other participants in the meeting, from the left: Joseph Ellwanger; Rose Dotson, singer, who became the accompanist during high school and college and then a medical doctor; Howette Flippin, singer, who became a teacher. On the extreme right, Marilyn Crump Miller, singer, who became director of the choir during her college years and who ultimately, in 2012, became an ordained Lutheran pastor.

Many of the youth and their families saw Cross Church as "our church," if they were not active in some other church. The program gave Cross Church a positive, pro-family, pro-community image in the larger community that exists to this day. I was at the Milwaukee City Hall one day in 2004, to make a request of a committee, and at the break, one of the committee members, a city alderman, made it a point to seek me out and asked, "Do you remember me?" I confessed in an often repeated line of mine: "I remember the face, but not the name."

"I'm Willie Wade," he said. "I worked in your summer programs for a couple of years. That's part of the reason I'm an alderman today."

Another city alderman who became President of the City Council and served as interim mayor of the City of Milwaukee for a few months, Marvin Pratt, was speaking at a public event. When he saw me in the audience, he added to his remarks: "I want to give credit where credit is due. My very first job after graduating from Marquette University was as Assistant Director of the Youth Center at Cross Lutheran Church, and Pastor Joe over there, was my mentor."

Concern for Youth

The fact that Cross Church had a reputation for concern for youth in the community already in the late 50s, when Cross still had a parochial school and was one of the first Lutheran schools to accept African American children, was an important factor in developing in the congregation a deeply-rooted interest in the enrichment of all youth, not just the youth of the congregation. When the Cross parochial school was closed for financial reasons in 1965, it was significant that the congregation employed a youth minister, John Hushman, and annually received two or three Prince of Peace Volunteers (a program of the Lutheran Church—Missouri Synod similar to the Peace Corps) for the specific purpose of maintaining youth-serving programs.

That kind of intentional interest in helping to develop the potential of all youth contributed to the development of other youth-serving programs and attracted individuals and families to Cross Church because of its reputation for being a "youth-oriented" congregation.

Gloria Wright came to Cross Church already in the mid-60s because she saw the interest of the congregation in the youth of the community. She planted a Girl Scout troop at Cross. She developed relationships with several families in the community, whose daughters formed the backbone of the Girl Scout troop. Many of those girls came to Cross Church, were baptized, confirmed, sang later in the Cross Youth Choir, and became important leaders in the congregation, in the larger Church, and in the community.

A similar story could be told of the Cub Scout and Boy Scout program that existed at Cross Church for years. The scouting programs not only pushed youth toward positive goals and self-development, but pushed the congregation to recruit and train adult leaders, without whom a scouting program cannot exist. Without a doubt, a key to some of the youth programs at Cross, particularly the Girl Scout program, and later the Youth Choir, was the persona of Gloria Wright and her many gifts. She possessed the love, the vision, the creativity, the tenacity, the integrity, the discipline, the determination, the faith, and the hope that produced the fruits of some amazing programs and brought forth the best in scores of young people.

As significant as the gifts of one person, such as Gloria Wright, are in the outreach to youth and in their development, equally important is a congregation that wholeheartedly endorses the youth outreach and programming to the extent that members of the congregation step up to the plate and become leaders in the programming and to the extent that the congregation unabashedly and creatively weaves youth ministry into the worship and the budget and the mission and the culture of the congregation.

Youth Choir, the Centerpiece

The Cross Youth Choir, started in 1969, and continuing for more than 30 consecutive years, served as a visible reminder to Cross members, every time they sang in the Sunday worship, that youth ministry was an integral part of who we were, not an add-on to the program and the budget, dependent on available dollars and on repeated votes of the Church Council.

Quite often, there is a centerpiece to youth programming in a congregation, a component of youth activities that holds the main drawing power and around which other youth activities tend to revolve. For Cross Church, that centerpiece was the Youth Choir. We had basketball teams, tutoring programs, scouting programs, summer youth programs, even a youth newsletter produced by the youth themselves. But the youth choir was the centerpiece that held most of the drawing power and that helped shape personalities and nurture youth on their way to discovering who they were and where they were going in life.

The advantage of having the Youth Choir as the centerpiece to youth programming, rather then a basketball team or even a summer youth program, was the fact that the youth choir, singing songs like *Ain't Got Time to Die* or *I'm Mighty Grateful* or *I Made a Vow*, in the midst of worship, were getting in touch with God, with God's word for their lives, with their own heritage, with the faith of the ages, with their own congregation, with the struggles of God's people, at a depth that many people never reach. The one drawback to the centrality of the Youth Choir was the turnoff that it presented to the youth who didn't have an interest in singing in a choir or who thought they didn't have the gift of singing. The choir director worked hard to communicate to the youth that no one, not even monotones, would be turned away from the choir.

There are many stories from the vast experiences of the Cross Youth Choir, especially from their many concert tours, to the West Coast, to the East Coast, to Florida, to Texas, to Canada, to small towns in Wisconsin, stories that demonstrate the powerful impact of the choir on the congregation, on the larger Church, and on the youth themselves.

One of the most powerful stories comes from the early years. The Youth Choir began singing in the Sunday worship in December, 1969. Slowly the choir drew singers and built up its repertoire. In the summer of 1971, the Lutheran Church–Missouri Synod convention was to be held in Milwaukee. There was a Sunday evening in the schedule that was purposely left open for people attending the convention to be able to "do their own thing." Members of Cross wanted to communicate to the larger Church that it was not only possible for congregations to reach out to racially changing neighborhoods, but that it was the Church's calling to do so and that it was an enriching experience not to be avoided. Somehow the idea emerged that the Cross Youth Choir should schedule a concert for that Sunday evening that was free for the delegates, in the hopes that some of them would attend the concert.

The planned concert was truly a leap of faith. There were various reasons why delegates could decide not to attend the concert: They might not get the word about it. There was another concert by a well-known Lutheran choir being offered close to the convention center. Cross Church, on the other hand, was at least a mile and a half from the center. And, above all, there were dozens of activities for the convention delegates to choose from that Sunday evening.

Amazingly though, Cross Church was filled to overflowing that hot July Sunday evening, with about 400 people, including a strong representation from the congregation and the community, and with at least 200 people from the convention.

The 20-plus members of the Cross Youth Choir were presenting their first concert and were understandably nervous about the event. But they were dressed in their dashiki robes. Their parents and Cross supporters were present. And the sanctuary, including the balcony, was packed. They sang their hearts out all the way through to the last song, "To Be Young, Gifted and Black." They sang that last song with such fervor and conviction, after a diverse program of folk songs, black spirituals, Gospel songs, and traditional hymns sung to a new beat, that the audience spontaneously stood and gave the choir a thunderous ovation that seemed to last at least two or three minutes.

The youth in the choir knew before that evening that they were youth and that most of them were black. But what they really discovered that evening was that they were gifted and that they did not have any reason to be ashamed of being young or black. As a matter of fact, they could be proud of that.

We reminded the youth again and again of what they learned that hot summer night, that they were truly gifted, and we challenged them to continue to develop those gifts and to use them for the common good of all. Gloria Wright, Marilyn Crump Miller, and the youth choir directors after them, were constantly challenging choir members to assume responsibility for themselves, for the choir, for the congregation, and for God's world.

We realized that if we wanted youth to be leaders of tomorrow, we needed to give them leadership opportunities today. We encouraged youth to serve on all the committees of the congregation, and we added two slots to the 12 slots on the Board of Elders that would be reserved specifically for youth to serve as full-fledged Elders. We saw a bit of humor in adding youth to a board that seemed to be reserved only for "elders." But we realized that elders do not have a monopoly on wisdom and faith and love. Furthermore, we saw the need to train youth in the discipline and the experience of leading in all aspects of worship and in spiritual care and concern for sisters and brothers in Christ, which describes the main responsibility of the Elders at Cross Church. So youth and adults, members and non-members, who gather for worship at Cross, see youth reading the lessons, leading in prayer, serving Communion, and assisting the pastor and other Elders in the awesome responsibilities of leading in worship. Such participation in the total life and responsibilities of the congregation definitely gives youth a sense of belonging, a sense of ownership, and a deeper opportunity to hear the call of the Spirit in their own lives.

Youth in Recovery

As effective and significant as summer youth programs and a youth choir might be in a congregation, such activities must not be seen as the be-all and end-all of a congregation's outreach to youth. There are too many youth in the congregation, and specifically in the larger community, who still need to be reached with relevant programs that meet their interests and their needs. What is needed, of course, is an adult or two who see the need, have a vision, and whose faith and passion move them into action.

One day in the early 1990s, Cheryl Hayes, a member of Cross, came to me with her discernment and vision. She was a parent who saw the struggles of her own children when she had been a substance abuser and consequently emotionally detached from her children precisely when they needed her. Now that she was in recovery, she saw the damage that had happened to her children, and she saw the damage that was happening to children in similar circumstances, in her extended family, in the congregation, and especially in the community. Her vision was to offer children and youth with a parent, close relative or friend, who was addicted to alcohol or other drugs, to be able to come together and share their frustrations, their anxieties, and their discoveries in an accepting atmosphere, under the guidance of a sensitive, knowledgeable adult, and in a setting where youth could trust that their stories and concerns would go no further than the group.

The result of Cheryl's vision was the formation of a group that called themselves PEPCI (Persons Expressing Problems Challenging Ideas). The group was similar to Ala-Teen and met weekly for the purpose of venting personal tensions, receiving support and love, and gaining strength and perspective to continue on their journey of education and spiritual and emotional growth. Their closing prayer at the end of each meeting was the famous "Serenity Prayer," used throughout the recovery community:

> *God, grant me the serenity to accept the things I cannot change, the courage to change the things I can, and the wisdom to know the difference.*

Sponsoring a group like PEPCI, of course, is bringing young people together in the church building, who come from a variety of backgrounds, from rather solid families (but where there is a substance abuse issue) to very dysfunctional families, and from youth working hard on their educational pursuits to youth caught up in gangs and experimenting with drugs themselves. The explosive situations that can result from such a diverse group are challenging for the youth themselves, for the adult facilitators, and for members of the congregation. However none can deny that it is precisely youth who are caught up in the drug culture, because of a substance-abusing parent or a drug-abusing/drug-pushing peer group member, who should be the object of concern on the part of a congregation or people centering their lives in the Gospel.

CHOICES and Challenges

It was in the late 1980s that Venice (pronounced "Venus") Williams came to Cross Church as Youth Director. She had all but finished her academic work at Valparaiso University in the School of Deaconess Ministry. An African American woman who had grown up in Pittsburgh in the one Lutheran congregation located in the African American community, Venice was full of energy and of the Spirit. She had a heart for the Gospel, for the Church, for the African American community, for racial diversity and equality, for youth, for women, for the whole human family. We had made initial contact with each other at Valparaiso University when she showed up at a forum on the significance of the Sanctuary Movement of the 1980s, a forum where I was a speaker. On behalf of Cross Church, I invited her to test the waters in youth ministry at Cross Church.

Venice came to Cross and poured herself into youth ministry, and the whole ministry, at Cross for over five years, before she moved to a position in youth ministry with the Urban Coalition of the Greater Milwaukee Synod of the Evangelical Lutheran Church in America. As a result of her passion for youth, especially youth at the edges, Venice instituted some programs that are still in existence at Cross and other urban congregations in Milwaukee.

A program that bears the stamp of Venice's passion and creativity and that has been spawned in other congregations is CHOICES, a program designed especially for middle school and high school girls, whose choices during those adolescent years are so pivotal for shaping the rest of their lives.

CHOICES is designed to give adolescent girls the opportunity to sit down together around a healthy meal, prepared by youth and adults, served on brightly designed china and on lively decorated tables, and then have conversation with each other and with invited guests about topics that are crucial for teenage girls to know about and talk about, hot topics that seldom get discussed in the bright sunlight of a caring, truthful, enriching setting. The experience of engaging in healthy conversation and building relationships around a tasty, nutritious meal is designed to give girls a taste of positive, quality, family time together, an experience that many youth, in middle-income families as well as low-income families, often do not have. It is hoped that girls who experience the nurturing power of such table talk will continue the practice in their own families when they have made that big choice of having a family.

A spin-off out of the CHOICES program at Cross was the launching of a similar program called "Challenges," offered to boys in the same age range. The program is not exactly the same as CHOICES. It lacks the emphasis on the table setting with the brightly designed china, but the basic elements of food and sit-down conversation with each other, with a guest, centered on topics of crucial importance to middle/high school boys growing up in the "hood," is at the heart of the program. Finding the men who would take on the responsibility of such a regular, weekly program was no small challenge. But Craig Dent, Wayne Porter, and Michel Copeland stepped up to the plate and continued to reach out to boys in the congregation and in the community for several years. It is not coincidence that two of the three leaders are men who grew up at Cross Church and were nurtured by the scouting program, youth retreats, the Youth Choir, the summer programs, and Youth Confirmation.

Both the CHOICES and Challenges programs are envisioned and implemented with outreach to youth at the edges in mind. Milwaukee has one of the highest teen pregnancy rates and high school dropout rates in the country. Both of those facts should compel people whose lives are centered in the Good News of God's love for all people, to reach out to youth who don't believe that their lives are valuable and who often think that marriage and a job are highly unlikely and that they may not reach the age of 20 because of the high level of violence in their community. CHOICES and Challenges are two proven models, among others, that can enable congregations to actually walk with young people who are truly at the edges.

Youth Work Program

Another youth outreach and empowerment model used by several congregations of the Lutheran Coalition is the youth work program. The number of youth involved varies according to the amount of funding that congregations are able to collect and to allocate to the program. Usually the numbers are 20 to 40 youth.

The youth programs vary from congregation to congregation, but they concentrate especially in the summer months with 10 to 20 hours of work per week. The expectations of the middle/high school youth who work in the program are high. There are incentives and sanctions on such things as reporting for work on time, quality and quantity of work, attitude toward work and toward supervisors and fellow workers, and participation in Sunday worship and youth Bible class.

Besides nurturing positive work habits and a positive attitude toward holding down a job, the youth work programs provide many other values for the youth, the congregation, and the community. Much of the work that is done is lawn care for senior residents in the neighborhood and beautifying vacant lots and public areas around the church, thus building a sense of community pride and belonging among the youth and forging relationships between youth, congregation, and community.

Usually there is heavy investment of time on the part of the pastor in the program, thus giving the pastor an opportunity to walk with youth in another setting besides Confirmation.

Most of the youth work programs have strict guidelines on how much of the money will be paid out on "pay day" and how much will be put aside in a savings account that is accessible at the end of summer, to enable youth and parents to purchase back-to-school clothes and supplies. There is also an educational element in the program nudging youth to develop a sense of stewardship of money, teaching them how much to set aside for God, for savings, for school needs, and for personal recreation.

Tutoring Program

After-school tutoring programs are also excellent avenues for reaching youth at the edges, to meet real needs of young people, to provide human links with partner congregations, and to provide positive activities for young people who otherwise might be hooking up with the wrong people at the wrong time.

As clear as the rationale for after-school tutoring is, we found out at Cross Church over the years that the challenges and the obstacles are ever-present in the midst of the great opportunities. Getting students to the program on a regular basis is a rock-bottom challenge, and the next biggest challenge is motivating the students to believe in themselves and in the possibility and the joy of learning. Obviously the ability, the creativity, the dependability, the experience, and the unconditional love of the tutors is essential, along with appropriate and exciting materials and an atmosphere that inspires and re-assures students day after day that they can learn and that there are amazing rewards, immediate and long-range, that await every person who actively travels the journey of study and learning.

It is impossible to carry out an effective after-school tutoring program without developing an ongoing relationship between the congregation and the local elementary school, its principal, and the teachers. What a wonderful occasion it is when congregation and school discover the mutual enrichment that can happen when congregation and school walk together and work together. The school advertises the after-school tutoring program. Teachers and tutors communicate with each other. Children discover that there are people out there who care about them. The needs of teachers and students show up in the congregational prayers. The congregational justice committee advocates for certain changes or budget needs that benefit the school. It is amazing what happens when a congregation and a neighborhood school actively work together on behalf of the education of children, especially those who are struggling with the learning process.

Venice Williams, the Director of Youth Ministry at Cross Church for several years, was the coordinator of the after-school tutoring program there. In that capacity, she often went to the local Siefert School to visit the classrooms of students in the tutoring program. The children invariably brightened up and enthusiastically welcomed her presence in the classroom. The relationship between student and tutor, in this case, Venice Williams, was deepened. Motivating the students in the tutoring program became measurably easier. And relationships were forged between students and Venice Williams that lasted for years.

Confirmation Class

Whatever the youth outreach or youth empowerment program might be in a congregation, one of the "signature" youth programs of a congregation must be the youth confirmation class. Unfortunately youth confirmation classes have gotten a bad rap among many pastors. It is at the bottom of the priority list, or the enjoyability list, of many pastors. There may be as many reasons for this as there are pastors. My hunch is that many confirmation classes are filled with youth who are more pushed there by parents than drawn there by an inner desire for spiritual growth. That is not to knock parental expectations and encouragement, especially from parents who are examples of spiritual growth enthusiasts themselves.

There are ways to forge the youth confirmation class culture in a congregation to be the positive, life-giving, community-building, leadership-nurturing, identity-clarifying, commitment-strengthening, vision-raising, rite of passage that it can be in the eyes of the congregation and the youth.

It is very Lutheran and very Christian to plan the Confirmation class experience as a Scripture-anchored time together, a rare time of the week for most youth, when deep questions are raised and Scripture is turned to, as though it is the deep well of spiritual truth and fresh water for parched throats and dehydrated spirits that it truly is. With 45 youth Confirmation classes under my belt, in two urban, predominately black, congregations, I can say that youth usually approach Scripture with a sense of expectation when the study is facilitated with a sense of awe and expectation and with relevant, probing questions.

The more diverse the Confirmation class, the more interesting and exciting the sessions together can be. The diversity can include such variables as youth from single-parent and two-parent households, youth from families where neither parent is connected with the congregation, youth from middle-income and low-income households, youth from different racial/ethnic backgrounds. The recruitment that would produce such diversity would have to be carried out intentionally by youth leaders and pastor among all the youth programs connected with the congregation.

Youth confirmation in the traditional Lutheran congregation is a process and a part of the congregational culture that is actually on a par with Baptism in the minds of some of the third- and fourth-generation members. And among those who recognize that Baptism is definitely more important than Confirmation, there still is built into their Lutheran culture the conviction that youth Confirmation is an important milestone, yes, a "rite of passage." After all, it is that moment when a baptized child who has been nourished on the Word of God, stands up before the congregation and testifies to the faith that is within them.

For a non-traditional Lutheran congregation, such as a predominantly African American congregation, however, youth Confirmation is often not seen as such a vital part of the spiritual growth process of young people. Consequently, it takes some intentional effort to build youth Confirmation into the fabric of the congregational self-image.

Early in the 1970s already, we developed the practice at Cross Church of having each confirmand prepare and present a personal testimony to his or her faith in Christ, based on a specific Bible verse, in the worship the Sunday before their actual Confirmation. This practice required some struggles for all the youth. There was the struggle of "What do I really believe?" And "How do I put it into words?" And "Can I really say this before the entire congregation?"

The practice also required some extra time on the part of the pastor. It meant at least one, sometimes two or three sessions with each confirmand, to help the young person probe the meaning of the Bible verse for his or her life and to lead the confirmand to write it out in a clear, articulate manner. I found, however, that the sessions with each confirmand gave me an excellent opportunity to talk with each youth on an individual level in a way that was never possible in the midst of the class session.

We also developed the practice of each Confirmation class planning, designing, and crafting a banner with a theme, thought up and voted on by the class, and then displaying the first names of each confirmand very prominently on the banner.

I remember some of the themes on the banners: "We're high on Christ." "Growing in the Spirit." "We've come this far by Faith." "Strengthened by Fire." "Overcoming Violence Working for Peace." "We're the light of the World." "Fill my Cup." "Alive in the Spirit." "I made a Vow."

When Pentecost, the day of Confirmation, arrived, the banner would be hung near the altar for everyone to see, and the banners from the previous four years would be brought out of storage and hung up along the sides of the sanctuary. The banners would remain for every worshiper to see for at least three months. The banners, with the names of all the youth emblazoned on them, gave each confirmand an added sense of his or her importance in the Body of Christ at Cross. And congregational members had their memories jogged regarding the names and the importance of the youth.

Learning From Youth: Birgmingham 1963

It was September 15, 1963, in Birmingham, Alabama. We had gotten the heartbreaking, stunning word between Sunday School and worship, that the Sixteenth Street Baptist Church had been dynamited and that four girls had been killed, including Denise McNair, the daughter of our Sunday School Superintendent, Chris McNair. In a state of shock, we went ahead with the worship. I was leading the youth choir up the steps from the fellowship hall to the sanctuary for the processional, when I overheard conversation among the youth behind me. "I wonder whether they'll try to blow up our church?" asked one of the youth. "They can't do that," another responded, "we haven't been confirmed yet." Still another youth got her theology right and added: "But we have been baptized."

Actually, I was proud of all three of the young people, who were expressing some important aspects of their faith. The first youth expressed a sense of real concern for the Church and the gathering of believers. The second youth expressed appreciation for Confirmation. And the third youth clearly recognized that Baptism is the sacrament that gives us assurance that we belong to God.

It is this amazing depth of faith in children and youth that Jesus was referring to when he said that we need to receive the kingdom of God like a little child, or we'll never grasp it or really enter it. Recognizing the depth of faith, and the depth of discernment, of children and youth, congregations would be the richer and the stronger if they regularly and intentionally had ways of tapping that faith and listening to the witness of the youth.

One of the ways to share that witness of young people with the congregation I discovered somewhere along the way, and I know other pastors have discovered it as well. I would regularly ask the members of the youth Confirmation class a question that would draw on their faith view. I would ask each class member to write down their personal response. We would talk about the responses in class. And then the next Sunday, I would share some of their responses as part of the sermon. What a wonderful way to share the witness of young people with the congregation. The responses of the youth often astonished the members of the congregation. Not only did the testimonies of the youth enrich the faith of the congregation, they gave those who were really listening a deeper understanding of a day in the life of a youth, what youth think about, what they experience, what they are troubled by, and what they believe and hope for.

I had the youth respond to such questions as: “What can you do to help Milwaukee overcome violence and become a more peaceful city?” “Think of an adult in our congregation whom you love and respect and explain why that person means so much to you.” “How would you answer, if some person at your school asked you why you go to church or to Confirmation class or sing in the choir?”

I will never forget the witness of youth shared at Hephatha Church, Milwaukee, inspired by Pastor Mary Martha Kannass, in her children's sermon the Sunday before Martin Luther King’s birthday. After talking with her students about King’s “I Have a Dream” speech, she had asked them to think about the kind of world they thought God wants and the kind of world they dream about.

All of the answers were deep and revealing. I cannot forget three of the answers: “I dream of a world where every child can walk to school and to the store without being afraid of being shot.” “I dream of a world where every child knows who their father is.” “I dream of a world where there is no war.” How rich is a congregation who is reaching out to youth, walking with youth, listening to youth. Its members are catching a glimpse of the Kingdom of God.

CHAPTER 6

RAISING UP LEADERS

We have different gifts, according to the grace given us. If a person's gift is prophesying, let them use it in proportion to their faith. If it is serving, let them serve. If it is encouraging, let them encourage. If it is contributing to the needs of others, let them give generously. If it is leadership, let them lead with zeal. If it is showing mercy let them do it cheerfully.

–Romans 12:6-8

I was leading worship in the absence of Pastor Mary Martha Kannass at Hephatha Church, three years into my retirement from full-time parish ministry. We were singing the opening hymn, when Roxanne Tally, a sophomore at Mt. Mary College in Milwaukee, sat down next to me in the front pew and whispered in my ear, "I'm ready to read the first or second lesson, if one of the readers doesn't show up."

I was struck by the fact that this college sophomore was in church on a Sunday morning during the school year. But I was even more amazed that this young woman felt that much responsibility toward the congregational worship that she would offer to help out as a reader, if needed.

So two weeks later, when she and I showed up to walk in the Martin Luther King Scholarship All-a-thon, I decided I would walk with her and do an extended conversation to get to know her. She was very willing to talk with this septuagenarian, so we walked and we talked the entire five miles on that bright sunshiny Milwaukee Saturday morning in May. And my amazement grew.

"Do you have brothers and sisters who have gone on to college?" I asked.

"Well, I do have a brother and three sisters," she answered, "three of them older than me. But I am the first from my family to even graduate form high school."

"I am impressed," I said. "What is it that motivated you to finish high school and to go on to college when no one else in your family is on that track?"

"I've always wanted to make something of myself," she answered. "At first I wanted to become a lawyer because I thought I could help people that way. But now I'm preparing to become a nurse."

"What made you change your mind?" I asked

"When I started coming to Hephatha Church," she responded, "I saw how people care about each other and how we're constantly praying for people who are ill and people with problems. So I've decided I want to become a nurse, probably a pediatric nurse."

"I can't help but notice how you offered to read one of the lessons the Sunday I was leading worship," I continued. "And I noticed how you assist Pastor Mary Martha. You are definitely a leader. Is there anyone in particular at Hephatha Church who has had a strong influence on you?"

I expected Roxanne to probably name Pastor Mary Martha, who has a strong, personal relationship with all the youth at Hephatha. Instead, she responded quickly by naming Mrs. Wilson.

"Do you mean Hazel Wilson?" I asked, "Or do you mean her daughter, Sandra?" Hazel Wilson was an 80-year-old woman who had great difficulty negotiating the steps at Hephatha, but she was there every Sunday in her appointed spot, fourth pew from the front next to the center aisle, left side, until she simply was not able to get to church at all.

"Hazel Wilson," Roxanne continued. "When I was a junior in high school, soon after I started coming to Hephatha, Mrs. Wilson came to me and asked me whether I would help her prepare Communion each Sunday. I considered it an honor that she asked me. I knew how important Communion is in our worship at Hephatha. So I've been coming every Sunday before service to get Communion ready, especially now that Mrs. Wilson isn't able to do it."

"Not only are you a leader at Hephatha," I continued, "I understand that you are a leader at Mt. Mary College. Did I hear correctly that you are on the student council and that you ran for president of the student body this year?"

"That's right." Roxanne's face brightened as she spoke with a sense of pride. "Although I was only a sophomore, I ran against two juniors, and lost by only six votes. I'm sure I can make it next year."

The conversation went on and on, on that bright Saturday morning. No doubt about it. Roxanne Tally was emerging as a real leader, at Hephatha Church, in her family, at Mt. Mary College, in the world.

The Gift of Leadership

Part of the mission of the Church, and especially in urban congregations, is to raise up leaders, to empower people who think they have no power, to discover their power, and to use their power for the building up of the Body of Christ, and for the common good of all.

All through his letters to the first-generation Christians, Paul talks about the gifts God has given to every believer, and he constantly urges his readers to recognize those gifts, develop those gifts, and then use those gifts to build up the Body of Christ and to do the work of the Lord.

In Romans 12:8, Paul mentions "leadership" as one of the many gifts God has given to the people of God. And if someone has that gift of leadership, Paul urges them to exercise that gift "with zeal," not halfheartedly.

Paul may have in mind in Romans 12:8, the gift of leadership in the formal sense of presiding over a church council or committee or even leading worship, but the gift of "leadership" is much more expansive than that. In the broad sense, leadership is a gift given to every baptized Christian and to every person. It is that gift that often lies fallow in our lives, but it can be stirred to life and to action. It is that gift that enables a person to step forward, finish high school, and go on to college, when no one else in the family has graduated from 12th grade. It is that gift that moves a teenager to get to church a half hour earlier than almost everyone else to make sure the Communion elements are ready for congregational worship. It is that gift that moves an African American college sophomore to run for president of a student body that is predominately white. It is that gift that propels a college student to get up on a Saturday morning to participate in a five-mile walk to raise funds for Martin Luther King scholarships for central-city students.

There is no doubt that Roxanne Tally is a young woman who has discovered the leadership gift in her, and she is using that gift in some amazing ways. A very important question to probe is: "How did it happen that against all odds, she has broken through the barriers that are keeping thousands of young people from discovering, affirming, and using that same leadership gift that is inside of them?"

Without exception, every leader has had some important person(s) in his or her life who have recognized those gifts and encouraged that person to develop those gifts and to use those gifts in a very specific way. In Roxanne's case, it was a great-grandmother, who in a seemingly "small" moment of Roxanne's life, asked Roxanne to help her in a very important task connected with congregational worship. Who'd have thought that an "ordinary" non-professional woman, two generations distant from a girl with very limited horizons in her growing-up years, would have such an impact on a high school teenager's sense of self-worth and the development of her gift of leadership?

Hazel Wilson reminds us that every adult Christian has the potential and the responsibility of developing relationships with children and youth for the purpose of receiving their witness and, when the right moment of discernment arrives, to also encourage and call forth the gifts that we recognize in them. Pastors especially have this opportunity and responsibility.

Hazel Wilson was not the only factor in motivating Roxanne to become a leader at Hephatha Church. There was a caring pastor, Mary Martha Kannass, and a whole congregation of people who regularly live and breathe hospitality and affirmation and caregiving toward everyone, and especially toward children and youth. There was a pastor and a congregation who let Roxanne know that she was appreciated as she helped prepare Communion Sunday after Sunday, as she read one of the lessons in her own energetic, passionate manner, and as she assisted the pastor in leading worship. It was that caregiving culture of Hephatha congregation, after all, that convinced Roxanne to choose a career of nursing over her original choice of becoming a lawyer.

There is still a third factor in Roxanne's life that contributed to her leadership development. She participated in the Hephatha youth work program. In the youth work program, she worked at various jobs, especially helping to clean up yards and to plant flowers for senior citizens living near the church, and she helped clean the church and the church grounds. For Roxanne, this work gave her a feeling of contributing to the congregation and community and also nurtured a sense of pride in belonging to the church and the neighborhood, a solid foundation for wanting to be a leader.

Raising Up Another Leader: Craig Dent

Craig Dent started attending Cross Church in 1974, as a seven-year-old, when his older sister, Tracy, brought him with her to Sunday School. (Tracy had begun attending Cross at the invitation and encouragement of "Auntie" Virginia Walker Riley, the pied piper who was responsible for bringing two or three dozen family members and community contacts to Cross Church.) His journey at Cross Church is helpful in understanding some of the many dynamics involved in raising up leaders for the Church and the community.

Raised by his hard-working mother, along with his older sister and brother, in the Parklawn Housing Project, Craig quickly found Sunday School, and a little later, Junior and Senior Confirmation class, to be the spiritual nurturing and the peer group experience that fed his soul and provided the positive community that every growing child needs, especially if the pull of the neighborhood is to the streets and to the gangs. In a conversation with Craig, in his mid-forties, he called up the names of Wayne Porter, Joel Ellwanger, Rexanne Andrews, and a dozen other contemporaries who were essential, he said, in keeping him on a positive path through his challenging adolesence and early twenties. His participation in the Cross Youth Choir, the cross-country choir tours, the youth retreats, the YES (Youth Ever Serving) Group activities, the Cross summer youth program, the Sunday youth Bible class, and the Sunday morning worship were very formative, he added, in keeping those positive relationships growing, in broadening his horizons, and in developing his determination to be a leader in the congregation and in the community.

After graduating from high school, Craig completed two years at the University of Wisconsin-Whitewater and continued after that to take classes at Milwaukee Area Technical College. He married Trisha Brown in 1993, and together they deepened their relationships with old and new members.

As he searched for the right job to fit his gifts and his desire to serve his community, Craig worked various jobs—as a store clerk, machinist and as an aide at a rehab hospital. In 1996, Wayne Porter, a friend of Craig's from youth confirmation class days and a faithful member of Cross, suggested that Craig could live out his faith and serve young men and women from the community if he were to become guard at a local state prison. He applied for the job and passed with flying colors. He's worked in that capacity at the Milwaukee Secure Detention Facility since 1996. He says it's more than a job for him. "I really want to help men and women get past their tough starts in life, their bad choices and addictions," he states, "and get on the right path. I want them to know that they can be successful, even when it seems impossible."

When asked to serve on the Board of Elders in 1998, Craig said he would be honored to serve in that upfront spiritual leadership role because he knows firsthand how important Cross Church has been in his life and how formative the Gospel and the community of believers can be for any child, youth, or adult. After 15 years of continuous service on the Board of Elders, reading Scripture in the Sunday worship, serving Communion, visiting the homebound, Craig continues to serve in that vital role. "Among other things," he says, "I want boys and young men to see that God and church and Bible study are as cool for men as for women."

In 2001, when I saw Craig's deep concern for boys growing up in the poverty pockets of Milwaukee's central city, I asked him whether he would be willing to work with two or three other men to launch a weekly gathering for middle school and high school young men, from the community as well as the congregation. "The purpose of the group," I said, "would be to give the young men a safe place to talk over questions and problems, with input from slightly older men who have navigated the rough waters of adolescence in the 'hood.'" Not only did Craig accept the challenge, but he stuck with it for ten years.

There is no one factor by itself that led Craig to believe in Christ, to see his worth before God and his gifts, to be ready to take leadership in the congregation and in the community. But the love of his mother and older sister, the witness of "Auntie" Virginia, the formational experience of the two years of Confirmation classes, the positive experience and discipline of singing in the Youth Choir, the serving activities in the summer youth program and the YES Group, the personal counsel of a friend and brother in Christ, and the regular rhythm of the weekly gathering of the Gospel community at Cross, served as a channel for the Spirit to raise up Craig as a leader, hopefully for the rest of his life.

Lois Glover: A Leader in the Congregation and Community

A social service worker, Lois Glover worked hard, along with her husband, during the 1960s, '70s, and '80s and into the '90s, to see that their four children not only finished high school, but graduated from college as well. Lois's parents were both teachers in Arkansas. She grew up with a strong experience in a Baptist congregation, with a heavy emphasis on the importance of a college education, and with a clear example of a daily work ethic.

After an uncertain start at Cross Church, Lois returned to the congregation in the late '60s, where she saw a strong youth program emerging and the congregation becoming involved in social justice issues. She saw the Church, and Cross Church in particular, as an important nurturing community for her family and as a beacon of justice and hope for a neighborhood with economic and educational challenges. She invested herself in a leadership capacity at Cross Church, serving on the Board of Elders, on the Social Ministry Committee, and on the Caregivers Committee. A believer in the nurturing power of the Word and in the importance of building community, she was a regular participant in the Sunday morning Bible Class.

Lois Glover always had a sensitive conscience and regularly expressed anger over injustices and violence that happened in the city, or anywhere in the world. She spoke regularly at Bible classes and at Social Ministry Committee meetings about the rising toll of drugs and crime in the community, the lack of family-supporting jobs, and the difficulty that ex-offenders returning from incarceration have in finding housing and jobs. She was incensed that the government can find money for prisons and wars and yet has difficulty coming up with funding for education and drug treatment. She was a woman who looked at the world around her and felt deeply that much should be changed.

When Lois heard that Cross Church would be one of the eight founding congregations in MICAH, an interfaith organization of congregations that would work on justice issues, she was one of the first members of Cross to get involved. She helped form Cross's MICAH Core Team and quickly became its chairperson. She went to MICAH trainings and to the week-long training of the Gamaliel network to strengthen her leadership skills to better understand the finer points of organizing people and money to bring about change.

A firm believer in working hard on anything worthwhile, Lois worked very hard to organize members of Cross to work with other MICAH members on such campaigns as shutting down drug houses, negotiating with banks to set aside $500 million for home buyers in the central city, and securing more City of Milwaukee jobs for central city residents. She worked especially hard at getting as many as 100 members of Cross to participate in the annual MICAH public meeting, where 1,200 MICAH members gather to celebrate victories, lift up leaders, and call public officials to accountability on various issues.

It was not surprising that WISDOM, the state-wide organization MICAH was part of, selected Lois Glover as president in 2003. In that capacity, she presided over Executive Committee meetings and led large WISDOM rallies in Madison. She spoke at one very large Rolling Thunder rally in Milwaukee in 2004, with nearly 4,000 participants, urging people to "value their vote and vote their values" in the 2004 presidential/congressional elections.

I'm sure that Lois Glover never dreamed of leading a statewide organization composed of 130 congregations and 100,000 members. She undoubtedly never thought that she would be addressing audiences numbering 500 and 1,000 and 4,000. But she carried out her leadership responsibilities thoughtfully, prayerfully, and competently. After all, she had arrived at this point in her journey of leadership step by step: from thoughtful parenting to dedicated social service work to assisting in worship to carrying Communion to shut-ins to chairing the Cross MICAH Core Team to turning out 100 Cross members for public meetings, to rallying hundreds and thousands to speak and act and vote for justice.

It was Lois Glover following the Spirit's lead. And once again, it was nurturing parents with high expectations, and a congregation who encouraged leadership training and development, that brought that latent leadership gift in Lois Glover, to full fruition.

Empowering People

Although the stories of Roxanne Tally, Lois Glover, and Craig Dent are amazing stories of leadership development, there are hundreds of other such stories at Cross Church and Hephatha Church and other congregations that may not be quite as eye-catching, but are equally miraculous and

Spirit-led. There are many who thought they had few, if any, gifts, who saw themselves as having very little to give others, and powerless to change anything, who discovered along their journey that they had many gifts, that they had much to give to others, and that they even had the power to make changes in themselves and in the world around them.

Developing people's gifts, especially the gift of leadership, is not an insignificant dimension of the mission of the local congregation. It is one of the major thrusts of every program of the congregation: youth programming, committees, boards, auxiliaries, councils, choirs, and ministries. Each of these congregational components has goals to fulfill, and one of the goals must be the development of the gifts of everyone involved. As pastors and congregational leaders evaluate the accomplishments of each program, they should evaluate the development of the gifts of the participants.

"Empowering people" (raising up leaders, developing the gifts of the people) is a major goal of organizing. It could just as accurately be a key phrase in the mission statement of a congregation. I believe that's what Jesus had in mind for his 12 disciples. And that's what he has in mind for all his disciples today.

CHAPTER 7

OVERCOMING SEXISM: THE ONGOING SAGA

In the last days, God says, I will pour out my Spirit on all people. Your sons and your daughters will prophesy, your young men will see visions, your old men will dream dreams. Even on my servants, both men and women, I will pour out my Spirit in those days, and they will prophesy.

– Acts 2:17-18

I had been pastor at Cross Church about three years when our congregation received notice in 1971, from the President of the South Wisconsin District of the Lutheran Church–Missouri Synod (LCMS), the church body Cross Church belonged to at the time, that our congregation was in danger of being dropped from membership in the LCMS, and I was in danger of being removed from the clergy roll. We had transgressed against two important rules of membership. First, we had invited Reverend Ernest Glenn, Pastor of Christ Presbyterian Church, located three blocks from Cross Church, to preach at our joint Thanksgiving service. Such ecumenical worship according to LCMS practice was forbidden, since the LCMS was not in "doctrinal fellowship" with the Presbyterian Church USA.

Secondly, Cross Church had elected women to serve on the Board of Elders. Elders in the LCMS tradition assist the pastor in leading in worship, distributing Communion, and carrying out pastoral visitations. According to LCMS practice, only men are permitted to do pastoral work.

So the congregation had to decide whether we were going to back off these two courses of action, or whether we would move ahead with these plans, and

Marilyn Miller narrates a special reading at the Declaration of Sanctuary service, at Cross Church, Sept 15, 1983. She was Director of the Cross Youth Choir at the time. Her journey at Cross Church began as a Girl Scout in the 1960s and led to ordination as a Lutheran pastor in 2012.

risk loss of membership in the LCMS and loss of the financial subsidy we were receiving from the South Wisconsin District of the LCMS.

The Church Council, after prayerful discussion, decided that both of these courses of action had a Biblical basis and were in keeping with the mission of our congregation: to proclaim and to live the Good News of God's love in Jesus Christ to as many people as possible, as effectively as possible. So we decided that we would take risks for the sake of the Gospel and not reverse our decisions.

Women in the Church

Passing up the matter of ecumenical work and worship, which will be considered in another chapter, the focus here is on the other issue: the role of women in the Church. I am tempted to let the topic go, because the predecessor bodies of the Evangelical Lutheran Church in America, as well as most Christian denominations, approved women's ordination in the latter half of the twentieth century, and it seems that the issue has been resolved. But nothing could be further from the truth. Overcoming sexism is still an ongoing saga in the Church and in the world.

In all of the denominations that have approved women's ordination, there are still congregations who will not consider calling a woman pastor. There are still girls and young women who are growing up in congregations and never witnessing a woman leading the worship, administering the sacraments, proclaiming the Word. There are entire denominations that do not permit women's ordination.

Furthermore, it is crucial that the Church understand and remember how it came about that entire denominations were radically transformed in regard to the role of women in the Church. If we are going to be open to radical transformation now and in the future, we dare never forget how transformation of monumental proportions has recently taken place and is taking place in many congregations now.

A small step that Cross Church took on its journey of overcoming sexism was to elect women to the Board of Elders. A very small step indeed. But we were suddenly challenged by the LCMS District leaders to be sure that this was more than simply going along with the flow of the cultural changes taking place in the country in the '70s. The threat to drop Cross Church from membership in a church body that Cross had belonged to since Cross's beginning in 1870, and a Church body that was now providing a financial subsidy to help us maintain a Gospel witness in the central city of Milwaukee, pushed us to be as certain as is humanly possible, that this was the right thing to do, not in spite of our faith in Christ and in the Gospel, but because of it.

As we looked at Scripture, it seemed clear that the New Testament Church, though it was emerging in the midst of a patriarchal, male-led culture, was preaching and practicing a new culture in the Church that affirms male/ female equality and was beginning to encourage and accept the gifts of women as readily as it encouraged and accepted the gifts of men.

It was the apostle Peter who was the main preacher on that first Pentecost Sunday (Acts 2). He quoted the Old Testament prophet Joel in that radical Pentecost sermon: "Even on my servants, both men and women, I will pour out my Spirit in those days, and they will prophesy." Acts 2:18. The term "prophesy" in the Bible does not refer to predicting the future as much as it refers to publicly proclaiming God's Word and applying it to people's lives. Women, as well as men, according to Peter, can expect to be filled with the Holy Spirit, and the Church should be ready to accept Spirit-filled women who are gifted and called to "prophesy," to proclaim the Word of God publicly.

Although Jesus' 12 disciples were all men, he had many women followers with whom he engaged in theological conversation and who were affirmed for their faith and their witness, such as the Samaritan woman at the well, Mary and Martha, the woman healed of the issue of blood, and the Syro-Phoenician mother whose faith was greater than he had found in Israel. One of the women disciples of Jesus, Mary Magdalene, was directed by the risen Lord to take the crucial message of his resurrection to the 12 disciples.

Paul is given credit for being a first-generation Church leader who caught the amazing vision of the Gospel that calls into being a new community that shatters society's walls of race and class and gender. In Paul's letter to the churches in Galatia, he writes one of his most radical descriptions of the unifying and equalizing power of the Gospel: "All of you who were baptized into Christ have clothed yourselves with Christ. There is neither Jew nor Greek, slave nor free, male nor female, for you are all one in Christ Jesus." (Galatians 3:27-28.) The Church has struggled for 20 centuries to live into the truth of that vision. That soaring eloquence of Paul's was not simply a poetic statement for hymn writers to put to music. It is the description of how the Church is to transcend society's barriers and it is the power to become that new community.

We were convinced by the Spirit at Cross Church in 1971, that God had given several women the gifts to help lead in worship, to care for the sick, and to pray with and for God's people, the gifts expected of the Elders of the Church. And so we had a sound biblical basis, we insisted, for continuing with women on the Board of Elders.

Besides the Scriptural basis for women Elders, many on the Cross Church Council added another stone to the foundation of our position. It might be called the historical/cultural/reality stone. "Look at how many families in our congregation are headed by single women," a member of the parish council stated. "Women raise their children, support their families, make big and little decisions every day to keep their family going. How can we say to them that in the Church we will not permit you to nurture your sisters and brothers and to help the congregation make its big and little decisions regarding mission and outreach, as though you didn't have the gifts, the experience, or the ability to do such things?"

Many women have incredible gifts of spiritual discernment that are vital for the life of a congregation and its worship. Add that fact to the reality that almost every congregation everywhere has more women than men, and the net result is that a congregation looking for the gifts of spiritual maturity and compassionate caregiving will almost always wind up with the names of more women than men on their list. So the result will be more women than men on a Board of Elders, which is not bad at all, as long as the congregation looks for such gifts in all sectors of the congregation.

Ideally a Board of Elders, the board or committee that assists the pastor(s) in leading worship, in walking with members of the congregation, in ministering to the sick and chronically ill, and in distributing Communion in worship and to those unable to attend worship, should be as inclusive as possible: women, men, young, middle-aged, senior citizens, low-income, middle-income, Black, White, Hispanic, Asian, Native American, gay, lesbian, persons in recovery, ex-offenders. It is very important that everyone in worship, especially people who are taught by society that they don't count for much, recognize, as they observe the very people who lead worship, that in God's family, they do count and that they can, wherever their gifts fit, play a leadership role in the congregation.

It is not by accident that women are members of communities of faith in greater numbers than men. And certainly it is not because women are the "weaker gender," as sexist mythology might suggest. Quite the opposite, I believe. It is because so many women who experience the mystery of carrying an emerging life for nine months, go through the incomparable birthing experience, and then sense their vital role in nurturing and raising this child who is daily at their breast and on their knee, develop a profound sense of responsibility toward themselves, toward their children, toward their community and world, and toward God.

Faith is born of the Spirit, and it is strengthened on the anvil of life experiences, one of which is the awesome experience of women who travel the unique journey of birthing and mothering.

African American Women as Leaders

In addition, some African American women, I do believe, have an extra dose of spiritual adrenalin in their veins that has resulted from their experience of slavery and marginalization right up to the present. It was the slave mother who knew she had to be the strong, nourishing parent for the long haul, because the father would likely not be very present in her children's lives. If the father was from another plantation, he would not be permitted to live with his family. The more cruel reality was that the father could be sold any day to another slave owner. And, of course, quite often, the father was the plantation owner himself.

Although we are four or five generations from slavery, unfortunately there are conditions of joblessness, drug addiction, drug selling, gangs, and incarceration that fuel the instability of the family, especially wherever there is concentrated poverty (40 percent or more in a given neighborhood). In such conditions, it is the mother who either is completely demoralized and gives up on life and its meaning, or who rises out of the ashes of seeming hopelessness and musters extra strength and courage, to keep the family together and to try to raise her children and her grandchildren to experience the love of God and a loving community and to live out the meaning and the purpose of their lives.

Lula Williams, a member of Cross Church since she was 20, raised her five children at Cross Church. All five were baptized and confirmed. Two of them were active in the youth choir, and all of them experienced the love and the mentoring of various members of the congregation. Two of the children got caught up in drug abuse, and Lula, drawing on her spiritual adrenalin, decided to raise the three children of her drug-addicted daughter, who was unable to raise her children. Raising three grandchildren who were emotionally and psychologically impacted by the drug-abusing mother, was a daily challenge for a dedicated, no-nonsense grandmother.

Lula Williams would be the first to tell you that her regular weekly worship with the community of believers at Cross has been essential for her own spiritual nurture and sanity. She would also be quick to add that her participation on the Board of Elders for some 20 years has been a source of strength for her. It provided a special opportunity for her to serve her Lord and her congregation in a way that gave her life meaning beyond the crucial and demanding job of parenting three challenging grandchildren.

Many a Sunday morning shortly after the start of the service, we saw Lula ease down the aisle on the south side of the sanctuary with three grandchildren in tow, and then she would struggle mightily to keep awake. Little did she realize that she was doing far more than fueling up for her important day-to-day calling. She was providing real inspiration for those of us who knew her, and knew that she was coming straight from her third-shift job and from her tough job of grandparenting. And she was reminding us why we had to continue the struggle to keep an urban congregation going in the face of financial shortfalls and why we could not back off of including women on the Board of Elders.

During the days that Cross Church belonged to the Lutheran Church-Missouri Synod, women were not supposed to hold any office on the Church Council or to vote in a congregational meeting. However, about 1970, women at Cross Church began voting in congregational meetings and holding offices, such as Treasurer, Secretary, and Education Chair.

In 1976, the Association of Evangelical Lutheran Churches (AELC) was formed by pastors, leaders, and congregations that left the LCMS because of LCMS prohibitions against women's leadership, among other reasons. Cross Church agreed with the leadership of the AELC, that the Gospel frees us to transform the practices of the Church when they inhibit the life and the outreach of the Church and its witness to the Good News of Jesus Christ. So it is no surprise that Cross Church was in on the formation of the AELC and became an active member of the English Synod of the AELC at its founding assembly.

As a result of the free air of the AELC, Cross Church, in 1980, called Viviane Thomas-Breitfeld as Associate Pastor. That was a totally new experience for members of Cross Church. Even though the congregation had thoughtfully and prayerfully decided to continue the practice of including women on the Board of Elders, in the face of threats of expulsion from the South Wisconsin District of the LCMS, having a woman pastor who carried out all the liturgical and pastoral duties of an ordained minister, was another level above having women elders. Consequently, one man, an African American member of the congregation who had held leadership positions in the congregation over a period of ten years, left Cross Church because, he said, "I don't believe that it's right for a woman to be a pastor over men."

Virginia Walker-Riley

It was at the same time, in 1980, that Cross Church elected Virginia Walker-Riley as its first female congregational president. Sometimes she was called "The Woman in Red" because she usually wore something red, and sometimes even dressed entirely in red. She was among the first group of African Americans to be received as members of Cross Church in 1959. She quickly immersed herself in the life of the congregation, as far as an African American woman could go at the time. Virginia Walker-Riley became a dedicated leader of the Girl Scout troop at Cross and supported youth programming at the church and in the community.

Active as she was in the congregation, Virginia Walker-Riley was equally active in her large extended family and in the central city of Milwaukee. She regularly hosted a potluck feast in her two-bedroom apartment, inviting her "clan" and close friends every Christmas Eve and every Easter Sunday. It was a diverse gathering of 40 to 50. Always eager to witness the Gospel and extend the wide welcome of Cross Church to all people, she would purposely invite her pastor and his family to join this diversity of people and to lift the celebrative meal above simply a family holiday gathering. As a visiting nurse by vocation, she walked with people every day, offering medical advice, compassionate caring, and spiritual nurturing at every stop. She often referred persons to "Pastor Joe" for counseling or saw to it that people were picked up for worship on Sunday, or placed needy persons on the list for a Christmas basket.

A recipient of a warm welcome from many "old guard" members of Cross when she was received as one of the first African American members of Cross, Virginia Walker-Riley later saw many of these lifelong members of Cross die or move out of the neighborhood and leave Cross during the '60s and the '70s. She witnessed the transformation of Cross as it welcomed new members, white and black, during those same years, and as it moved its witness into the public square.

Because of her 20-year history as a faithful member of Cross Church who experienced the week-by-week transformation of Cross Church, changing from a congregation of "old-guard" whites sprinkled with a few African Americans to a congregation of African Americans sprinkled with some new white members, Virginia Walker-Riley was highly respected by young and old at Cross. She was an excellent choice by the congregation to lead it through its continuing transformation as part of the AELC.

As a sign of her leadership skills, Virginia Walker-Riley not only worked hard to sharpen Cross's witness to the Cross neighborhood. She also saw that it was in the self-interest of Cross Church and of all the urban congregations for Cross Church to be represented at the decision-making tables of the regional and national expressions of the Church. She often took off a day of work to participate in those policy-setting meetings herself. I remember returning with her from a regional meeting in Central Wisconsin, where she was the only racial minority person and the only lay representative of urban ministry. It was late winter, and we hit a patch of ice in the road. Our van careened out of control into a ditch, landing us on the side of our van. Fortunately, neither of us was hurt. Even such scary experiences did not deter her from making sure that Cross Church had a voice in shaping the new church body, the Evangelical Lutheran Church in America.

When Virginia Walker-Riley died of breast cancer in the 1990s, the church was packed at the time of her funeral, with members of her family (most of whom had joined Cross Church one by one over the years because of her witness), with community people, and with people from the larger church. There was no doubt in the minds of any of us that Virginia Walker-Riley loved her Lord, loved her congregation, and loved all people, especially those with special needs. What a loss it would have been for Virginia's family, for Cross Church, for the larger church, and for the community, if she had not been permitted by the church she loved, to exercise her gifts to the fullest.

Marilyn Crump Miller

One of the most gratifying stories that testifies to the profound value of Cross Church's affirmation of the gifts of women is that of Marilyn Crump Miller.

As a third and fourth grader, Marilyn Crump Miller started coming to Cross Church when she was simply Marilyn Crump and a member of the Girl Scout troop led by Gloria Wright. She attended Sunday School and Sunday worship and was confirmed in 1969. Neither of her parents went to college, and they never formally joined Cross Church, though they were often in attendance. They were salt-of-the-earth people who role-modeled for their children what it meant to work hard and to live on behalf of others. They supported their children in all of their participation at Cross Church and at school.

Marilyn Crump was one of those persons for whom every pastor and every teacher is profoundly grateful. Loaded with musical gifts, spiritual gifts, and intellectual gifts, Marilyn was a born leader. And it was a joy to see all of those gifts blossom.

Marilyn's three sisters and brother followed her to Cross Church. When the Cross Youth Choir started in 1969, Marilyn signed up. As a teenager, she sang with the maturity, the passion, and the spirit of an Aretha Franklin. Her three sisters had similar singing gifts. I used to say in those early days of the youth choir, "If none of the choir members show up for a singing engagement except the Crump sisters, not to worry. They'll sound like a 20-voice choir."

As gifted as Marilyn was in so many ways, she was never aloof and never above learning and growing. Her leadership gift blossomed when she stepped up to the plate and offered to become director of the Cross Youth Choir, after Gloria Wright stepped down for health reasons. Marilyn was in college. She had never had any formal training to be a choir director. But her leadership role in youth retreats, in choir concerts, in Sunday School teaching, as a youth member of the Board of Elders, and in leading worship, gave her a sense of self-confidence, an inner calling to witness to the Gospel, and a readiness to serve Christ, so that directing the Cross Youth Choir was just another step in her journey of discipleship, self-development, and growth in leadership skills.

Marilyn graduated from Concordia College and Cardinal Stritch University and first taught at Concordia College. She went on to work at the University of Wisconsin-Milwaukee as advisor to minority students in the School of Engineering. Through all these years of involvement with secondary education, Marilyn was faithful in leadership roles at Cross Church—as youth choir director, youth Bible class teacher, director of youth activities, and, above all, as a witness to the Gospel and a nurturing member of the Body of Christ.

Following an inner call to more involvement in the larger church, Marilyn left her post at the University of Wisconsin-Milwaukee, took a leap of faith, and became a staff member and ultimately Executive Director of the Lutheran Human Relations Association (LHRA), a pan-Lutheran organization dedicated to combating racism, sexism, classism, and every "ism" that breaks down the "beloved community" that God intended the human family to be. Marilyn's risky career change reveals not only her faith in God's leading, but also demonstrates a deep-felt desire to actively work at attacking racism in the Church and in society.

At almost the same time she became the first African American director of LHRA, Marilyn took another leap of faith in agreeing to run for the position of vice-president of the Greater Milwaukee Synod of the Evangelical Lutheran Church in America (ELCA). The position of vice-president of a synod in the ELCA is the highest office that a lay person can attain in the synod. The bishop is the "president" of the synod. But the vice-president is the officer of the synod who actually presides over the synod council meetings. As a sign of the respect that the synod clergy and lay delegates had for Marilyn's faith and leadership ability, they elected her over another very qualified candidate.

As if she had not poured enough of her soul into the lives of people and the mission of the Church, Marilyn felt the call to ordained ministry, completed her seminary work at Wartburg Theological Seminary, and was ordained into the ministry of Christ in 2012. She was immediately called to serve as pastor of the Lutheran Church of the Reformation in Milwaukee, just a little more than a mile from the congregation where her faith had been nurtured.

Cross Church found out over the years that Paul was right: "We are neither male nor female, for we are all one in Christ," and that encouraging, affirming, and celebrating the gifts of women in the Church to the fullest is one of the most important aspects of the Church's mission—for the good of the Church and of the whole world.

CHAPTER 8

RACE MATTERS: COMBATING RACISM AND CELEBRATING DIVERSITY

Here there is no Greek or Jew, circumcised or uncircumcised, barbarian, Scythian, slave or free, but Christ is all, and in all. Therefore, as God's chosen people, holy and dearly loved, clothe yourselves with compassion, kindness, humility, gentleness and patience. Bear with each other and forgive whatever grievances you may have against one another. Forgive as the Lord forgave you. And over all these virtues put on love, which binds them all together in perfect unity.

–Colossians 3:11-14

It was about 11:00 p.m. on a Saturday night, when I was still a bachelor pastor in Birmingham, Alabama. I had just finished running off the bulletin for the next day's service at St. Paul Church, and I was walking along Sixth Ave. South, from the church to the parsonage next door. I noticed that a man had evidently run out of gas, had left his car in the middle of the street and was standing behind the trunk of the car, pouring gas into the tank opening, right behind the license plate, above the middle of the rear bumper. I froze in my tracks as I saw a car traveling at a speed of about 40 miles per hour, proceeding down the middle of the street, heading straight toward the man filling his gas tank. I was sure that the driver of the oncoming car would stop or swerve at the last minute. But he didn't.

He didn't even slow down. He rammed into the back of the stalled car, pinning the man with his gas can between the two cars.

The collision of the two cars was so loud and the shrieks of the man pinned between the cars were so passionate that I knew the man would need an ambulance as quickly as possible, or he would bleed to death.

So I ran into the parsonage, turned to the Yellow Pages for "ambulance," and dialed the first ambulance company my fingers came to, noticing that the company was located not more than a mile and a half away. I explained the gravity of the situation and the location of the accident to the person who answered the phone.

I was relieved when the ambulance arrived within about five minutes. When the ambulance driver jumped out, opened the doors of the ambulance, pulled out the stretcher, placed it on the street next to the gravely injured man, the driver looked at the man and realized he was African American. The driver said apologetically, "I'm sorry, but I can't take this man. I can only take whites."

I looked at the driver in disbelief. "What do you mean, you can't take this man? He's so badly injured he needs to get help immediately."

"I'm sorry," the driver insisted."Our company has an agreement with the colored company that we take whites, and they take the colored."

The gravity of the injured man's condition and the damnable consequences of racial segregation in Birmingham were sending adrenalin throughout my body and passion and anger throughout my soul. I looked the ambulance driver straight in the eyes and I said emphatically: "If you don't take this man to the nearest hospital, you and your company will have a lawsuit on your hands, especially if this man dies. This is a life-or-death situation."

The ambulance driver hesitated momentarily, and then without any argument, placed the semi-conscious man on the stretcher and hurried him away to the nearest hospital. Regrettably, the man's injuries were so severe that he did not recover, and I attended his funeral the following Friday.

This emotional experience in 1962 in Birmingham gave me a profound taste of the racist structures and policies that had been developed and enforced over the years during slavery and since slavery was ended in 1865. It was just one of scores of experiences that indelibly impressed upon my soul, the harshness, the pervasiveness, and the demonic nature of racism

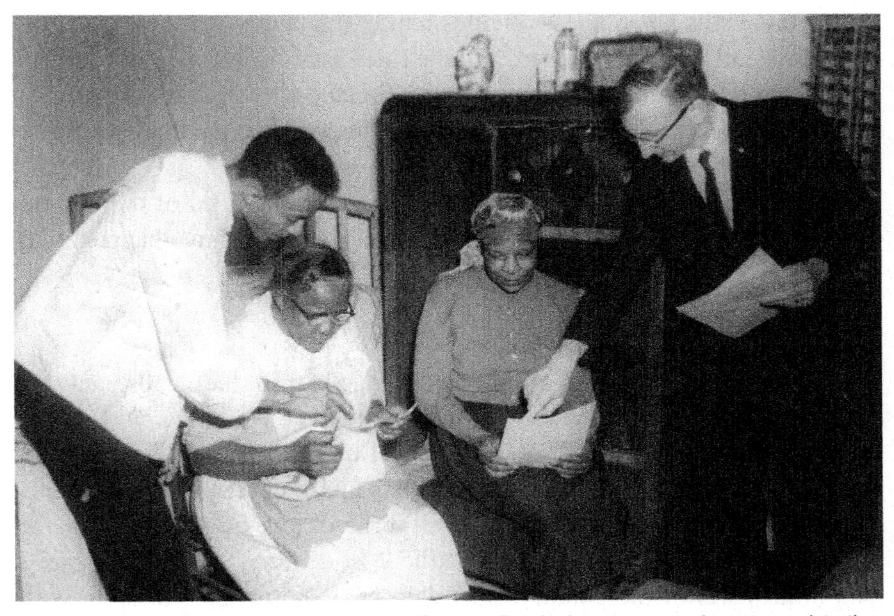

Joseph Ellwanger and a student from Miles College, Birmingham, as part of a voter registration drive in the fall of 1965, are assisting two women to register to vote. Following the passage of the 1965 Voting Rights Act in August, 1965, voter registration drives were conducted in black communities all over the South, resulting quickly in the election of African American leaders at the city, county, state, and federal levels and compelling white elected officials to become more accountable to the black community.

and all the policies and attitudes it had spawned over the years. It is no wonder that Martin Luther King often spoke of the three most threatening demonic forces at work in U.S. culture to be materialism, militarism, and racism. That late Saturday night rendezvous with racism in front of my house in 1962 is a helpful image to understand racism then and now.

There we were in the middle of the street, the white ambulance driver, the black man dying prostrate in the middle of the street, a few African American spectators drawn by the noise of the loud crash, and a white pastor, burning the midnight oil. We were all together as human beings, hovering over a man who desperately needed medical help. There was no disagreement about that. Everyone from the ambulance driver to the youngest spectator knew that. That was the obvious, compelling human reality that night.

But there was a much less obvious reality that almost trumped the life-and-death call for help. Racism, and the rules established over the years to enforce racism, demanded that a white ambulance driver was not to transport a black person to the hospital. Racism dictated that the man should be left in the street until the "right" ambulance arrived.

It took an intervention by someone who was convinced of the wrongness of racism's rules, to thwart what ordinarily would have happened as the usual course of events.

Are the Days of Racism Over?

There are those who would say that my image is from the 1960s, and that this is the 21st century. The days of racism are over. Nothing could be further from the truth. That is not even true of blatant racism. The Southern Poverty Law Center in Montgomery, Alabama, keeps tabs on incidents of overt racism and has listed several verified acts of overt racism for every month of every year right into the 21st century. They report racist acts in all parts of the country, including cross burnings, leafleting with racist threats, distribution of racist periodicals, and occasional shootings and lynchings.

There is a "joke" in the African American community that you can be stopped and ticketed by the police for "DWB," Driving While Black. Blacks driving in and through white communities, often going to and from work, are sometimes stopped by police, not because they were speeding, but simply because they were "suspicious," since they were black persons driving in a white community.

It is true that great progress has been made in reducing overt racism. Lynchings have all but exited the landscape. The "N" word has not disappeared, but its usage has diminished greatly. Legal segregation and racial discrimination have been outlawed in public accommodations, employment, education, housing, the armed forces, voting procedures, and governmental entities. I know of no congregation that refuses entrance to people of color, as was the case into the 1970s.

This progress is not to be passed over lightly. We must pause to give God praise and thanks for some amazing transformation in our society and in communities of faith. And we certainly must give thanks for the incredible leadership, commitment, and sacrifice of thousands of men and women and girls and boys, who laid their lives on the line, and some of whom gave their lives, especially during the 1950s and 1960s, to free people of color from racist oppression and discrimination and to free whites from a false sense of superiority and from cultural deprivation.

The United States did not undo 250 years of slavery without a very costly war. And the U.S. did not undo 100 years of second-class citizenship for those former slaves and their offspring, without a very costly struggle for freedom and equality.

As the years pass, it is extremely important that all of us, black and white, gratefully acknowledge the price that was paid by the thousands who risked their jobs and their lives and demonstrated and went to jail, and by those who gave their lives, for freedom: Martin Luther King, Medgar Evers, Jimmie Lee Jackson, Viola Liuzzo, James Reeb, Jonathan Daniels, the four girls killed in the bombing of the 16th Street Baptist Church, Denise McNair, Carole Robertson, Cynthia Wesley, Addie Collins, and others.

I attended the Martin Luther King Day celebration in Birmingham, Alabama, in January, 2004. Of the 750 persons who attended the celebratory breakfast at the downtown civic center auditorium, there were approximately 50 whites who joined in the powerful event. In the afternoon rally, where I had the honor of speaking at the 16th Street Baptist Church, there were probably 30 whites in an audience of 400.

The optimist would say that having close to ten percent participation by Birmingham whites in a 2004 celebration of King's life and the dismantling of the racist segregated way of life that had dominated the South and much of the rest of our country, was a sign of progress. After all, Birmingham, Alabama, is where the KKK had intimidated whites and blacks with frequent bombings and Police Chief "Bull" Connor had ruled with an iron fist. I clearly remember that when I attended the nightly movement rallies in the 16th Street Baptist Church during the demonstrations in the spring of 1963, I was the only white person, other than the two detectives sent by Governor George Wallace to spy on the movement's activities.

So ten percent white participation in a Martin Luther King Day celebration is progress. However, in a metropolitan area where whites are still in the majority, the low percentage of white turnout is a sign of a racist attitude that does not see the elimination of racial segregation as a victory for the whites as well as blacks. And it is a reminder of the gulf that still separates many whites from blacks.

The Southern Christian Leadership Conference, the organization headed by Martin Luther King in the 1960s, had as its motto: "Saving the soul of America." The civil rights movement, as articulated by Martin Luther King, Ralph Abernathy, Andrew Young, John Lewis, C.T. Vivian, Wyatt T. Walker, Fred Shuttlesworth, and others, was seeking not only to lift the heel of white racist oppression from off the necks of people of color, but it was seeking to empower white Americans to be healed of their racism and their hypocrisy and to be able to live into the fullness of their own creed, that "all people are created equal."

It is not sufficient to express gratitude for the sacrifices of the freedom fighters of the 1950s and 1960s, as important as that is. It is also important for whites and people of color to learn from the lessons of the 1950s and 1960s, that the forces of racism do not roll over and die easily. The forces of racism are still at work, and therefore must continually be recognized and confronted in each congregation and community and in every generation.

If racism is to be challenged and overcome, the charge should be led by whites, who are the perpetrators of white racism, as well as blacks, who feel the brunt of its oppression. That is exactly the message that the "Concerned White Citizens of Alabama" tried to communicate to Alabama and to the nation when we marched in Selma on Saturday, March 6, 1965, all 72 of us.

Selma 1965

Let me share the story of our March 6 demonstration, for the sake of telling it from the perspective of a participant and for the sake of gleaning some meaning from it for the ongoing struggle against the deep-rooted racism in our culture.

In January, 1965, the SCLC launched a campaign in Selma, Alabama, to lift the severe discrimination that most African Americans experienced in attempting to register to vote, as well as in voting and in holding public office, in Selma and throughout the South. In Dallas County, where Selma is the county seat, one percent of the eligible African Americans were registered to vote in 1965. In neighboring Wilcox and Lowndes counties, with 80 percent African American population, not a single black person was registered. The evidence of discrimination against African Americans attempting to exercise their constitutional right to vote in the counties around Selma was undebatable.

As black citizens in Selma attempted to register to vote and were turned away in January, 1965, African Americans from all walks of life and of all ages began to march to the county courthouse in an effort to dramatize the need for local, state, and national officials to do something about this despicable, unjust situation. Pastors, domestic workers, students, even public school teachers who were at risk of losing their jobs, marched day after day.

The reaction of Sheriff Jim Clark to the non-violent demonstrations and the attempts to register to vote was a harsh, angry, "lock-'em-up" approach of arrest and jail time. By mid-February Clark had locked up over a thousand demonstrators, creating real problems in jail space. Children and youth who were arrested, were marched to a little-used, unheated barracks at the edge of the city.

Those of us who gathered regularly in the monthly meetings of the Birmingham Council on Human Relations, 90 miles north of Selma, heard the horror stories of mistreatment of those arrested, and especially of the unsanitary, health-endangering conditions the youth were experiencing in their makeshift, unhealthy jail house, with February temperatures below freezing at night.

Our soul was stirred by the brave stand that our sisters and brothers in Selma were taking to attain rights that were already guaranteed by the U.S. Constitution. We contacted the SCLC and asked how we might help. The SCLC sent Hosea Williams and Al Lingo to meet with us. At their suggestion, we began to devise a way of expressing solidarity with the courageous band of "freedom fighters" in Selma.

The white members of the Birmingham Council on Human Relations, the only bi-racial citizens' group in Birmingham at the time, decided that Alabama, and the nation, needed to see that there were white citizens in Alabama who agreed with the Selma voting rights campaign. So we sent out an invitation to whites throughout Alabama to join us in Selma on Saturday, March 6, to march to the Dallas County Courthouse to make a public declaration of our support of the voting rights campaign.

The time was short. People had only a week to respond to the invitation that went out to people on the mailing list of the Birmingham Council on Human Relations and its parent body, the Southern Regional Council, to Unitarian churches in Alabama, and to certain professors on the college campuses. Word of mouth from one justice-minded person to another was probably one of the most effective avenues of communication.

We weren't sure how many people would show up on March 6. This was not a Saturday "trip to the mall" nor a routine civic-minded demonstration. This was a group of whites identifying with what was perceived as a "black cause." This was a march to a county courthouse where the sheriff was known for his roughhouse tactics. This was a state where the KKK was notorious for its violent attacks on anyone, white or black, who advocated for racial justice, integration, and a change in the Southern "way of life." This was a county that had arrested over a thousand persons who had demonstrated for the very cause that we were supporting.

I don't know about the other 71 persons who participated in the March 6 demonstration of the Concerned White Citizens of Alabama (that's what we called our newly-formed organization), but I didn't sleep very well the night before our march. My wife, Joyce, who was four months pregnant with our first child, had signed up to go along. So I had a lot on my mind as we took off that crisp Saturday morning from St. Paul Church. Reverend Ervin Oermann, Lutheran pastor to the deaf in Birmingham, was the lone Lutheran colleague who committed to going on the demonstration and who rode with us.

We arrived without incident at the gathering point, the Reformed Presbyterian Church in Selma, a small black congregation, three blocks from the house where I grew up from eighth grade on, and where my parents were living at the time.

The gathering time at the Reformed Presbyterian Church was filled with various emotions. We were meeting most of our fellow marchers for the first time, each of us there with different life stories and from different motivations.

There were several, like myself, who were motivated by the love of Christ, to identify with our sisters and brothers and to join them in crying out to the authorities for the constitutional rights that were rightly theirs.

However, there was one motivation we all shared: We all felt we had to break the silence of "good" white people in the face of such glaring injustice and in the face of such sacrifice on the part of African Americans. We were determined to state publicly, unequivocally, at the risk of bodily injury and arrest, our support of the movement in Selma. We were speaking to the African Americans who were paying dearly for their disenfranchisement and for their struggle to correct it, to white Alabamans and Americans of all persuasions, and to the power structures of Dallas County, the state of Alabama, and the President and Congress of the U.S. Our message was simple: Let our African American sisters and brothers exercise their constitutional right to vote and hold office now, not someday in the uncertain future. And we were white Alabamans taking this stand.

We purposely went as an all-white group from Alabama to try to make it clear that this was not a "Negro problem," but a problem of our national integrity, a problem that all of us should embrace, especially since it was white office holders who had the power to make things right.

So there was a sense of deep solidarity among the 72 people who did show up from Birmingham, Tuscaloosa, Huntsville, and several other cities and small towns in Alabama. We knew that everyone present was there at some risk, all of us united in a common cause.

We were about ready to prepare ourselves for the ten-block march down Broad Street and for the action on the courthouse steps, when Reverend James Rongstad, Pastor of St. John's Lutheran Church, a white congregation in Selma, entered the fellowship hall where we were gathered, insisting that he had something to say to the group. He was a colleague of mine, since we were both pastors at the time, in the Lutheran Church-Missouri Synod, although we did not know each other and did not work together because our congregations were in different geographical clusters. We gave him the floor to speak, even though I could sense from the tone of his voice that he was going to be critical of our action.

I don't remember all the points of Rongstad's statement, but I do recall that he asked us: "Why are you coming from outside of Selma to tell us what to do? We didn't go up to Birmingham to tell you what to do when you were having your problems."

Rongstad was looking right at me as he asked the question. So I responded: "We're not simply pointing the finger at Selma. We're here today to speak to Alabama and to all of the United States."

I am sure Pastor Rongstad found it difficult to explain to his parishioners and other whites in Selma, what another pastor of his own denomination, was doing leading a demonstration in solidarity with those "black troublemakers." More than that, I am convinced that he was honestly struggling with the meaning of this moment in Selma's history. But he did not see how the Selma demonstrations were part of U.S. history, and as he struggled with the Church's role in all of it, he apparently came down on the side of those who believe that non-violent demonstrations are too confrontational and too problematic for Christians to participate in. I don't know whether he felt the deep injustice that needed to be redressed. I do know that if in his heart of hearts, he saw the clear justice issue at stake, it would have required a great deal of courage for him to have publicly taken a stand in support of the Selma voting rights campaign. And it might have cost him his pastorate. But as I ponder why he went out of his way to publicly oppose our planned demonstration, I have to conclude that either he hoped to persuade us not to march that day, or he wanted to be able to say to those who tried to associate him and all Lutherans with our action that day and with the movement for voting rights, that he was not one of us and he had even tried to stop us.

After Rongstad's departure, we focused on the mission for which we had come. Hosea Williams, for the SCLC staff in Selma, spoke encouragingly to us and tried to prepare us for various scenarios that could take place as we proceeded with our planned demonstration. He gave us directions on how to handle potential hecklers as we walked down Broad Street to Alabama Ave., how to handle possible violence on the part of KKK-types, and how to deal with arrest. He assured us that our presence in Selma as the first group of Southern whites to demonstrate on behalf of justice for African Americans would be significant in many respects. He assured us that there would be supporters from the SCLC staff and from the movement who would monitor our path and be there to help, if help was needed.

It was agreed that as president of the Concerned White Citizens of Alabama, I should lead the march and read our statement of purpose from the courthouse steps. It was also the group's decision that we should march two by two for protection. I thought it would be safer for Joyce to be toward the rear of the line, since she was four months pregnant. Even though the front of the line was seen as being potentially more dangerous and more publicity-prone, Marjorie Linn, a woman from Birmingham, boldly and proudly volunteered to march with me.

We set out, two by two, walking on the sidewalk, Jeff Davis Avenue, to Broad Street and then down Broad Street, the main avenue in Selma. We walked past the small, old Jewish synagogue, past the large Presbyterian Church and Hotel Albert at Dallas Avenue, and past the stores on Broad Street between Dallas and Alabama avenues. Folks along the way stared at us, wondering who we were and what we were about. We began to think that all our concern about potential violence would not materialize.

The atmosphere of a calm Saturday in Selma quickly evaporated as we turned the corner at Alabama Avenue to walk the block from Broad Street to the Dallas County Courthouse on the corner of Alabama and Lauderdale. There were people milling around on the sidewalk, looking in our direction, making it clear that they had been waiting for us. As the head of the march came to Lauderdale Street, we saw to our right that the street was filled with white men, perhaps 150 or 200, the type that you could guess were members of the Ku Klux Klan. Some of them had in their hands bats and pipes the length of a baseball bat. They had parked two cars in the middle of the street, positioned in such a manner that the foul-smelling smoke they were managing to pump out constantly from their tailpipes, just three or four feet from us, was aimed at our line of march.

When I saw the threatening mob with angry faces and with hands clenched around pipes and baseball bats in the middle of the street, my fear was that there was no presence of the county sheriff or the city police. We braced ourselves for the worst.

As I looked straight ahead across Lauderdale Street, I was surprised to see several Dallas County deputy sheriffs standing on the corner in full uniform, with the look on their faces that seemed to say: “We’re in charge of this intersection, and we’ll handle the situation as we please. We knew you were coming, and this smoke screen and menacing mob is a part of our Dallas County welcoming party.”

In spite of the mob and the smoke screen, we kept on moving forward, until Marjorie and I could go no further. There were several sheriffs’ deputies blocking our path, one of them nonchalantly smoking a cigar, and another with a piece of paper in his hand, as if the paper had some special significance.

The whole line of march had to stop as the deputies confronted us. Ironically, this left Joyce and the others toward the rear of the line of 72, in a much more vulnerable position, right in front of the "welcoming party," with their pipes and bats and their catcalls like: "You nigger-lovin' trash!" and "Why don't you go back home where you belong?"

Dallas County Sheriff Jim Clark, famous for his tough talk and for his violent outbursts, was out of town on that particular Saturday, or we probably would have been confronted by him. The sheriff's deputy with the paper in his hand seemed to be the deputy in charge. He looked me in the eye and said, "I have a telegram from your boss, Reverend Homrighausen." He had some difficulty pronouncing the name. He proceeded to read from the telegram sent to Sheriff Clark:

> *The demonstration being led today in Selma by the Reverend Joseph Ellwanger does not have the official endorsement or sanction of the Lutheran Church—Missouri Synod. In no way does the Reverend Joseph Ellwanger represent the Church in an official capacity.*

"Now what do you say to that?" the deputy asked of me, as though he had me pinned to the wall.

I had no idea where the deputy was going with this reading from the surprise telegram and his question of me. However, I responded quickly and with a matter-of-fact tone of voice: "Well, President Homrighausen has a right to his own opinions, but we are here today to stand in solidarity with our brothers and sisters who are asking for their voting rights, and we would like to proceed to the steps of the courthouse to make our statement."

I halfway expected the deputies to arrest us, or possibly try to turn us around and disperse us, or simply block us from proceeding further, leaving most of the group at the mercy of the threatening mob to our right. But surprisingly, the deputies stepped aside and permitted us to proceed to the courthouse steps.

I walked halfway up the flight of a dozen or so steps, and the rest of our group gathered at the foot of the steps. I read the entire statement that had nine short paragraphs:

> *We as white citizens of Alabama have come to Selma today to tell the nation that there are white people in Alabama who will speak out against the events which have recently occurred in this and neighboring counties and towns.*

We deem it a tragic retreat from the American principle of 'no taxation without representation' when citizens of Alabama, Negro and white, must undergo a college level examination to be able to exercise their right as a responsible, law-abiding, taxpaying citizen, to vote.

We are horrified at the brutal way in which the police at times have attempted to break up American citizens who are exercising their constitutional right to protest injustice. And we are shocked at the inhuman way American citizens of Dallas and other counties in Alabama have been treated when taken prisoner in the recent demonstrations.

We are sickened by the totalitarian atmosphere of intimidation and fear officials have purposefully created and maintained to discourage lawful assembly and peaceful expression of grievances against the existing conditions.

THEREFORE: As citizens of the United States of America and of this state of Alabama we do by our presence here affirm our faith in the abiding principles upon which our nation and our state are founded and for which our forefathers died. We are immovable in our determination that this be a 'nation under God with liberty and justice for all.'

We urge that the governor of our state and all elected officials, state and local, use their power and prestige to see that all open and subtle intimidation of persons seeking to register to vote be removed.

We request that, since many citizens have for so long been given the clear picture that they are not wanted in this registrar's office, the state and local officials owe it to these citizens systematically to inform them that they are welcome and that they are encouraged to register and vote. We ask that not only the federal government but our own state legislature go on record against the current 'college test' type of a registration form in favor of a simple information blank and that assistance be made available to fully understand or fill out the form.

We finally plead for federal help in terms of laws and registrars if these injustices are not removed forthrightly.

After reading the statement, we sang the first stanza of *America* as our prayer for Selma, for Alabama, and for the whole country:

Oh beautiful, for spacious skies,
For amber waves of grain,
For purple mountain majesties,
Above the fruited plain.
America, America, God shed His grace on thee,
And crown thy good, with brotherhood,
From sea to shining sea.

No sooner had we started singing than the marauding crowd in the street, with bats and pipes in hand, began singing their version of *Dixie*, to counter our fervent hope of brotherhood.

The strains of *Dixie* had scarcely started, with a distinct edge of mockery, when a strong chorus of *We Shall Overcome* from across Alabama Avenue formed a counterpoint to *Dixie* and created a powerful symphony of solidarity with our plea for voting rights for all and with our hope for "brotherhood from sea to shining sea." A crowd of four to five hundred African Americans, who had been laying their lives on the line for the past two months for a national voting rights act, had gathered on the grounds of the federal building across the street from the courthouse, to demonstrate appreciation and support for this motley crew of white folks who broke the barrier of quietism and spoke with their bodies and their voices, for voting rights for all.

Although the three groups gathered at the courthouse intersection were all engaged in song, the tensions were mounting. Wilson Baker, Chief of Police in Selma, known for his attempts to deescalate tensions that sometimes mounted at the climax of a demonstration, seemed to appear from nowhere and approached me as I dismounted the courthouse steps and prepared to lead our group back to the church from which we had launched our march.

"Joe," he said in a quiet voice as he stood at my side, "I think you'd better take the group back by Church Street instead of Broad Street. The group in the street is getting out of control."

I was surprised he called me "Joe." I had never met him before. However, he knew my parents and my brother, David, and so in typical Southern familiarity, he addressed me by my first name. I think he was trying to communicate that he came not to hinder, but to help.

I had to make the decision quickly. We certainly did not come to look for bloody confrontation, so I headed around the corner and along Church Street back to Knox Presbyterian Church.

We debriefed quickly because people wanted to get out of Selma before dark. We were all grateful that only one person had been hurt by the mob, a photographer who had been knocked to the ground and whose camera was smashed. We felt we had accomplished our mission. We had read our statement. The press was there to get the word out. And we were very grateful for the visible, vocal support of the local movement folks, who had every right to be relaxing from two months of costly struggle, even as some were preparing to start back up the next day. (It's possible that some came just to see with their own eyes whether white Alabamans would actually show up to publicly stand with them and their cause.)

It was about 3:30 p.m. when Erv Oermann, Joyce, and I left Selma and headed back on State Highway 22 toward Maplesville, Clanton, Highway 31, and Birmingham. Highway 22 from Selma to Highway 31 at Clanton is a distance of about 30 miles, 30 miles of winding, up-and-down roadway with little shoulder room, few turnoffs, and long stretches of woods crowding either side of the road and often forming a canopy over the highway. Under ordinary circumstances, it's a picturesque stretch of asphalt. However, on March 6, 1965, it became ominous, as two cars that had trailed us out of Selma pulled up alongside of us, swerving as though they would purposely sideswipe us or try to scare us off the highway. Undoubtedly they were from the "welcoming crowd" in the street next to the courthouse. It was a scary moment. It was not clear whether they had weapons, whether they simply wanted to scare us, or whether their real goal was to push us off the road into the ditch. I was driving. Joyce was in the front passenger seat. Erv Oermann, in the back seat, was so frightened that he crawled down into the foot space between the front and the back seats so that he was not visible to someone looking in from a passing car. I decided my best strategy was to keep my eye on the road, not let them scare me into swerving off the road, and hope that they would neither try to fire a gun into our car nor try to push us off the road by physical contact or by pulling in front of us and then making a sudden stop.

Either they didn't want to damage their own cars, or they decided they had had enough fun for the day. Thankfully, after a few miles of taunting us by pulling alongside of us and then trailing very close behind us, then repeating their tactic two or three times, they finally pulled off the road at Maplesville, and we never saw them again.

The drive the rest of the way into Birmingham was thankfully uneventful, and filled with some animated conversation about the day's events and some audible sighs of relief.

It was dark as we pulled up to St. Paul Church and home. We were surprised to see lights on in the fellowship hall of the church and cars parked alongside of the sanctuary. After all, it was Saturday night and nothing had been scheduled for the evening. The three of us checked out the church hall and discovered tables set with food. Several congregation members facing us began clapping as we entered, and Ricky Bentley, a high school student from the congregation, with his trumpet firmly fixed on his lips, began playing an unforgettable rendition of *When the Saints Go Marching In.*

Joyce and I had not been commissioned by St. Paul to demonstrate for justice in Selma on March 6. We had talked with leaders of the congregation about our plans. But because the event grew out of the Birmingham Council on Human Relations and the newly-formed Concerned White Citizens of Alabama, the action did not get approved by any board at St. Paul Church. Even though I was acting out of my faith and out of my deep experience of walking with my African American sisters and brothers, and we had gotten affirmation from those with whom we talked, it was not a foregone conclusion that all the leadership at St. Paul would wholeheartedly endorse the action. There were certainly African American leaders in Birmingham and throughout the country, who were convinced that non-violent demonstrations were too confrontational, too disruptive, and were not the way Christians should go about working for change.

However, it became very clear, the night of March 6, when Joyce and I were welcomed back with a meal and a trumpet salute, that St. Paul congregation affirmed our action and deeply appreciated our witness that day.

The support of St. Paul leadership became even clearer when Arthur J. Horne, on behalf of the Board of Elders and the congregation, wrote a strongly-worded letter to Reverend Edgar Homrighausen, asking him to visit our congregation at his earliest convenience to explain why he had sent the telegram to Sheriff Jim Clark, "reprimanding Pastor Ellwanger for his actions on March 6."

Here is a portion of Arthur Horne's letter to Reverend Homrighausen:

> *Your actions (sending the telegram to Sheriff Clark) are a slap in the face of all the members of St. Paul and Black Lutheran Christians throughout the world. We further feel that your statement, as a leader in the Lutheran Church, has bridled the tongues of other Lutheran Christians who feel the urge to stand up and be counted against the evils of segregation that have oppressed God's people for over 300 years.*
>
> *You see, Pastor Homrighausen, Joe Ellwanger is more than just a pastor to us here at St. Paul and this community, that for reasons you must have heard about, has so much fear and distrust for any thing the white man teaches or preaches.*
>
> *Joe Ellwanger has come into our community and dwells among us, shares our burden of segregation with a kind of love only God can give...*

President Homrighausen did respond to St. Paul's invitation to speak with them by inviting St. Paul's Council to come and speak with the Church Council of his congregation in Cullman, Alabama, an all-white town about 60 miles north of Birmingham. This was a strange response to a congregation that was hurting from a public action of their district president. At best, we could only guess that President Homrighausen wanted St. Paul members to hear the pushback his members were giving him regarding the civil rights demonstrations in general, and the March 6 demonstration in particular, and maybe, just maybe, he wanted his members to hear what their black sisters and brothers were thinking and experiencing. But it was not the direct conversation with their district president that St. Paul members were looking for and needing at that moment. St. Paul congregation never did get an opportunity to talk with him, in a conversation that could have given both sides an opportunity to bare their souls and possibly to have begun a discernment process on how the Church could deal with racial gaps and get at the roots of racism.

Those of us who did go to the courthouse steps in Selma were grateful that the Associated Press picked up the story, so that the *New York Times* and newspapers in small-town USA as well, printed the story on March 7 and March 8. Since my name was mentioned as the leader of the demonstration, I received scores of letters in response to the event, almost all of them favorable and almost all of them from people of faith, expressing gratitude that the Church was associated with this public stand for justice.

Of course, the day after March 6 went down in history as "Bloody Sunday", the day that 500 men, women, and children started across the Edmund Pettus Bridge, intent on starting their 50-mile walk to Montgomery. Led by John Lewis and Hosea Williams, the column of determined marchers barely reached the other side of the bridge when they were met by sheriffs' deputies on horses and state patrolmen with tear gas, cattle prods, and nightsticks. The marchers were ordered to stop and given two minutes to disperse. Within 30 seconds, the phalanx of Sheriff Jim Clark's deputies and Governor George Wallace's patrolmen moved up the middle and along both sides of the column of marchers, mowing them down with all their instruments of brute force in hand. Several of the marchers were hospitalized, and miraculously no one died, as the marchers staggered back to Brown Chapel AME Church from which they had started.

Fortunately, not only was the Associated Press there to get the story out across the country the next day. There was television coverage that was telecast on the Sunday evening news that very night. Much of the nation was shocked at the obvious brutality to men, women, and children who were exercising their freedom of expression and demanding the rights already guaranteed to them in the U.S. Constitution.

The Voting Rights Act

The call went out from the Southern Christian Leadership Conference and from Dr. King himself, urging clergy of all faiths and community leaders to gather in Selma that Tuesday in solidarity with the 500 who had been brutalized on Bloody Sunday and in solidarity with the call for a national Voting Rights Act.

An indication of how deeply Bloody Sunday had struck the conscience of the nation, and the faith community especially, were the hundreds of pastors, priests, rabbis, nuns, and a few political and union leaders, who dropped everything on the Monday morning following Bloody Sunday, and headed toward Selma.

It was not easy to get to Selma. You either had to drive to Selma, or fly to Birmingham or Montgomery and rent a car to drive the rest of the way. A group of about 20 clergy from Chicago chartered a plane and flew to Birmingham Monday evening. A half dozen brought their sleeping bags and bedded down in our front room Monday night. We headed to Selma Tuesday morning by car. No one knew what the action plan was, once we got there. We had the general gut feeling that all of us would pick up where the 500 had left off on Sunday, that we would cross the Edmund Pettus Bridge and head toward Montgomery, if law enforcement officers would let us. But no one really knew the plan.

We were there to tell the nation that the cause of the 500 who were stymied on Sunday was no trivial one that could be postponed for another generation or two. It was a cause supported by leaders from all over the country, and it needed to be acted on with a sense of urgency. When we arrived at Brown Chapel AME Church, the appointed gathering place, at about 1:00 p.m., the sanctuary (that held about 500) was filled to overflowing and the street in front of the church was packed with what appeared to be another thousand, waiting to get word as to the plan of action. As I was part of the crowd that was growing by the minute, someone came up to me and asked, “Are you Reverend Ellwanger?”

I responded with a surprised voice, “Yes!”

“Well, they want you to speak, since you led the march on Saturday.”

I was really taken aback. I knew that the 500 who had faced the tear gas and cattle prods and horses on Sunday were the heroes. But I realized more and more, as I followed the young man who had come to get me, through the crowd into the packed church and up to a waiting seat in the chancel, that the small, belated appearance of 72 white Alabamans the previous Saturday had not gone unnoticed, and did have a small part to play in the growing momentum of the movement for a strong national Voting Rights Act.

I was humbled to sit with the movement stalwarts who had given so much over the years: Martin Luther King, Andrew Young, Ralph Abernathy, Fred Shuttlesworth, Hosea Williams, and others. I don’t remember exactly what I said when I was introduced. I do remember that the appreciative assembly gave me and the other 71 Concerned White Citizens of Alabama an amazingly strong crescendo of applause and spontaneous verbal affirmation. I was beginning to learn how to speak "off the cuff" and from the heart, as I said: "We were not very many last Saturday. We could only muster 72 white Alabamans to stand up publicly in solidarity with the call for a strong Voting Rights Act that so many of you have been laying your lives on the line for. But I want you to know that there are many other white Alabamans who agree with us and with you. I am here today to march with you. Together, with God's help, we can win. We will have a Voting Rights Act. And all the people of Dallas County, Wilcox County, Lowndes County, and all the counties across this nation will be able to vote and to hold office. I am humbled and proud to march with you all today."

That "Turn Around Tuesday" after Bloody Sunday saw the largest number and percentage of white participation in a civil rights demonstration in the South to that date. Martin Marty, writer for *Christian Century,* was there to record the event, and he noted in his article in the next issue of the *Century* that he was grateful for some Lutheran involvement in the justice movement.

Eventually that Tuesday afternoon, Dr. King spoke to the assembly and then led the diverse group of some 3,000 people to Broad Street and across Pettus Bridge. Suddenly the long column stopped. Those of us toward the front saw King and Abernathy kneel in prayer. Then the massive column reversed and returned to Brown Chapel. We found out later that King, after much agonizing, had decided to abide by a court injunction and wait for a hoped-for favorable court decision permitting the Selma-to-Montgomery march. The favorable decision did come a few days later.

The call for a strong Voting Rights Act was gaining more steam as the week of March 7 wore on. A call for people of faith from all over the country to converge on Washington, D.C. on March 12, went out from the National Council of Churches under the leadership of Robert Spike. A small interfaith group of 15 leaders from around the country was asked to join in a meeting that same day with President Lyndon Johnson at the White House, to urge him to push for a Voting Rights Act. The Lutheran Human Relations Association (LHRA) received an invitation to send a representative, and I was chosen to go, because of my involvement with the march of the 72 white Alabamans in Selma on March 6.

When President Homrighausen heard that I was planning to go to Washington to talk with the President about the Voting Rights Act, he made it a point to call me, asking me not to go. He said I would be going just for the sake of ego and publicity. Apparently he concurred with many white Southerners who dismissed the authenticity of the entire civil rights movement as one massive publicity stunt in which the leaders were vying for the spotlight. Little did he realize that I enjoyed the pastoral side of my calling so thoroughly that I found it difficult to carve out time for these prophetic forays.

However, as I looked at the denominational representatives from all over the country slated to be part of the National Council of Churches group, I saw that I was the only white Southern clergy, and I thought that it was important for President Johnson to hear from a white Southerner in support of voting rights legislation. So Joyce and I traveled to Washington D.C. to be part of this response to Bloody Sunday and part of this historic dialog with the President about the first major voting rights legislation since women's suffrage.

Joyce and I were amazed as we walked into the huge sanctuary of the Lutheran Church of the Reformation in D.C., where the main rally was being held. Over 2,000 persons had gathered from all over the U.S. in preparation for going to talk to their legislators about supporting voting rights legislation. The sanctuary was packed, and as several of us, who would be part of the delegation to visit the President, walked down the aisle to proceed to the front of the sanctuary for presentations, the entire assembly stood and applauded for three or four minutes.

The applause was especially for Reverend Robert Spike, Ex-Director of the National Council of Churches, and me, because we had been in Selma and participated in the "Turn Around Tuesday" march over the Pettus Bridge just three days before. Little of this Spirited enthusiasm for voting rights legislation would have germinated and reached this level of broad-based, biracial, national support, had it not been for Bloody Sunday and the evening news clip showing men, women, and children walking across a bridge, pleading peacefully for voting rights and then suddenly being mowed down unmercifully by law enforcement officers.

I remember meeting the other members of the group of 15 at the visitors' entrance to the White House and then proceeding to the Oval Office, which did have a massive oval-shaped table. I don't remember what others said to President Johnson, but I still have the notes that I made for myself, so I know what I said to President Johnson:

> *I am a white Lutheran Pastor serving an African American congregation in Birmingham. I want you to know that 71 white Alabamans joined me last Saturday in Selma, asking for a strong voting rights bill. There are many, many more whites in Alabama who support that position.*
>
> *But what I want to be sure to tell you is that a voting rights bill is needed desperately. My parents live in Selma. I grew up there. I've been to Wilcox and Lowndes counties, where not one single African American is permitted to vote. There are African American pastors, colleagues of mine, who cannot vote. This is not right. Something has to be done to correct this immediately. We need you to lead the way.*

In the flurry of the President's busy daily schedule, I don't know how impressive our presentations were. But I do believe that he got a clear message that religious leaders around the country, led by ordinary people crossing a bridge, risking their lives for a voting rights act, were downright serious about this call for voting rights legislation.

Selma to Montgomery March

We soon heard that Federal Judge Frank Johnson had granted permission for the Selma-to-Montgomery march to take place. Remarkably, or shall we say "miraculously," the march took place over five days, March 21 to 25. On the last day, March 25, people were invited to join the smaller group of 300 that had walked the 48 miles to the edge of Montgomery. The scene was surreal. About 15,000 people from Alabama and all over the country marched up Dexter Avenue and sat on the boulevard, facing a stage that had been erected in front of the Alabama Capitol, flying the flag of the Confederacy and with the defiant Governor George Wallace sitting in his office.

Joyce and I were sitting on Dexter Avenue right in front of Dexter Avenue Baptist Church, where Martin Luther King had been pastor ten years before, at the time of the Montgomery Bus Boycott, 1955-56, at the start of the civil rights movement, and at the formation of the Southern Christian Leadership Conference.

There was an air of victory that day as King gave the speech climaxing the historic march. He talked about the voting rights bill that must be passed and the dramatic transformation that would take place, especially in the South, once voting rights were actually guaranteed.

At the end of the event, the names of 16 Alabama leaders, almost all ministers, who had participated in the demonstrations in and around Selma, were read off. These were the persons who were to represent the march and meet with Governor Wallace to present a declaration asking for his support of voting rights. I was totally surprised when my name was read off as the only white member of the delegation.

Years later, I learned that my younger brother David, who at the time was an assistant attorney general with the State of Alabama and whose office was on Dexter Avenue overlooking the scene of the celebration at the end of the Selma-to-Montgomery march, was watching the event, along with a couple of co-workers. When his co-workers heard during the announcement that one of the ministers in the delegation to see Governor Wallace was white, one of his peers said angrily to the other; "I'd like to get a hold of that traitor and castrate him." (Actually, he used graphic street language in place of "castrate.")

A few days later, on March 30, the group of black ministers and I met with Governor Wallace. It was a meeting filled with tension. Here was the governor who had stood in the door at the University of Alabama in Tuscaloosa and vowed, "Segregation yesterday, segregation today, segregation forever." Now he was talking with the leaders of the forces that had led the struggle for ten years to end segregation, and he was being asked, in effect, to join them in putting nails in the coffin of segregation. I didn't say much. Reverend Shuttlesworth and those who had invested so much of their lives in the struggle, were the ones to lead the presentation of the petition and raise the questions. However, it was an honor to be included, and I welcomed the opportunity to complete the visible symbol of the vision of diversity and unity that Dr. King and the SCLC leaders had always lifted up during the long struggle to end racial segregation.

The flurry of demonstrations and actions in March of 1965 was so hectic, so draining, so exhilarating, so amazing, so unbelievable, that it almost seems impossible that all that happened between March 6 and April. And what is equally amazing is that President Johnson and Congress worked hard on a strong Voting Rights Act in April, May, June, and July, and got it passed and signed by August, 1965. There is no doubt that that Voting Rights Act of 1965 has been pivotal in bringing down the walls of *de jure* (legal) and *de facto* (actual) segregation in all parts of our country, particularly in the South.

Selma 2005

I was in Selma for the 40th Anniversary of Bloody Sunday and the Selma-to-Montgomery march in March, 2005. I was eating lunch in the desegregated St. James Hotel on Water Street and engaged in conversation with Reverend C.T. Vivian, one of the charismatic leaders of the Selma demonstrations, who was in his eighties in 2005 and who was also having lunch at the hotel. He came over to our table and in the midst of the conversation, he exclaimed: "You know, Joe, if we were able to transform this country as radically as we did, by our non-violent demonstrations here, there is absolutely no aspect of our country's problems that we could not solve if we set our minds to it, if we stay committed, if we're willing to work for it non-violently, and if we trust God. That's what Selma has taught us."

With Reverend C.T. Vivian, I believe that the events of Selma 1965, are instructive, decades later, to all those engaged in the struggle against racism and the struggle for justice. That is the chief reason I have shared my piece of the Selma experience in great detail.

Learning from Selma

So what does the Church learn from the events in Selma in 1965? This is a crucial question.

Certainly, Reverend C.T. Vivian is correct. We learn that people of faith who organize around a justice issue and who act non-violently to raise up the issue and call for change, can bring about significant transformation of society, often far beyond our own expectations. Certainly the 500 deeply committed persons who bravely walked across the Pettus Bridge on March 7, 1965, had only a vague vision of the amazing results that would sweep this nation, thanks to their humble, brave action on that fateful Bloody Sunday.

Furthermore, Selma teaches us that people of all faiths are called by God to be concerned about justice issues, not just about the spiritual life of individuals, as important as personal faith and the fruits of faith are in each person's life. The reality that 50 percent of the people of Dallas County (the percentage of African Americans) and 80 percent of the people of Wilcox County, had no voice in their government and were robbed of their dignity as human beings, was an intolerable injustice that people of faith should have been deeply concerned about, not in spite of their faith, but because of their faith.

This "working for justice," Selma teaches us, must be more than an intellectual stance on the part of a few religious leaders. It must be part of the warp and woof of the liturgical and organizational life of the community of faith. Issues of poverty, availability of health care for all, racial discrimination, and instances of "warring madness" should be part of a congregation's regular fare in their prayers, in sermons, and in Bible study. Justice issues are not simply "political" issues. They are also spiritual, moral, and theological issues that every person should be struggling with as part of their worship, prayers, and daily life, even as they struggle with their personal addictions, their relationships, their spirituality, their losses, their weaknesses and strengths, and their daily priorities.

The white congregations—and some black congregations—in Selma did not participate in the movement's call for voting rights for all. They did not even mention the issue in their prayers or their worship or in their Bible studies. The religious leaders did not see justice issues as part of the mission of the Church or of concern to individual persons of faith.

Some congregations and clergy did mention the movement for voting rights in sermons and Bible studies, either dismissing the movement as inconsequential or as downright wrong.

There were many colleagues, President Homrighausen included, who in various ways said: "Joe, we agree with your goals of justice, even of racial integration, but we disagree with your methods of achieving your goals. Demonstrations, even non-violent demonstrations, are too confrontational. They cause more harm than good."

President Homrighausen states that position in the last paragraph of his telegram to Sheriff Jim Clark: "Insofar as his (Ellwanger's) goal is freedom for all under just legislation, we agree. But we do not concur with, or sponsor, his philosophy or action of demonstration in this instance."

Homrighausen certainly had the right to intellectually disagree with the methodology of people putting their lives on the line for human dignity and voting rights. But as the public voice of the Church, to publicly disparage the methods of those struggling to lift the oppressive indignities in Selma and elsewhere, was giving aid to the oppressors, as surely as was the silence of the Church and of good people.

Participating in public demonstrations is difficult for most people of faith, because they've never done it before and because it seems to be at odds with their understanding of the spiritual life. Their view of the life in Christ is that it is to be a life of reflection, of inner and outward peace. Yes, of "quiet."

The preference for "quiet," in place of publicly standing over against injustice, is called "quietism."

Selma teaches us to break though the quietism of our human nature and our various denominational traditions, as well as our temptation to simply intellectualize or to criticize, and instead to take a public stand against injustices. It is not a matter of choice between a quiet reflective faith in God or a public demonstration of concern for some justice issue. It is a both/and. It is the Jesus who spent the night in prayer who was the same Jesus who publicly overthrew the money changers' tables in the temple, calling the scene a "den of thieves."

This combination of inner reflection and outward prophetic action calling for a change, is the paradox of the life of faith, which results in an inner tension, the struggle to know and to discern God's will, and an outer action that creates/reveals a "tension in the community." That is what was happening in Selma in 1965. As African Americans in Dallas County were asking for the right to vote, Sheriff Jim Clark, Mayor Joe Smitherman, and the white power structure of Dallas County resisted the call for change by arresting hundreds of demonstrators and attacking them with cattle prods, horses, and tear gas on Bloody Sunday.

Selma was full of tension in February and March, 1965. It was not a comfortable time in Selma. Many blacks and almost all whites saw these tensions as totally negative and to be avoided at all cost. The obvious tensions in Selma were the major reason why Pastor James Rongstad showed up on March 6 to tell us to leave Selma. I think that the tensions in Selma over the voting rights issue were the main reason why President Homrighausen sent a telegram to Sheriff Jim Clark, a most unusual action on the part of a church official, to disavow official church support of our action on March 6. He was certain that the causes of the tensions in Selma were the demonstrators. If the demonstrators would go away, there would be no tensions. So obviously the demonstrators were causing the tensions.

Suppose that the white power structure had told people, as they came to register to vote: "Sure, come right in and register. That is your right as a U.S. citizen. We're glad you're taking your civic responsibility seriously." What would have happened? There would have been no arrests. There would have been no tension in Selma caused by black demonstrators. It was not the demonstrators in Selma who created the tensions. Rather, the white power structure's resistance to doing the right thing created the tension.

What Selma teaches us is that tensions that result from authorities refusing to do the just thing, when people non-violently call for justice to be done, cannot be avoided. It is precisely that tension that brings to light the injustice of the situation and moves people and officials of conscience to act on behalf of justice. It was the tensions of Bloody Sunday, and the weeks leading up to Bloody Sunday, that moved people from all over the country, and Congress, and the President of the United States, to finally pass a strong Voting Rights Act to address the underlying injustice.

As Martin Luther King often stated in his speeches: "True peace is not the absence of tension, but the presence of justice."

But it was more than the tension of Bloody Sunday and the demonstrations that caught the attention of people of conscience around the country. It was the undeserved suffering of the men, women, and children on Bloody Sunday.

It was the commitment of the people who went back to the Dallas County Courthouse again and again, risking arrest, risking the loss of their jobs, risking mistreatment and name-calling by the law enforcement officials, and many actually being arrested, that made a deep impression on people following the news from Selma. Such deep commitment, such innocent suffering, such sacrifice made it clear to people of conscience that this was an issue of profound importance, an issue that deeply affected people's lives.

Selma teaches us the validity and the power of non-violent demonstrations in working for justice. Non-violent public demonstrations are not always necessary to achieve a greater degree of justice, and there are various ways besides demonstrations to speak the truth to power, to hold up an injustice for the public and authorities to see. However, Selma teaches us that non-violent public demonstrations, direct action, and civil disobedience are tools not to be shunned by people of faith seeking to do justice and working for peace.

Sometimes that is the only method of effectively catching the attention of the public and authorities, of holding up an injustice for everyone to see, and holding up a vision for people to implement.

It is true, however, that law enforcement personnel today have learned to handle demonstrations, including civil disobedience, more professionally, and media often conspire to keep demonstrations out of the news entirely, with the result that the public and power structure officials either don't get the message, or they conclude that the issue is not that important.

As miraculously powerful as the Selma demonstrations were in reaching the conscience of the nation, of Congress, and of the President, and of bringing about actual changes in the voting law, in voting procedures, and ultimately in the racial makeup of local, state, and national governmental leadership itself, there is still much residual racism left. Racist attitudes, racist systems, and advantages that have accrued to the white majority over 250 years of slavery and 100 years of second-class status for persons of color, do not disappear overnight.

The raw hatred and abuse of law enforcement officers, the appearance of white mobs with baseball bats and steel pipes, and the viciousness of sheriffs' deputies and state patrolmen on Bloody Sunday are the reminders to us that the roots of racism run deep, and the carbon monoxide of our racist culture is in the air we breathe daily. As people of faith, we have to work constantly at detecting, rooting out, and overcoming racist attitudes and behaviors and policies, as surely as we work at detecting and rooting out all demonic attitudes and practices.

Combating racism includes, among other things, educational approaches in religious and secular curricula that underscore the unity of the human race and the many gifts that different racial and ethnic groups and individuals bring to the table. Anti-racism workshops can be helpful in leading whites to see the privileges and advantages of whites in Western culture, and the concurrent disadvantages of persons of color.

Whites who are not personally prejudiced toward African Americans often approach issues such as equal job opportunity, police brutality, and equal opportunity for secondary education, from a more intellectual perspective than persons of color, who approach such issues from more of an experiential, gut level.

President Homrighausen, for instance, in his telegram to Sheriff Jim Clark, stated that "the Church condones no discrimination." He would insist, I am sure, that he was not a racist and that he held no prejudice toward persons of color. But there is no indication in the telegram that he felt the pain and the oppression of African Americans, many of whom were pastors, teachers, and members of congregations in his jurisdiction. And his very action that day, of distancing himself from me and from our action to bring about change, bolstered Sheriff Clark and the racist system of segregation that kept persons of color in "their place" as second-class citizens. Alas, it is quite possible for persons not to exhibit racist, prejudiced attitudes toward people of color, and yet at the same time, support a policy or a system, by our silence or by our rationalizing, that is racist in its impact and harmful toward persons of color.

Likewise, the debate has been going on for decades regarding affirmative action in equal opportunity to jobs and to secondary education. Opponents to affirmative action argue from a theoretical and intellectual level that academic and written tests should be the sole determining factor in college admissions and hiring decisions. The fact that tests have seldom been the only deciding factor in the past is overlooked, and the unlevel playing field created by 250 years of slavery and 100 years of second-class citizenship is swept aside as irrelevant.

Not only does the religious community have the responsibility to take major leadership in naming and combating racism in the faith community and in society, but it has the responsibility of creating communities of faith that model the inclusive, non-racist attitudes and policies that result in multiracial, inclusive congregations.

Racism is one of the most insidious, demonic forces at work in U.S. culture. It is one of those forces that will probably never disappear from the face of the earth, especially from the U.S. It can pop up in Pewaukee, Wisconsin, as easily as in Philadelphia, Mississippi, or in New Orleans. The faith community, and especially the Church, is called to be vigilant, and more than that. It is called to be pro-active in detecting it, combating it, and uprooting it at every level, in personal attitudes and in systemic policies, inside and outside the Church. And yes, we are called to put our lives on the line in the public square, to uproot the vestiges of 250 years of slavery, 100 years of segregated, second-class citizenship, and 400 years of white privilege, white domination and overt and subtle violence. The integrity of the Church's witness depends on it.

Chapter 9

GAY/LESBIAN MINISTRY: A BLESSING, NOT A BURDEN

As they traveled along the road, they came to some water, and the eunuch said, 'Look, here is water. Why shouldn't I be baptized?' And he gave orders to stop the chariot. Then both Philip and the eunuch went down into the water, and Philip baptized him. When they came up out of the water, the Spirit of the Lord suddenly took Philip away, and the eunuch did not see him again, but went on his way rejoicing.

–Acts 8:36-39

When you drive up to Cross Lutheran Church, Milwaukee, for the first time, you will notice the outstanding landscaping around the sanctuary, the office area, and even along the outside edges of the parking lot next to the church. You don't have to raise plants as a hobby or to be a horticulturalist, to be struck by the beauty of the plantings, the variety of colors, the careful blending of the flowering plants with the green/red/yellow foliage of the shrubbery. There it is, in the central city of Milwaukee, in the " 'hood," as some African Americans would describe it. Summer or winter, it will catch your eye.

You might conclude that the congregation, looking creatively at how it could communicate to the people of the neighborhood that God is a god of beauty and that this congregation wanting to bring the beauty of God into the lives of the people, decided to set aside a few thousand dollars to carry out this amazing landscaping project around the church. Or perhaps you might guess that a devoted member of the congregation died and left some money for this specific purpose.

Timothy Hansen speaks at a "Coming Out Sunday" at Cross Church, following the congregation's decision in December, 1991, to become a "Reconciling In Christ" congregation. "Coming Out Sunday" became an annual observance at Cross Church, in an effort to help both gay and straight congregational and community members deal with the effects of heterosexism and homophobia that are part of the culture of the faith community and of the nation.

The true story behind the beautiful plantings is that a gay couple started coming to Cross Church in the mid-1990s and found it to be a community of people who were not perfect, but who exhibited love and acceptance of all people, including gay and lesbian persons. They saw that the congregation was trying to bring healing and empowerment to the neighborhood and city around them. They soon joined the congregation, after years of estrangement from the church. They were so deeply touched by the acceptance, the spiritual enrichment, and the opportunity for service that they found at Cross Church, that they planned the landscaping, purchased the scores of shrubs and plantings, and then lovingly planted each of the shrubs one by one. They painstakingly weeded and pruned and watered them for years.

There is only one way to describe this extravagant outpouring of money and time and energy. It was clearly an investment and labor of love. It was their way of exclaiming: "Thank you, God, for your love, and for the love that we have found in this place."

Newer members of Cross Church probably don't know the story behind the beautiful landscaping, but for those who do, it is a powerful reminder that ministry with gay and lesbian persons is not a burden to be borne, but a blessing to be celebrated and a blessing that enriches the entire congregation.

Most congregations do not easily come to the point of consciously, openly engaging in ministry that reaches out to gay and lesbian persons. In fact, the majority of congregations follow a "don't ask, don't tell" philosophy. They insist that they welcome all people, and they may add that they're pretty sure that there are some lesbian or gay persons in their congregation. But they don't talk about homosexuality, and they would not consider blessing same-gender couples in a public commitment ceremony in a worship service, as part of their ministry with gay and lesbian persons.

Then, of course, there are many congregations, from Pentecostal to Roman Catholic, in which it is openly taught, sometimes in an even-toned voice and sometimes in shrill, haranguing tones, that homosexuality and the "homosexual lifestyle" are sinful. According to that viewpoint, there are three ways to deal with your "sinful condition," if you self-identify as lesbian, gay, bi-sexual, or transgender (LGBT). You can repent of your "homosexual tendencies," and ask God to give you the strength to be heterosexual. Or you can go to a therapist and get help to be "healed" of your homosexuality so that you can become heterosexual. Or you can simply live a celibate life and never express your sexuality.

My Journey of Awareness

My personal journey of awareness and commitment to gay/lesbian ministry outreach and to justice for the LGBT community has been a slow, steady, rewarding journey.

I grew up in a family (1930-1940s) where homosexuality never came up in the conversation and at a time in U.S. history when I do not recall any media coverage of homosexuality or of gay/lesbian persons in the news. The only references to homosexuality that I recall during my high school/college/seminary days (1946-1958) were conversations in which my classmates sometimes referred to certain male students as "fairies." To my knowledge, there was no physical abuse shown toward students with "gay characteristics," but the labeling of the students carried with it varying degrees of verbal abuse. I do not recall any discussion of homosexuality in any class that I took through college and seminary. Of course, there was very little discussion of heterosexuality, except for clear warnings in "pastoral theology" classes against sexual intercourse before marriage, sexual promiscuity, adultery, and divorce. These actions were generally described as irresponsible and unloving and contrary to God's will for a responsible, loving expression of one's sexuality (which was assumed to be heterosexual for everyone) within the committed bond of marriage.

I was never confronted with anything related to homosexuality in the first years of my ministry, which consisted of my year of internship in Kansas City, Missouri, 1955-56, and my first call as pastor of St. Paul, Birmingham, Alabama, starting in 1958. However, in 1963, I was presented with some of the darker side of our society's views of homosexuality.

It was in November, 1963, that I received a phone call from someone at the Birmingham City Hall, asking me to come to his office as part of an investigation. He was vague about the nature of the meeting, and I didn't push him for more information, as I should have. I went to his office, not realizing that it was a little bit like Daniel going into the lion's den. I had some of Daniel's faith in a God who watches over God's own. But I didn't have a full appreciation of the ferocity of the lions. I had no sooner sat down in the appointed office than the officer informed me that this was a very serious matter that we were about to discuss and that I was the one who was about to be charged with a very serious crime.

My mind was running at a fast clip. I was trying to imagine what heinous crime I was about to be charged with. I had participated in some of the mass meetings and in some of the planning meetings of the demonstrations held in the spring of 1963 in Birmingham and I had been the lone white person in some picket lines that the Inter-Citizens Committee, led by Reverend C. Herbert Oliver and Reverend J.L.Ware and the Alabama Christian Movement for Human Rights, led by Reverend Fred Shuttlesworth, had set up to walk in front of the main downtown department stores. The picket lines were calling attention to the fact that the department stores had not hired African American clerks, as they had promised to do in May of that year, as part of the settlement agreement at the end of the demonstrations. I knew that I had not committed any crime in participating in these efforts that were crucial to progress on the civil rights front. But I also knew that the white power structure of Birmingham, and the KKK, were downright angry that any white person would be in solidarity with African Americans in their attempt to change the status quo. I thought maybe the DA would dredge up an old segregation law and try to stick me on some obscure Alabama law against whites and blacks meeting together.

As I was trying to imagine what they were going to charge me with, I saw a police officer lead into the room an African American man, about 30 years old, in the drab coveralls that immediately labeled him as an inmate of the county jail.

The officer looked at me and spoke in a serious tone of voice: "This prisoner reported that last week, when he was cleaning the men's room on the first floor of City Hall, you made a pass at him, tried to have sex with him, and he had to push you away and run to get away from you. Isn't that right, Charlie?"

"Yassuh, boss man," the trusty said nervously.

"Well, what do you say to that, Ellwanger?" the officer asked.

"This must be a joke," I responded. "I haven't been in the City Hall in months, and I've never seen this man before in my life."

"Well, that's his story, and I'm afraid we're going to have to charge you with attempted sexual assault. We'll set up a court hearing and send you the papers in a week or two."

The inmate left the room with that look on his face that said: "Well, I did what the man told me to do, but I sure don't know what's happening."

I left the room in total disbelief, wondering where this would lead. I shared the threat with only a handful of people whom I trusted. I shared it with Reverend Karl Lutze at a Lutheran Human Relations Association Board Meeting in North Carolina, two days later, and he promised to help me get legal assistance if I needed it. Having served as a pastor in the African American community of Muskogee, Oklahoma, in the 1950s, he had no difficulty believing that white law enforcement officers in the South were quite capable of using their position of power to intimidate anyone trying to bring about change in "our Southern way of life."

When I shared my situation with a colleague, who was a Lutheran pastor and a seminary classmate, and a pastor in a white suburb of Birmingham, his response, in a caring tone of voice, was: "Well, Joe, if you really have those urges, I can help you get some counseling." I figured that if a colleague and classmate believed the DA before he believed me, 99 percent of white folks in Birmingham would do the same. I also got an "enlightened" view of homosexuality from a clergy person who was taking a calm, sensitive approach to advising someone who, he believed, had homosexual "urges." His perspective was that such a person should get counseling to get his sexuality straightened out.

I decided that I would not share my story with my congregation until I actually got a notice of a court hearing. Likewise, I decided I wouldn't seek legal help until I had some official papers in my hands.

About a week after the shocker experience at City Hall, I got a call from the DA's office: "You know the charges that we're ready to make against you. Well, I've talked with some of the people here at City Hall, and we're ready to make it easy on you. If you leave town in the next few weeks, we'll drop the charges. What do you say to that?"

"Well," I responded. "If you think you can get me to leave town this way, you're wrong. I have done nothing wrong. This is a trumped-up charge, and you know it. I love my congregation and my work here. There's no way I would leave."

The conversation ended rather abruptly, and that was the last I heard from the investigator at the City Hall.

I have never solved the mystery of who was really behind this abuse of power by the DA's office. Was it Police Chief Jamie Moore? Was it the downtown merchants who resented the pressure being put on them to live up to their agreement after the demonstrations in May of that year? Was it elements of the KKK within the Birmingham Police Department? Was it one of the KKK claverns that thrived on pulling off bombings, cross burnings, and maneuvers of all sorts? Was it some downtown power broker who had the ability to direct the police department and/or the DA's office to do his bidding?

Whoever was behind this Machiavellian attempt to achieve the goal of maintaining the status quo, the experience taught me that you dare not blindly trust officials to do the right thing.

The incident had the side effect of adding to my very limited understanding of things connected with homosexuality. In actuality, I learned nothing about homosexuality or about people struggling with their sexuality or about gay/lesbian persons trying to live out their sexuality and their lives in a responsible, healthy manner. But I learned in a gut-level experience what our prevailing culture thought about homosexuality at the time and what the culture was "teaching" people about homosexuality.

Whoever concocted this fairly sophisticated plot to get Ellwanger out of Birmingham, was banking on Ellwanger being so fearful of a public hearing or a trial in which he would be tarred and feathered with the reputation of being a homosexual, that he would leave town rather than risk such a fate. That is homophobia at its worst. And it is homophobia that feeds anti-gay hatred, stereotypes, and misinformation. I'm sure that most of the law enforcement officers, the jail personnel, the prisoners, the business people, the KKK faithful, and anyone who knew about the plot got a kick out of pinning the label of "nigger-loving homosexual" on this young clergyman. They reinforced each other's views that being homosexual is about as low as you can sink in the mire of perverted humanity. I've often wondered what horrendous impact this scenario may have had on the African American trusty, who may or may not have been gay, beyond the experience of the manipulation of the authorities in forcing him to be part of their nefarious plot.

Probably very few of the folks involved in this plot were ever taught by their parents, their teachers, or their pastors, that lesbian and gay persons were human trash whose sexual orientation was sinful, despicable and morally reprehensible. Yet they all had this view in their heads and in their guts, as if they had taken it all in with their mother's milk and with the unspoken cultural taboos that they had breathed in, at the high school parties, the card games, the corner bars, and yes, at Bible class and church meetings.

If you ask people for a basis for their position that homosexuality itself is wrong and sinful, some will reply with a rationale from their understanding of nature: "Well, it's clear that God created us male and female, and it was God's intention that men and women marry and have children. Anything other than that is going against nature and against God. It's just plain wrong."

I suppose I could blame my lack of knowledge about gay and lesbian persons and my failure to consider outreach to such persons as part of the

Church's mission, on the silence of my teachers and pastors throughout my growing-up years, as well as on the silence of the media and the silence of the gay and lesbian community itself.

However, the silence was broken in June, 1969, when the Stonewall Inn, a gay bar in New York City, was raided by the police. The bar had been raided before, and the clientele had always acquiesced to police intimidation and arrest. But in June, 1969, the patrons at Stonewall Inn resisted. Windows and doors were broken. Rocks were thrown. People ran in the streets. Dudley Clendinen and Adam Nagourney, in their noteworthy volume *Out for Good*, a carefully documented history of the struggle to build a gay rights movement in America, describe the resistance at Stonewall Inn in June, 1969, as historic. They describe the historic significance of the Stonewall event in this way:

> *From that night the lives of millions of gay men and lesbians, and the attitude toward them of the larger culture in which they lived, began to change rapidly. People began to appear in public as homosexuals, demanding respect. And the culture began to react to them.*

In December, 1973, the American Psychiatric Association voted to remove homosexuality from its list of "mental disorders" in its *Diagnostic and Statistical Manual.*

Reconciling in Christ

So in the '70s and the '80s, the heretofore "invisible" community of lesbian and gay persons became visible and vocal. And the nation and the Church began to talk openly about homosexuality. Sometimes we talked with gay and lesbian persons, not just about them. As an active member of the Lutheran Human Relations Association (LHRA), I was drawn into the dialog about homosexuality and the conversation with gay and lesbian persons in the '80s. The LHRA was one of the first religious organizations to take a clear stand: the Church is called to welcome gay and lesbian members on the same basis that they welcome any other members and the Church is called to work for the elimination of discrimination against gay and lesbian persons in society.

It was the strong position of LHRA on homosexuality that moved the adult Bible class at Cross Church, to undertake a study of homosexuality, with the understanding that at the end of the study, Cross Church would decide whether they would become a "Reconciling in Christ" congregation. As a "Reconciling in Christ" congregation, Cross Church would openly welcome gay and lesbian persons who profess a faith in Jesus Christ to participate in the total life of the congregation.

Because Cross Church was to make an important decision, a decision that would undoubtedly be fraught with emotions and differences of opinion, we encouraged every confirmed member to participate in the study leading up to the decision. The study consisted of weekly sessions starting in September and concluding at the middle of December.

We looked at all the Bible passages that seemed to address the issue of homosexuality.

We saw that the passages in Leviticus and Deuteronomy were set in the midst of the "purity codes" that Jews were supposed to follow to make it clear to each other and to the tribes around them, that they were followers of the true God and that they were different. There are no Jews or Christians who currently follow the strict requirements of the purity codes, especially the requirement that people are to be put to death for various infractions of the purity codes, such as "cursing one's father or mother" or "committing adultery with another man's wife" (Leviticus 20), or a woman "for whom no proof of virginity can be found" at the time of marriage (Deuteronomy 22).

We saw that the sin of the people of Sodom (Genesis 19) was not the expression of love and commitment between two gay men, but the attempt of a group of heterosexual men to gang rape the visitors at Lot's house as an act of intimidation against the "foreigners" at Lot's house. We saw that Jesus did not address homosexuality or homosexual acts at all, though he did speak against divorce.

We noted that Paul's warnings against homosexual practices, as well as the Old Testament warnings, were made against the backdrop of a cultural understanding that everyone is heterosexual and that anyone who expresses homosexual attitudes or actions is willfully acting in an unnatural and detestable manner. There was no word for homosexuality or any thought about the possibility of some people having a homosexual orientation in their psycho-physical makeup and possibly in their genes.

We noted that a Gospel-centered Church and a Gospel-centered Christian has the love of God and Jesus Christ himself at the center of their faith and their life, not a set of rules. The role of the moral directives of Scripture such as the Ten Commandments, is to give followers of Christ important signposts to help them see the direction they are to go, as they seek to live their lives in Christ, for Christ, and for Christ's purposes. The one commandment, among the Ten Commandments, that deals with sexuality ("Thou shalt not commit adultery") points us in the direction of expressing our sexuality in a responsible, committed, and loving manner, with someone to whom we commit ourselves for life. If we accept the testimony of almost every gay/lesbian person, that their sexual orientation is as mysterious and powerful a discovery, usually around puberty, as it is for heterosexuals, then the directive of the commandment is equally challenging for straights and for gays: that is, to express their sexuality within their natural, God-given orientation, responsibly, lovingly and ultimately in a lasting, committed relationship with another person.

We did grapple with Scripture as we prepared for our congregational decision. And "grapple" is the right word. There was plenty of back and forth sharing between people with different views and interpretations. However, we realized that we needed to talk with gay and lesbian persons, not simply about them. At the time, in 1989, Cross Church did not have any openly gay or lesbian members. We knew of three members of Cross who we were almost certain were gay, but they were not "out," so we invited three gay and lesbian members from a neighboring ELCA congregation, Village Church, to share their stories with us. They made it clear to us that their sexual orientation was a self-understanding that emerged from within them as they grew up. They each had different accounts of difficulties they encountered along the way, with friends, and with pastors and congregational members, and all three testified to what a freeing, empowering experience it was to find a congregation where they did not have to hide that part of their identity, where they did not have to fear being demeaned, and where they were assured of God's love, acceptance, and forgiveness. They spoke with excitement about the roles that they filled in their congregation: Sunday School teaching, singing in the choir, assisting the minister in leading worship, and participating on the Church Council. It became obvious to us that there was much more to their identity than their sexual orientation. And it became clear that they led productive lives, using their gifts to build up sisters and brothers in their congregation, and to contribute to the common good in the larger community.

I recall that the question was raised during our congregational discussions: "What will we do if we become a 'Reconciling in Christ' congregation, and a couple comes to the pastor and asks to have a commitment ceremony at Cross?"

The response from someone in the group didn't answer the question precisely, but it seemed to satisfy the questioner: "We can't really answer that question now. We'll have to cross that bridge when we get there. We've got a lot of growing to do as a congregation. But if two gay members of our congregation asked for a blessing on their partnership, we'd have to struggle with that request with a whole lot of love, remembering they're our sisters and brothers"

I added: "As their pastor, I'd have to counsel them in much the same way I counsel any couple. It is a very important question. The way we respond to such a request will communicate an important message to the gay and straight community."

After three months of weekly discussion, the time came for the annual congregational meeting, the second Sunday of December, the date we had agreed we would vote on whether to become a "Reconciling in Christ" congregation. The issue was not played down as just another item on the agenda of the annual meeting. We saw the decision as an important juncture in our congregational journey and a defining moment as we discerned our mission and our identity. I focused the sermon in the Sunday worship on the issue, stating: "If gay and lesbian persons received their sexual orientation from the hand of the Creator, just as heterosexual persons do, and that is the truth that gay and lesbian persons have shared with us in our sessions these past weeks, then we are called by the Gospel to receive them as sisters and brothers in Christ, as we would receive anyone else."

I went on to say: "Paul affirms in his profound declaration in Galatians 3:28: 'You are neither Jew nor Greek, slave nor free, male nor female. For you are all one in Christ Jesus.' He does not add: 'You are neither gay nor straight.' But he could have. Within the Church of Paul's day, there was a strong tendency for Jews to discriminate against Greeks, for free people to discriminate against slaves, for men to discriminate against women. We could certainly say in today's Church, straight folks tend to discriminate against gay and lesbian persons. Paul would say that in the Body of Christ, there should be no difference in the way any of these groups of people are received and treated, for we are all one in Christ Jesus."

I closed my message by stating passionately: "I don't know how the vote will turn out today. No matter how the vote turns out, though, and no matter how you vote on this issue, I want you to know that I will love you and continue to be pastor to each of you with the same unconditional love after the vote as before the vote."

All confirmed members of Cross, including teenagers, were eligible to vote. So we had a broad spectrum of voters. When the vote was tallied, there was an overwhelming majority of 72 votes for becoming a Reconciling in Christ congregation and 14 votes against. We were grateful that the vote was not a squeaker. That would have left people with the feeling that "We haven't really decided this matter yet." Or persons on the "losing" side would likely have said: "The vote would have been different, if so-and-so had been here."

All One in Christ

The Sunday after the vote, I arrived at church at my usual time, about an hour before service time. I walked through the sanctuary, and I noticed a beautiful spray of flowers in front of the altar, with a lengthy wide ribbon flowing from the basket onto the red carpet covering the chancel floor. I walked up to the flowers to see if there was a card indicating the donor and/or the occasion for the flowers. There was no name, but the wording on the ribbon said: "ALLELUIA! WE ARE ALL ONE IN CHRIST!"

I quickly got the message, as did all morning worshipers who had been at the previous Sunday's congregational meeting. But no one seemed to know who was so ecstatic and grateful over the welcome mat that had been rolled out for gay and lesbian persons. It was not until Monday that I discovered the exuberant donor of the flowers. It was Tim Hansen, Lutheran Volunteer Corps worker who was doing his year of service with Project RETURN, a reentry ministry to assist men and women coming out of prison, started by

Cross Church and housed in the Cross Church building. Tim Hansen soon thereafter joined Cross and stayed on after his year of volunteer work to serve as Director of Project RETURN for two years. At the time, I saw Tim almost every day, since we had adjoining offices. I knew of his capable, dedicated service to Project RETURN and to ex-offenders, but I had no idea that he was gay until we took the vote and he placed the flowers before the altar.

Tim Hansen brought home to many of us at Cross Church a reality factor in the homosexuality debate that is often overlooked: The vast majority of lesbian and gay persons are working every day at jobs that contribute to the common good of all. Often these jobs are aimed at empowering people at the edges, to get back on their feet and to live into their potential. Their invisibility as gay/lesbian persons is a sign that their sexual orientation is only one piece among many that contribute to their total identity. But their invisibility as gay/lesbian persons is also a sign of the massive pressure of our culture that makes it difficult for gay and lesbian persons to be open about that part of who they are.

After our congregational decision to become a Reconciling In Christ congregation was made, there was a feeling of relief that the vote was finally taken, and the uncertainty of where the congregation stood on this "hot button" issue was behind us. However, there were some of us who realized that this decision would mean very little in terms of spiritual growth or in terms of outreach to lesbian and gay persons in the congregation and in the community, unless we planned something that would continue spiritual nurture in the congregation and would communicate to the gay/lesbian community our genuine welcome and hospitality.

"Coming Out" Sunday

An informal committee that grew out of the three-month study before the vote included Tim Hansen and several others who were eager to live into the new vision for the congregation. The group came up with the idea of a "Coming Out" Sunday, to be observed the Sunday before the national "Coming Out Day," which is October 11.

One important piece for the special Sunday was to have a lesbian/gay person tell his or her story as a "Contemporary Witness," a dynamic that was often included in the Sunday worship format at Cross. The witness slot usually came after the Second Lesson, and gave a congregational or community member an opportunity to witness to their struggle, their faith, their victory, and in turn, to perhaps encourage/challenge the congregation to grow or to act.

A second aspect of the Sunday was the "coming out" gathering after the service, during the regular Adult Bible Class time, where gay and straight people would be encouraged to "come out" with their experiences and struggles. It could be the testimony from a heterosexual person, sharing his or her "aha" experience that led that person to overcome the homophobia of our culture, or from a gay/lesbian person testifying to his or her inner, as well as outer, journey.

A third aspect of the special focus Sunday was the publicity in the gay community, as well as the total community, utilizing the print media especially, to invite gay and straight people to join a congregation that is attempting to live out the Gospel in a way that encourages gay and straight to wrestle with an issue that has been essentially off the radar screen for most Christians or has been talked about in misleading, judgmental ways that demean gay/lesbian persons and fail to bring the healing light of the Gospel to bear on it.

At that first "Coming Out" Sunday, Tim Hansen bravely volunteered to be the person to share his story in the Contemporary Witness slot in the service. He had never publicly told his story, and he had never dreamed of making himself so vulnerable in a worship service in the midst of his own congregation, among people he would be seeing on a weekly basis.

I don't know how well Tim Hansen slept the night before his testimony at the service. I know I had a few butterflies in my own pastoral heart, not knowing what kind of reaction the congregation and the community would have to this bold, extraordinary witness.

Tim started at the beginning of his own journey of self-awareness. He told of feeling "different" and "unique" even before his teens. Then as he moved through adolescence, the pressure all around him was to date girls, even though the strong pull inside of him was an attraction to boys, not to girls. He looked around at his friends, his family, his congregation, for someone to talk to, about this inner struggle, but found it very scary to even think about broaching the subject to anyone. He asked God to forgive him and to transform him into a "normal" man who was attracted to women. He started attending different churches to see whether he could get some spiritual help somewhere. When he was in England during his college years as a foreign exchange student, he attended a Pentecostal church, where they prayed for the Holy Spirit to heal him of his "sinful" urges. He waited and prayed for the change, but it never came.

Tim returned to Minnesota and was living at home. When the inner struggle reached a fever pitch, he felt frustration and shame and guilt, to the point of bargaining with God: "If you transform me, I will serve you forever. I will do whatever you call me to do." Still the change did not come. In desperation, he actually attempted to end his life, feeling unworthy and guilty and condemned, with no sign of healing or change or transformation in sight.

With the intense inner struggle continuing, Tim was awakened one night, he said, in the middle of his sleep, with a bright light throughout the room. Startled out of his sleep by the light, he heard a voice say: "I love you as you are. You are my child."

"From that point forward," Tim stated, in an emotion-driven voice that quivered with authenticity, "I have felt at peace with God and with myself. I know that I am loved by God as I am. I have been healed, not as I expected. My sexual orientation has not been transformed. But I have been transformed. I am forgiven and loved by Christ. And I do plan to serve Him wherever he calls me."

When Tim finished his short, but profoundly moving story, there was a moment of silence. The kind of silence you experience when you stand before an awesome sight, when you sense that you are standing on holy ground. And then the entire congregation stood and applauded and applauded and applauded. There was no doubt that the Spirit was in that place.

After the worship, about 40 persons gathered for the adult sharing. After the courageous testimony of Tim, the stage was set for others to come out with stories that had never been publicly told before. Gay and lesbian persons identified with Tim, especially in his fears of talking with people about his struggle, his sense of guilt and shame, and his experience of deep depression. They were deeply grateful for their experience of acceptance and warmth and the presence of Christ in the service. Straight persons shared stories of how they had overcome, or were in the process of overcoming, the homophobia of our culture, to accept lesbian and gay persons as they are. Doing this kind of unique sharing on a taboo subject in the midst of a black and white group of people, made the sharing even more profound.

Unfortunately, there were a few members who had boycotted the service. But the majority of Cross's members were there, along with many visitors, both gay and straight. There was no doubt that the Good News of God's love in Jesus Christ was communicated and celebrated in a powerful, creative way. And there was no question in the minds of the Worship Committee and Evangelism Committee that "Coming Out Sunday" should be observed every October.

There were those members of Cross who asked: "Why do you feel compelled to have a 'Coming Out Sunday'? Why not simply talk about Jesus' love? Why do you have to talk about gay and lesbian persons in the worship?"

We had to answer that question for ourselves, as well as for our critics. We concluded that it's the very reluctance to address the subject matter that requires us to focus on it. Otherwise, both the Church and the world conclude that there is something inherently wrong and unclean and perverted about gay and lesbian persons. That's what our homophobic culture teaches us. There are thousands of church bulletin boards around the country that boldly state "Everyone Welcome." Yet, given our racist and homophobic culture, every African American and every gay/lesbian person who passes one of those signs, says to himself or herself: "But that welcome doesn't include me."

Even though "Coming Out Sunday" is still outside the comfort zone of some members of Cross, there is a strong consensus among the leaders of Cross that the special focus Sunday is a powerful witness to the Gospel of Jesus Christ and to the Reconciling in Christ position of Cross Church. As a result, Cross Church has observed "Coming Out" Sunday every year since that first moving experience in 1990.

The "Coming Out Sunday" observance has varied from year to year. It has included lesbian/gay ELCA pastors, representatives of PFLAG (Parents and Friends of Lesbians And Gays), and leaders of Lutherans Concerned of North America. At times, it has included an afternoon program, in an effort to make the event as ecumenical as possible and to draw people who would be engaged in their own congregation on a Sunday morning, but who might attend an afternoon event.

I remember one of those Sunday afternoon events that drew a very broad spectrum of people, including some picketers from local fundamentalist churches and from the radical Baptist Church in Kansas headed by Fred Phelps. Two of the picketers came inside the church before the program started and cornered me on the landing of the stairway leading down to the fellowship hall, where the program was about to start.

One of the picketers glared at me and yelled: "You are going to burn in the hottest place in hell because you are the shepherd appointed by God to lead your people. And you are going against the Word of God."

The other picketer chimed in: "You don't deserve to be a pastor. You are the scum of the earth."

The scathing, hateful tone of the accusations made it impossible to carry on any kind of conversation, but I managed to squeeze in a short response in as even-toned a volume as possible: "I just want you to know that God loves you in spite of your hate and your failure to understand the Gospel." I somehow pushed by them and joined the group downstairs to get the program going.

The picketing and the hateful yelling and denunciations were a good experience for all of us, as horrendous as the impact was for all who were there. It was an in-your-face reminder of the venom that many gay/lesbian teenagers and adults growing up in fundamentalist churches often experience from the pulpit, and a heart-wrenching jolt to all of us to be more determined than ever to stay the course nudging and nurturing the Church to live out the Gospel in such a way that gay and straight church folk and non-church folk, catch a glimpse of the healing, affirming light of the Gospel of Jesus Christ.

Because of the public witness of "Coming Out Sundays," and because of the palpable warmth of the people at Cross Church, and due to the witness of LGBT persons at Cross, gay and lesbian persons were joining Cross Church, not in droves, but five or six each year, following that first "Coming Out Sunday."

Blessing a Commitment

Two men who had come to know each other and to love each other as they both came through a demanding, challenging drug treatment program together, came to Cross Church at the invitation of a mutual gay friend who was a member of Cross. David Nordstrom and Joseph Rogan were amazed at the empowerment and the healing that they experienced as they heard the Good News of God's unconditional love in Jesus Christ and as they experienced acceptance and community at a depth that they had never experienced before.

Soon after they started coming to Cross, David and Joseph asked for an appointment to see me. When the two of them sat down to talk with me, they were ecstatic about their experience of the love and acceptance they felt in the congregation. And they were very clear about the power of the Gospel experienced in the sermon and the liturgy and the weekly participation in Holy Communion for their personal journeys of recovery and self acceptance.

After a half hour of deep personal theological conversation about Scripture and the Gospel and Jesus Christ and the Church, David and Joseph got to the question that was obviously on their hearts: "Would you be willing to conduct a service of blessing for the two of us, as we commit ourselves to each other for life? We have come to know each other over the past months. We have had our disagreements and our tensions. But we have come to love each other as we have never loved anyone before. And we believe that we have enough in common, our faith in God, our common struggle to stay in recovery, and now our commitment to the Gospel and to the Church, that we are ready to make that lifelong commitment to each other. Neither of us ever dreamed of finding a church where we could celebrate this commitment publicly. But this is a congregation where we feel so welcome and where our presence together is so affirmed, that we are bold enough to ask you whether this would be possible."

I caught my breath. I knew that this moment would come some day. Here it was: 1993. More than three years since we had declared ourselves as a Reconciling in Christ congregation. I thought to myself: I could not have asked for a more authentic request for blessing a commitment ceremony. This was not a gay couple shopping around for a pastor who would conduct a ceremony for them. This was a couple who had come to our worship and our congregational family, had tasted of the Gospel and of the Holy Meal, and in the experiential context of the Gospel proclaimed and the Body of Christ lived out. They had asked for their promises to each other to be blessed by a pastor and a people with whom they were walking and with whom they were experiencing community.

I responded in much the same way that I would respond to a heterosexual couple who had asked me to officiate at their vows in the context of the congregation, but with the added awareness that this would also be very different from any marriage ceremony celebrated at Cross Church in its 123-year history. "Yes," I answered, "I'd be honored to plan such a ceremony with you. It is clear that you have a loving, caring relationship with each other, and you have much in common with each other, the kind of things that can keep a relationship together for the long haul. You have been worshiping with our congregation and have entered into the worship and the life of the congregation in a way that indicates your commitment to Christ and to Christ's Body, the Church. However, I am going to ask you whether you are ready to fully identify yourselves with the community of believers at Cross, before the ceremony, so that it is clear to yourselves and to the congregation that your vows and your commitment ceremony are not just in the Cross sanctuary, but also in the context of the life of the congregation." They both agreed and gladly joined Cross Church with the next group of new members.

Joseph and David saw the importance of the ceremony, first of all, for themselves. But they also saw its importance for families, for the Cross congregation, for the LGBT community, and for anyone who would hear about it. So they planned it thoughtfully and prayerfully. And I entered into the planning likewise, thoughtfully and prayerfully.

I wanted the congregation not only to be aware of the ceremony, but also to know they were invited and encouraged to participate as fully as possible. I brought the ceremony to the attention of the Board of Elders, the group of 12 elected persons responsible for the spiritual life of the congregation, alongside the pastor. I did not ask for a vote or for their permission. But I wanted them to have a healthy discussion of what was involved as Cross Church was breaking new ground. It was one of the Elders who in the course of the discussion, said it well: "We really decided this when we became a 'Reconciling in Christ' congregation. We said then that we would accept gay and lesbian persons as brothers and sisters in Christ, without questioning or condemning their sexual orientation. So if we truly accepted Joseph and David as our brothers in Christ on the day they made profession of their faith and joined our congregation, then we cannot condemn them for wanting their vows to each other to be made in our presence and to be blessed by God. Nor can we refuse their request just because there might be some people who are uncomfortable with it all. We should surround them with our love and support, as we would for any couple from our congregation."

I knew that I owed it to our Synod Bishop, Peter Rogness, to let him know what we were planning to do at Cross Church. After all, he was our spiritual overseer. I didn't want him to be blindsided or caught by surprise if someone were to talk to him about it. But I didn't want him to be put in a position of being asked to grant permission to Cross Church to do this. I wanted this commitment ceremony to be seen for what it was, an expression of Cross's ministry, a very natural extension of its outreach to the gay/lesbian community. That's exactly what this special worship was all about.

In celebrating with David and Joseph, Cross Church was not trying to score any political points or to take sides in the culture wars that were going on. We were trying to be true to the Gospel that is for all people, and we were trying to be the community of believers that gives support to its members, especially at those milestone moments in their lives when they want to praise God for God's overflowing, unconditional love and when they feel the need for strength beyond their own.

Fortunately, we had a bishop who did not try to micromanage the ministries of congregations. Nor was he fearful of taking risks for the sake of the Gospel. Nor was he trying to be a people pleaser. Most importantly, he had been an urban pastor and knew from experience that walking with people at the edges of society often results in different learning and in non-traditional expressions of ministry. Bishop Rogness was known to respond when asked about congregations conducting same-gender commitment ceremonies: "I trust my pastors."

I will not forget the date of David and Joseph's ceremony. It was on the 29th wedding anniversary of Joyce and myself: Sept. 18, 1993. I had asked the Cross Praise Choir to sing so that there would be visible congregational participation in the celebration. I had asked one of the Elders to be the assisting minister, as I always did in a wedding, to make it clear that the couple was not only receiving the Pastor's blessing but the congregation's blessing as well. Joseph and David had asked my wife, Joyce, to represent their families and the congregation, in speaking a word of affirmation and wisdom, in addition to my homily.

Joseph, who has a natural flair for the beautiful and the artistic, saw to it that the sanctuary was converted into a veritable garden of green plants and blooming flowers. Joseph's large family and David's smaller family were fully represented. Many friends from the LGBT and recovery communities were there as well. Their vows were surrounded by music, singing, Scripture, testimony, and that special assurance of Christ's presence in the Lord's Supper. That is the way Joseph and David wanted it: Their love for each other surrounded and strengthened by the love of their families, their friends, their brothers and sisters in Christ, and the love of Christ Himself.

Life went on after Joseph and David's ceremony. The sky did not fall. The economy did not collapse. The world did not end. However, life at Cross was changed. We had moved from "accepting gay and lesbian persons as sisters and brothers in Christ" to affirming two gay brothers in Christ as they committed themselves to each other for life. That's a little bit like Euro-Americans moving from accepting African Americans or Hispanic Americans or Native Americans as sisters and brothers in Christ to accepting a very specific African/Hispanic/Native American as a son-in-law or daughter-in-law. It's moving from the general to the specific, from the philosophical to the personal, from the distant to the close-at-hand.

Open Sharing

So there were some serious questions and concerns expressed by a few members of the congregation: "How could we let something like that happen at Cross?" And there were some who made it clear that they weren't struggling over whether this was acceptable for a congregation to do. They stated emphatically, "That just wasn't right!"

The Board of Elders discussed the reactions of the congregation and decided that the issue was not something that should be discussed underground and only on the congregational grapevine. The concerns, the questions, and the emotional criticisms needed to be shared openly in the presence of all of us, in the light of day, and in the context of sisters and brothers speaking the truth in love, to one another. Otherwise, there would be people who would say: "We never got a chance to say our piece." There would be people at Sunday morning worship who would be trying to guess who said what to whom. There would be people avoiding one another and distancing themselves from their sisters and brothers.

So we put out a notice in the Sunday bulletin and in a mailing to the congregation, that anyone who had concerns of any kind about Joseph and David's commitment ceremony, should come to an open congregational sharing session, set for a weekday evening in the fellowship hall.

We had no idea how many people would come or what the results would be. We felt led by the Spirit to hold this sharing session, and we simply put it in the hands of the Lord, hoping that people with strong feelings of any sort would be there.

Our hopes were fulfilled. There were about 50 people present, from one end of the spectrum of feelings to the other. David and Joseph were there. People who were angry and outraged were there. People who attended the commitment ceremony were there. And people who hadn't attended were there. Most of the Board of Elders were there. African American members and white members were there. It was a very diverse group of people.

We sat in one huge circle of chairs, taking up two-thirds of the floor space of the fellowship hall. We wanted everyone to be able to see everyone else as each person spoke. After reminding everyone that we were all baptized members of the Body of Christ at Cross and that our purpose every day, and that night, was to build one another up in the faith, speaking the truth of God's Word and of our feelings to one another in love, I laid down two ground rules for our conversation that night:

1. Each person was to be given one opportunity to express his or her feelings, doubts, convictions, fears, and hopes, so that no one would go away saying: "I didn't really get a chance to say what was on my mind." So I asked people to think about what they wanted to say because they would have only one opportunity to speak to the group, but everyone would be asked to speak, and they could speak as long as they wanted.

2. No one would have a chance to rebut another person. This was not a debate. This was not one side trying to prove the other side to be wrong. This was the community of believers at Cross, gathered at a critical moment in their life together, listening to each other, sharing with each other, being with each other, trying to understand where the other person was standing, so that we might continue our journey together with honesty, with sensitivity, and with love.

I asked whether anyone had a problem with the two ground rules. No one did. So we began what proved to be about two hours of amazing honesty and openness.

There were three or four persons who expressed deep doubts about the Church blessing gay or lesbian couples in their commitment to each other. They didn't think it was God's will. But with David and Joseph in the circle, along with many others who had celebrated with them, no anger or venom was directed at anyone. I do not recall that anyone spoke that evening of leaving Cross Church over this.

There were two or three persons who spoke emotionally of originally feeling that gay unions were wrong, but that they were coming to see things differently as they saw the positive relationship between David and Joseph and as they thought about it and prayed about it.

There were three or four gay and lesbian persons, besides David and Joseph, who said that they had attended Joseph and David's commitment ceremony. They were overwhelmed with joy and gratitude that there was a congregation where they were not simply tolerated, as long as they remained in the closet, but a congregation where they could openly live as individuals or as couples, and know that they were totally accepted for who they were.

There was one African American woman who spoke of her brother who was gay, and who had experienced much isolation because of it. She said she felt proud to be part of a congregation where she could openly talk about her brother without fear or shame.

Joseph and David shared their joy over the ceremony and the affirmation they felt from the congregation. They spoke of the powerful witness to God's love that the service had made for certain members of their families and for some of their friends, both gay and straight. They expressed disappointment and hurt to know that their ceremony had been received so negatively by some.

When it came my turn to speak, I reminded people of how we had come to this point in our life together: "When we were preparing to vote on whether to become a Reconciling In Christ congregation, someone raised the question: 'What would we do if we were asked to do a commitment ceremony for a gay or lesbian couple?" And someone in the group answered: 'We'll cross that bridge when we come to it.' Well, we have crossed that bridge. As the pastor who performed the ceremony, I can say that I felt that not only I, as the pastor, but we, as a congregation, were led step by step to this point. I believe that it was a positive witness to God's love for all people. It may not be seen as a sign of Christ's love by some people, just as Christ's affirmation of lepers and tax collectors and prostitutes was not seen as a sign of God's love by some. But I believe that this ceremony was grounded in the Gospel, and supported by the Gospel, and a visible exhibit of the Gospel for people to see."

We literally proceeded around the circle from one person to the person sitting to their left, to the person to their left, and so on. There were tears. There were groans. There were halting phrases and flowing phrases. A closing prayer by one of the Elders, asked for God's Spirit to help us walk together as a congregation, listening to each other, loving one another unconditionally, and seeking to discern God's will.

No one left the sharing session in a hurry. In fact, most people made it a point to seek out another person to hug and with whom to share God's peace. Many people made it a point to go to someone with a differing point of view, to affirm the other as sister or brother in Christ. Everyone agreed that even though the sharing revealed how different some of our views were, the overriding experience was one of catharsis and unity.

Four or five persons left Cross because of their opposition to the commitment ceremony, just as there were four or five who had left because of our decision to become a Reconciling in Christ congregation. However, there were six or seven persons who strongly opposed the ceremony, but who felt such strong ties with the congregation, with its diversity, with its Gospel-centered openness, with its youth ministry or with its social justice focus, that they felt more pulling them to stay at Cross than pushing them to leave.

A Blessed Journey

We went on, after the Joseph/David ceremony, to have many more such celebrations. Most of them were ceremonies where at least one of the persons speaking his or her vows, was a member of Cross, or was closely connected to Cross. The ceremonies were definitely a witness to church folk and to non-church folk of the inclusiveness of God's love. At one such ceremony I remember hearing one person in attendance at the practice, as she looked around at the Cross sanctuary, state incredulously: "You know, I haven't been in a church since I left home for college 20 years ago, and I never thought I would ever set foot in a church for this sort of occasion." And then there was the beautiful ceremony in which two women, both of them active members of Cross, spoke their vows to each other. One of them came from a strong Wisconsin Evangelical Lutheran Synod (WELS) background. In fact, her father was a rostered teacher in WELS. The whole family came to the ceremony and to the reception afterward. The father expressed his gratitude for Cross's ministry and for providing a church family where his daughter and her partner could find a spiritual home where they could be themselves, grow spiritually, and fulfill Christ's mission. (WELS, along with the Lutheran Church-Missouri Synod, takes an official position that any expression of a homosexual orientation is sinful.)

Most of the gay and lesbian persons who have joined Cross are white, though not all. That puts a heavy responsibility on some black members of this predominantly African American congregation to explain to friends and family members why they belong to that congregation with so many white, gay members. On the other hand, it is noteworthy that so many white gay and lesbian persons have not only attended Cross Church, but have joined Cross and become involved in its ministry, singing in the choir, teaching Sunday School, serving on the Church Council and on the Board of Elders. Not only is Cross Church predominantly African American, it is located in the heart of central city Milwaukee, where street people and low-income persons come every week for assistance and some come for Sunday worship. It's situated where your car can be broken into, the license plate removed, and on occasions, the car can be stolen, while you are attending a meeting or participating in choir rehearsal or worship. There are a handful of ELCA or UCC (United Church of Christ) congregations outside of the central city, where gay/lesbian persons are fully welcomed. And still there are about 30 LGBT persons who have joined Cross Church. Why?

I have not polled the lesbian/gay members of Cross to scientifically arrive at an answer to that question. But I have heard enough comments and gotten to know most of them well enough, to have some fairly clear answers.

One of the most basic reasons why gay and lesbian persons have been drawn to Cross is their experience of injustice as gays and lesbians, even though they can "blend into a crowd" in a way that a person of color cannot. They can identify with the experience of prejudice, stereotyping, hatred, and irrational prejudice, and so they find at Cross a sense of community and a dedication to working at justice issues, all in the context of Gospel-centered worship and soulful music.

In every outreach made by an individual or a congregation to a distinct culture or community of people, the individual or congregation is enriched. Again and again we found this to be true in our outreach to the LGBT community.

In planning a commitment ceremony for two gay men, I was surprised that they had chosen two unusual Scripture lessons for their service. One was Isaiah 56:3-5, and the other was Acts 8:26-40. Both of the Scripture passages speak of eunuchs being accepted by God. The men had read commentaries, trying to find passages that spoke positively of gay and lesbian persons. They knew that the common understanding of homosexuality during the era of the writing and the formation of the Old and the New Testament scriptures was a belief that everyone was heterosexual and that homosexual behavior was therefore a perversion of one's sexuality and identity. They discovered, however, that there are some Bible scholars who believe that the term eunuch describes not only those men who had been castrated, but those who had no interest in women. I discovered that there is, therefore, the possibility that "eunuch" is a term that in Biblical times could also have referred to a gay man. Although this understanding of the term "eunuch" in Scripture is not widely accepted or known, I discovered that this understanding is held far beyond the two men for whom I had the privilege of conducting a commitment ceremony.

Whether or not a person believes that the term "eunuch" encompassed gay and lesbian persons at the time the Scriptures were written, it is clear that eunuchs were considered outcasts, in much the same way that gay and lesbian persons are treated today by a huge portion of our society. And it is powerfully re-assuring to gay and straight persons that both Isaiah and Luke, the writer of Acts, go out of their way to make it clear that eunuchs are included as first-class citizens in the Kingdom of God. In Luke's account in Acts 8, of the dramatic story of the conversion and baptism of the "influential official with the Queen of Ethiopia," Luke did not need to use the term "eunuch" to identify this important official. But Luke insists on telling his readers that the Ethiopian official was a eunuch and that he was baptized, after confessing his faith in Christ. No other questions were asked. It seems that Luke wants us to know that the Kingdom of God also includes people with a sexuality that is different from "mainline" heterosexuals.

In 2006, the state of Wisconsin voted to amend the state constitution to declare that marriage can only be between one man and one woman and that no other type of relationship similar to marriage would be recognized, effectively eliminating health insurance coverage and hospital visiting rights for lesbian and gay persons committed to each other in civil unions. Non-gay persons can have only a faint understanding of the alienation and hatred felt by gay and lesbian persons as a result of that vote. I am convinced that that amendment will be repealed. The question is not whether, but when.

There are thousands of fundamentalist and mainline congregations that are bathed in anti-gay teachings on a regular basis. There are thousands of fundamentalist and mainline congregations that are willing to accept lesbian and gay persons as members under a kind of "don't ask, don't tell" policy that refuses to deal with what it would mean to accept them and their family units with honest conversations, genuine affirmation, and the blessing of their committed partnerships.

There are growing numbers of congregations that are actively reaching out to lesbian and gay persons, welcoming them as brothers and sisters in Christ, and celebrating their commitment ceremonies with them. That journey may seem for some congregations to be a burden, and may seem to be very divisive. But for congregations that are seriously walking with people at the edges and for whom the Gospel is more a call to costly discipleship and risk-taking than it is a call to quiet maintenance of the status quo, such a journey is a blessing, for pastor and people, for gay and straight, for the religious and the non-religious community.

Since 2006, three major denominations (the Episcopal Church, the Evangelical Lutheran Church in America, and the Presbyterian Church USA) have joined the United Church of Christ and the Unitarian Universalist Fellowship, in approving the ordination of persons in same-gender committed relationships. A few states now recognize gay marriages and/or offer marriage benefits to persons living in same-gender partnerships. Openly gay and lesbian persons are now able to serve in the armed forces.

Of course, there is still considerable resistance to acceptance of openly gay and lesbian persons, and especially to gay and lesbian marriage. There will continue to be controversy over the issues. However, not only does the younger generation have less difficulty with the issues, but the mounting number of laws affirming the rights of gay and lesbian persons, the growing witness of the Church, and the blowing of the Spirit will continue to free gay and straight persons to live into the unifying vision of God's kingdom.

CHAPTER 10

GIFTS FROM ABROAD: REFUGEES IN OUR MIDST

Keep on loving one another as brothers and sisters. Do not forget to entertain strangers, for by so doing some people have entertained angels without knowing it.

–Hebrews 13:1-2

Bounheua and Thongba Bouakongxaya and their daughters, Khampheua, Khampanh, and Thoy, came to Cross Church as refugees from Laos via Thailand refugee camps, in 1972. We had no idea how this experiment would work out. It was a leap of faith on the part of the congregation.

There were plenty of unanswered questions that we could raise as reasons why not to take this risk. They were all brought up at the Church Council meeting the night we made the decision to sponsor the family: "Would this endeavor cost Cross hundreds of dollars in unpredictable expenses? Would we be able to find the volunteers to take them to various resources, such as clinics and schools and governmental offices, to get them launched in a new culture and a new setting? Would we be able to communicate with them, since neither adult spoke much English? Would this time-consuming project siphon precious time and energy of pastor and people from the crucial mission of a relatively small urban congregation struggling to reach out to its neighborhood and to grow spiritually and numerically? Would outreach to Asians from abroad possibly hinder Cross's outreach to African Americans in the neighborhood?"

There were no certain answers to the questions raised. However, there were enough voices on the Church Council who believed "we can do it," that we voted to move ahead with the project. In fact, there was some positive growth that took place during the process of making the decision. "These are refugees," some insisted, "who have left everything behind and have come to this country with nothing more than the clothes on their back. It is our Christian calling to help them get a fresh start here."

Others added: "Instead of taking away from our mission and our congregational life, this experience and this added diversity will almost certainly enrich us and make us stronger."

The experience was enriching. The Bouakongxayas moved into the custodial apartment above the church office and Bounheua and Thongba served as custodians of Cross Church, until Bounheua's health no longer permitted him to do the work.

There were several members of Cross who offered to accompany the Bouakongxayas and to advocate for them as they learned the English language and familiarized themselves with a new country and a new culture.

The Bouakongxayas fit the mold of most refugees in many respects. They were extremely grateful for the roof over their head, the job that brought in more income than they had ever experienced, and the sense of community they felt from the congregation, especially from the dozen or so persons who escorted them to doctors' appointments, governmental offices, and the like. They worked hard to please their benefactors.

Soon after their arrival, the Bouakongxayas started attending Sunday morning worship, even though they had difficulty understanding the English. Within a few months, they expressed interest in joining Cross Church. I set up several sessions with Bounheua and Thongba, to communicate to them the basics of the Christian faith and especially the Good News of God's love in Jesus Christ. I soon had the honor of baptizing the parents and the children. Some 40 years later, they were still active members of Cross Church.

But that's not the whole story. A few months after their arrival, the Bouakongxayas told us of a cousin of Thongba's, Khane Khotsombath, and her husband, Bounlam, who would be able to come to the U.S. if they had a sponsor. They asked very cautiously and very sensitively whether Cross Church would consider sponsoring them. They even offered to house them in their own two-bedroom apartment.

The experience with the Bouakongxayas had been so positive that the Sponsoring Committee and the Church Council had very little discussion before they came to the decision to sponsor the Khotsombaths.

Bounlam and Khane, like Bounheua and Thongba, were in their late twenties, but with no children. They helped with the custodial work and took over the entire responsibility of caring for the church and office, when Bounheua's health caused them to leave the custodial apartment and move into their own place about a mile from the Church. Soon after their arrival, the Khotsombaths followed the lead of Bounheua and Thongba and joined Cross Church.

Refugee Ministry and Neighborhood Outreach

The outreach to refugees from Laos, even though it could be squared with the Gospel mandate to "go to all nations," seemed to be totally unrelated to Cross's outreach to its neighborhood, made up of African Americans. However, most individual Christians and congregations discover that they reap unexpected dividends from taking a leap of faith that on the surface seems almost foolish.

About three years after the arrival of the Bouakongxayas, we noticed that the apartment complex three blocks south of the church had attracted 25 to 30 Laotian/Hmong families, along with 25 to 30 African American families. Our evangelism teams canvassed the entire complex, inviting all the families to worship, Sunday school, and after-school tutoring. We didn't get a record response, but we did make contact with the Manikham family, a Laotian family with three very bright daughters in elementary school. Mrs. Manikham was a committed Christian, active in a Laotian congregation on the south side of Milwaukee and active in trying to organize Laotian/Hmong families in the apartment complex. The three Manikham daughters—Soumontha, Inthava, and Somthavin—started coming to Cross Sunday School, worship, and after-school tutoring. The three girls soon were baptized and later confirmed. It was clearly an advantage to have the Bouakongrayas as members of Cross when the three Manikham girls took that leap of faith and walked those three long blocks to Cross Church. They maintained their relationship with Cross Church through high school, until each of them went off to college, to marriage, and to destinations far beyond Milwaukee.

A second surprising connection between refugee ministry and neighborhood outreach at Cross occurred after Khamphuea Bouakongxaya graduated from Carthage College, a Lutheran college in Kenosha, 40 miles south of Milwaukee. Khamphuea had majored in elementary education and had applied for a teaching position in the Milwaukee Public Schools.

Khamphuea had no control over where she would be assigned to teach. With 152 elementary schools in Milwaukee, her chances of being assigned to any of the three schools close to Cross Church were extremely slim. No one was more surprised than Khamphuea herself, when she received the assignment to teach at Siefert School, the school closest to Cross Church, a school attended by several Cross children and many neighborhood children.

To this day, neither the Bouakongxayas nor members of Cross Church fully realize the vital role that the Bouakongxayas have played in Cross's neighborhood outreach. And it all happened because the Social Ministry Committee and the Church Council of a financially-strapped urban congregation stepped way out of the box by engaging in refugee ministry. The Holy Spirit took care of the rest.

We realized that there were many members of Cross who had a more distant relationship with these quiet, humble people from half way around the world. We observed special black history services, especially during Black History Month, and we held services with a focus on the role of women in the Church and in our nation's history, especially during Women's History Month. We observed "Coming Out" Sunday to more fully appreciate the stories of gay and lesbian persons. And we held youth services and men's day services, to more fully appreciate the gifts of men and youth. So we decided we would observe an "Asian Gifts" Sunday.

We invited the Laotian pastor from the Laotian Christian Church to preach, as well as members of the Laotian congregation to join us in our worship. In a small way, we tried to let the Bouakongxayas and the Khatsombaths know that we appreciated them, their gifts, their culture, and their people. And in a small way, members of Cross were nudged to notice these quiet, faithful members of Cross and to openly and publicly celebrate their witness and their gifts in our midst. We helped children, youth, and adults come to recognize that not all Asian people are "Chinese" and that there is even a difference between Laotian and Hmong, even though they all come from the same country of Laos. We also nudged a few more people to reach out to these Laotian sisters and brothers to get to know them and to know their amazing journeys to the refugee camps, to the U.S., to Milwaukee, and to Cross Church.

If the journey with the Bouakongxayas and the Khatsombaths had been the only chapter in the story of Cross's refugee ministry, it would have been enriching and nurturing enough, for the congregation to be truly grateful for the experience, with all of its unexpected fruits. But there were several chapters yet to come.

Political Refugees Seek Sanctuary

In 1982, a group of concerned persons in Milwaukee began forming to relate to the tide of refugees arriving in the United States from El Salvador and Guatemala. Most of the Salvadorans and Guatemalans arriving in the U.S. were political refugees, rather than economic refugees. They were not coming for a greater income for themselves and their family. They were fleeing a dangerous situation in their country, where their very lives were threatened if they were to remain.

Civil wars were raging in El Salvador and Guatemala, and government soldiers, with training and equipment from the U.S., were arresting, torturing, disappearing, and assassinating anyone who appeared to have connections or sympathies with the guerrillas, or who raised questions about government policies. Labor union leaders, teachers, priests, catechists, and university professors were especially at risk.

U.S. immigration officials were routinely sending these political refugees from Central America back to their home countries, even though the U.S. had an official policy, in line with United Nations policies, of protecting refugees who had reasonable fear of persecution if they remained in their country of origin.

The Milwaukee groups concerned about Central American political refugees were contacting congregations in metro Milwaukee to try to recruit them as sanctuary congregations or as congregations that would publicly endorse any sanctuary congregation.

A member of Cross, Carolyn Jackson, became active on the Milwaukee Sanctuary Committee and invited me, and others at Cross, to become active with the committee. I attended some of the meetings and came to realize the grave dangers that hundreds of Salvadorans and Guatemalans were facing as a result of our country's policies of returning at-risk refugees and of endorsing governmental repression in Central American countries.

Two high-profile events had fueled concern for Central American refugees and for justice and human rights advocates in Central America. Salvadoran Archbishop Oscar Romero was assassinated by Salvadoran military on March 24, 1980, while celebrating the Eucharist, and on Dec. 2 of the same year, four Catholic Church women were raped and assassinated by Salvadoran military near the main Salvadoran airport. There was no doubt in anyone's mind that the military repression in El Salvador and in neighboring Guatemala was at horrendous levels.

There were individuals and groups around the U.S. who were looking for ways to make a strong witness against the repression and the persecution happening in Central America, as a result of the financial and military aid of the U.S., and under the direction of the U.S. State Department—all in the name of "fighting Communism." Milwaukee was blessed with a Catholic Archbishop, Rembert Weakland, who was deeply concerned about the Central American repression. And Milwaukee was blessed with a Catholic lay leader, Ruth Chojnacki, who gave leadership to local organizing that led to the launching of the Milwaukee Sanctuary Movement in 1982.

It was on a cold, rainy night, December 2, 1982, the second anniversary of the murder of the four church women in El Salvador, that St. Benedict the Moor Catholic Church, Milwaukee, and Cristo Rey Catholic Church, Racine, declared themselves as sanctuary congregations in a service of prayer and celebration at St. John Cathedral in downtown Milwaukee. Cross Church was well represented at the service, having voted to become an "endorsing" sanctuary congregation. That meant that we were not, at the time, receiving any refugees into sanctuary at Cross, but that we stood with our sisters and brothers at St. Benedict and at Cristo Rey, and would do everything in our power to defend them and the refugees in sanctuary, if they were arrested or taken to court by the Immigration and Naturalization Service.

Publicly receiving several Guatemalan and Salvadoran refugees into sanctuary was a bold act of civil disobedience on the part of the two sanctuary congregations and the endorsing congregations. It was especially bold on the part of the refugees, whose names were read out at the service that night. There was a sense of "holy tension" all through the service. The refugees who were being received into sanctuary were present in the service, wearing bandanas over their faces below their eyes, to avoid recognition, as the press took pictures for the next day's papers in Milwaukee and around the country. People of faith were standing in solidarity with their Central American brothers and sisters, at risk of reprisals from their own government.

Archbishop Weakland spoke for all those who supported the sanctuary movement when he stated: "We truly believe in the sanctity and sacredness of all human life. I had to weigh this act of civil disobedience with the very real threat to these people's lives if they were to return to their homeland."

Rachel Parra, secretary of the parish council at Cristo Rey Church, spoke with a tremor in her voice at the Dec. 2 service: "We take this action after much prayer and deliberation. It is our belief that the current policy and practice of the United States government with regard to Central American refugees is illegal and immoral. If this is indeed a country based on the inalienable rights of every person to life, liberty, and the pursuit of happiness, we, as American citizens, have the right to call on our government to respect these rights when they are violated."

With the endorsement of Archbishop Weakland and the dramatic service publicly declaring sanctuary being held at the cathedral church of the Milwaukee Archdiocese, the sanctuary movement in Milwaukee was off to an auspicious beginning.

One by one, congregations around the country declared sanctuary. A momentum was building, and Milwaukee-area congregations that had endorsed the two initial sanctuary congregations, were asked to consider declaring sanctuary themselves. Cross Church had leaders like Carolyn and Tom Jackson and Pat and Ellis Coleman, who were led by the Spirit to bring the challenge to Cross to become a sanctuary congregation.

Declaring sanctuary was a much bolder step than endorsing another congregation. It would mean receiving a refugee into sanctuary, taking responsibility for housing, and being vulnerable to possible legal action by the INS.

Richard R. Caemmerer Jr., world-renowned artist, is holding up the Sanctuary Cross, which he designed and assisted in constructing, with the aid of Latin American children and adults, as well as children and adults from Cross Church. The Cross stood in the chancel of Cross Church, reminding worshipers that Cross Church was a Sanctuary congregation.

A Leap of Faith

It was during the summer of 1983 that the Cross Church Council considered whether or not we would declare sanctuary. The pragmatic questions were raised: What would happen if the INS picked up our refugee and charged Cross Church with "harboring an illegal alien"? Would Cross Church be fined some exorbitant amount of money, like $500,000? Would Pastor Joe or the congregational president be arrested? Would legal assistance be available?

There were no clean answers to any of those questions. We saw that declaring sanctuary would require a real leap of faith. So the deeper question began emerging: Why would Cross Church take such risks, especially since the move seemed to have nothing to do with a predominantly African American congregation's mission of proclaiming and living the Gospel in a poverty neighborhood?

One council member, an African American man who had served in the U.S. Army and who was an active member of the Army Reserve at the time, spoke very strongly against the move: "How can we consider taking a step that is illegal and contrary to our own government's policy? All the unrest in Central America is a result of Communists trying to take over the countries. And we have to stop Communism."

After some lengthy debate, it was Ellis Coleman, an African American member of the Board of Elders, who became very emotional and impatient with the back-and-forth discussion. "I can't understand why people are hesitating with this decision," he said. "Many of us in this room have foreparents who made it to freedom back in the days of slavery, precisely because some people of faith took the risk of going against their government and offered protection to runaway slaves making their way to freedom on the Underground Railroad."

There was silence after that moving statement. There was no more debate. With one dissenting vote, we made the decision to declare sanctuary, with the service of celebration to be held on September 15, 1983.

Celebration of Sanctuary

We chose September 15 as the date for declaring sanctuary for two reasons. September 15 is observed as a freedom day in parts of Central America and because September 15, 1963, was the infamous day on which four

Jorge (assumed name), from Guatemala, at right, with unnamed colleague at the lectern on the left, tell their stories of threats to their life and harrowing journeys to the United States, seeking safety. They are speaking at the service inaugurating sanctuary at Cross Church, September 15, 1983, when Jorge was received by Cross as "refugee in sanctuary."

girls were killed in the bombing of the Sixteenth Street Baptist Church in Birmingham, Alabama. We wanted people to see that the complicity of the South's power structures in the intimidation and violence perpetrated against blacks in the 1960s in the U.S. South was similar to the complicity of the U.S. government's support of intimidation and violence against *campesinos*, church workers, and anyone in Latin America who was resisting the government-sponsored repression in the 1980s.

We tried to plan the declaration of sanctuary celebration in such a way that we would raise consciousness in the Milwaukee area about our country's financial and military collusion with the assassinations, the disappearances, and the pervasive repression in Central America. We certainly wanted to bring to the light what the U.S. Immigration and Naturalization Service was trying to do behind the scenes, sending Central American refugees who had entered the U.S. to escape possible torture and death, back to those life-threatening situations. And we wanted to publicly announce our determination to protect Jorge (assumed name), a Guatemalan refugee, who had fled to the U.S. at the insistence of family and friends. He had received threats to his life because of his union activities. We hoped that our public, open declaration of protection for Jorge, would push the INS into avoiding an attempt to send Jorge back to Guatemala.

We surmised that the INS would not want to draw the federal government into a protracted, secret-divulging legal process with Cross Church and all of our ecumenical allies. This was a huge leap of faith, but for whatever reason, the INS did not attempt to arrest Jorge during the two years that he was in sanctuary with Cross Church, nor did the INS threaten or intimidate Cross Church for its public stand against INS refugee policies and U.S. policies in Central America.

The worship at Cross Church, celebrating Cross's declaration of becoming a sanctuary congregation on September 15, was a moving, never-to-be-forgotten celebration of faith and hope and courage. Our Association of Evangelical Lutheran Churches Bishop William Kohn and our English Synod Bishop Harold Hecht were both present to publicly endorse our congregation's action. Pastors and members of more than 20 other congregations from a variety of denominations joined in the celebration that filled our 250-capacity sanctuary.

Thirty pastors, priests, bishops, and congregational representatives gathered in the chancel area around Jorge, holding over him our outstretched hands. Jorge wore a bandana kerchief over the lower part of his face below his eyes to hide his identity from the pictures being taken by the press. We pledged our protection to Jorge and sought God's blessing. We knew we were not alone in our stand of civil disobedience and in our closer walk with sisters and brothers in Central America. Above all, we felt the presence of God's Spirit moving among us and through us.

Jorge lived in a small cottage at the rear of the lot where our house stood, a block south of Cross Church. Consequently we saw him and talked with him almost daily. Shortly after the powerful celebration of declaring sanctuary, Joyce and I invited Jorge to join us in our family meal one evening. I don't recall what was on the menu that evening, but I do recall that Jorge ate very little. Concerned about Jorge's lack of appetite, Joyce asked him whether he was ill or whether she could serve him something else that would meet his needs better.

"Oh, no," Jorge responded, "I'm feeling okay, and the food is great. It's just that I find it very difficult to eat very much at any meal. I keep thinking about my family in Guatemala, and I know how little they have to eat. I just don't feel right if I eat a lot of food, and I know my family is half-starving." What a powerful example of how immigrants, or anyone "at the edges," can nurture us and enrich our lives!

Without a doubt, of all the refugees with whom we walked, Jorge's presence in our midst for over two years, had the greatest impact on our life as a congregation and on my life as pastor and as a believer in Christ in the 1980s. When I think of the amazing things that have happened as a result of this walk with Jorge and this act of civil disobedience in declaring sanctuary and being part of the twentieth century Underground Railroad for Central American refugees, it is truly mind-boggling.

Results of Sanctuary

Let me list the most visible results of this awesome experience with Jorge and the sanctuary movement:

- We were drawn into some profound relationships with others in the sanctuary movement, especially with Roman Catholics who were active locally. There was Ruth Chojnacki, coordinator of the local movement, who was theologically and historically grounded. There were scores of sisters in various orders—Dominicans, School Sisters of Notre Dame, School Sisters of St. Francis, and others—whose commitment to sisters and brothers in Central America who were oppressed because of their authentic witness to the Gospel, was truly inspiring.
- New observances in our Sunday liturgies became part of our Cross tradition. The Sunday before March 24 became the special observance of the martyrdom of Archbishop Oscar Romero. The Sunday before December 2 became the commemoration of the martyrdom of the four church women brutally raped and murdered in El Salvador, December 2, 1980. The Sunday prayers lifted up by name refugees and congregations and priests and pastors and bishops who had now become part of who we were as a largely African American Lutheran parish in the low-income community of Milwaukee.

- Members of the congregation went on mission trips to El Salvador. Flo Seefeldt, an African American member of Cross and activist engaged in local issues, joined one of the study missions to El Salvador in 1985, and returned with gripping stories from the people she met. She was especially struck by the stories she heard at the *Fe y Esperanza* ("Faith and Hope") refugee camp. This was a camp sponsored by the small Lutheran Church of El Salvador. As she told the story of the camp, she stressed especially the act of faith and hope that the small, financially-strapped Lutheran Church of El Salvador demonstrated in undertaking the maintenance of a camp for several hundred refugees, housing and feeding them day after day. But she stressed even more the physical risk that church leaders, such as Bishop Medardo Gomez, and camp staff personnel, were taking, in accepting these refugees from the countryside. These were people who were fleeing the constant violence between the guerrillas and the Salvadoran military. Most of the refugees were suspected by the Salvadoran military to be guerrillas or guerrilla sympathizers. This put the church leaders and camp staff under constant surveillance and resulted in threatening visits and frequent arrests by Salvadoran police and military.
- To have members of our congregation visit El Salvador and walk with the people, ever so briefly, and then return to tell the real stories of real people standing up for their faith at great risk to themselves, was more than informative. It was food for the soul that gave us perspective and strength to walk more closely with the poor and to be willing to take risks for the Gospel.
- One of those mission trips to El Salvador was the call in 1987 to accompany the Salvadoran refugees who were taking the huge risk of returning from camps in Honduras to their original residences in and around Guarjila, against the advice of the Salvadoran military. I decided to go on that mission, and that is when I met Reverend Margaret Suiter, an ordained pastor of the American Lutheran Church, who, in spite of a painful struggle with breast cancer and with the prognosis of five years to live, was an assistant to Bishop Gomez, working especially with refugees and people struggling for survival in the conflicted areas of the countryside. I was deeply impressed by Margaret Suiter's vibrant, courageous faith and at the same time, disturbed to learn that she was about to lose her health insurance coverage because she did not have a call from a Lutheran congregation or from a Lutheran entity in the United States.
- I came back to Cross Church, from that unforgettable experience of accompanying refugees back home, with a determination to find a call for Margaret Suiter, so that she could maintain her health insurance and continue to fulfill her passion of witnessing to the Gospel by walking with the people of El Salvador. Time was of the essence. So I came to the Cross Church Council with a request that Cross Church issue a

call to Margaret Suiter to be Assistant Pastor at Cross Church, with the special assignment to serve as Minister of Accompaniment with the Lutheran Church of El Salvador. The Cross Church Council voted unanimously to issue the call to Margaret Suiter, with the approval of the English Synod of the Association of Evangelical Lutheran Churches (AELC), and with the understanding that Cross Church would seek financial support for Reverend Suiter's ministry from individuals and congregations around the country. Cross Church did not have the financial resources to provide a salary for her, and we never were able to provide the regular, full salary we had hoped to. But the authentic call from a Lutheran congregation enabled Reverend Suiter to maintain her health insurance, and for that she was very grateful, as were Bishop Gomez and the Lutheran Church of El Salvador.

- To this day, there hangs in the conference room of Cross Church a picture of Reverend Suiter, looking out of the driver's window of the pickup truck she was driving, loaded with supplies for the refugees returning to Guarjila, and smiling as though this was the fulfillment of her life and her calling. And it was.
- Cross Church considered it a privilege to have called Margaret Suiter as Assistant Pastor in charge of accompaniment ministry in El Salvador and to have been able to continue the health insurance coverage for a super-dedicated Lutheran pastor. That would have been dividend enough. But something more happened.

We saw the bold stand for the Gospel and for justice on the part of the Salvadoran Lutheran church and Bishop Gomez. We saw the great need of the Salvadoran Lutheran Church for moral, spiritual, and financial support during those tumultuous days. We saw that the trips to El Salvador and the firsthand reports from Reverend Suiter were putting a face on the otherwise-invisible devastating policies of the U.S. government in training, aiding, and supporting the repressive death squad activities of the Salvadoran military.

So we developed the idea of a partnership relationship between our Greater Milwaukee Synod and the Lutheran Church of El Salvador. The Evangelical Lutheran Church of America (ELCA) and its expression in southeastern Wisconsin, the Greater Milwaukee Synod, had just been formed in 1988. Cross Church was one of four Association of Evangelical Lutheran Church (AELC) congregations, in a sea of 140 American Lutheran Church (ALC) and Lutheran Church in America (LCA) congregations that formed the Greater Milwaukee Synod in 1988. But Cross Church was bold

Cross Church members, from left to right, Carolyn Jackson, Norman Kane, and Joseph Ellwanger, participate in the march in San Salvador, El Salvador, March 24, 1987, commemorating the seventh anniversary of the martyrdom of Archbishop Oscar Romero. Carolyn Jackson was instrumental in leading Cross Church to become a Sanctuary congregation in 1983.

to send a resolution to the second assembly of the Greater Milwaukee Synod in 1989, asking the synod to form a partner relationship with the Lutheran Church of El Salvador. We brought Reverend Suiter to Milwaukee to speak to the assembly. Even though she was experiencing a painful kidney stone attack, she spoke to the assembly clearly and passionately about the courageous witness of the Salvadoran Lutheran Church in the midst of a civil war. When the vote on our resolution was taken, the assembly was unanimous in declaring a partnership relation with the Lutheran Church of El Salvador.

It was years later that Peter Rogness, Bishop of the Greater Milwaukee Synod, 1988-2000, stated that it was the Greater Milwaukee Synod's decision to partner with the Salvadoran Lutheran Church that helped spark the ELCA initiative that has resulted in all 65 of its synods establishing specific partnerships with churches abroad.

Gradually, over the years, the partnership with the Lutheran Church of El Salvador has deepened the involvement of many congregations of the

People of faith from Wisconsin, including members from Cross Church, are shown participating in the annual solemn vigil at the gates of Fort Benning, Columbus, Georgia, where the School Of the Americas (SOA) is located. People of conscience coming from all over the world call for the closing of the School, run by the U.S. Army and funded by the Pentagon. The SOA teaches Latin American soldiers how to use terrorist tactics against their own people as a way of maintaining control and squashing democratic reform efforts.

Greater Milwaukee Synod in mission and ministry in amazing ways. Over 12 congregations of the Greater Milwaukee Synod have a partnership with a congregation in the Lutheran Church of El Salvador. The partnership between St. John's Lutheran Church, Brookfield, and Heroes of the Faith congregation in El Salvador, has resulted in the two congregations sharing volunteers for vacation Bible School both ways and in many mission trips both ways.

Mary Campbell, an attorney and member of Redeemer Lutheran, Milwaukee, felt a call to serve in the Lutheran Church of El Salvador and spent five years heading up the human rights mission of the Salvadoran Lutheran Church. She has returned to Milwaukee with an adopted son, Ricardo, and has offered invaluable leadership to the Greater Milwaukee synod's El Salvador Committee.

Michelle Townsend, a member of Cross Church, felt a call to serve the Salvadoran Lutheran Church while Mary Campbell was in El Salvador, and she assisted in the human rights work of the church there for over a year. This walk with the Lutheran Church of El Salvador and with the people of El Salvador played a major role in Michelle's decision to enter the Lutheran

School of Theology in Chicago and to take the journey of ordained ministry. She accepted a call in 2010 to serve as Associate Pastor at Cross Church, and since 2012 has been serving as the lead pastor.

Without a doubt, the steady involvement of my wife, Joyce, myself, and several members of Cross, in the national efforts to close the School of the Americas, now called the Western Hemisphere Institute for Security Cooperation, in Columbus, Georgia, is closely connected with our congregational involvement in the sanctuary movement and our sponsorship of Jorge. Our close-to-the-ground walk with Bishop Gomez and the pastors and the people of the Salvadoran Lutheran Church, convinced us beyond the shadow of a doubt, that our country's training of Latin American military personnel, especially at the School of the Americas, was directly responsible for most of the assassinations, torture, and repression carried out by the military in El Salvador. Even though the officers involved in the murder and rape of the four church women, the assassination of Archbishop Oscar Romero, the massacre of the 800 villagers in El Mozote, and the six Jesuit priests, along with their housekeeper and her daughter at the University of Central America, were almost all trained at the School of the Americas, the United States has never required the government of El Salvador to reprimand the officers involved in these vicious crimes against the people of El Salvador.

Members of Cross Church have gone year after year to the School of the Americas Watch annual demonstration at the gates of Fort Benning, calling for the closing of the School of the Americas and calling for a Congressional investigation of U.S. foreign policy that trains military officers in terrorist tactics to be used against their own people. Joyce has been moved so deeply by our country's complicity in the savage repression against the people of Central America that she committed an act of civil disobedience in 2002. She walked onto the grounds of Fort Benning, where the School of the Americas is located, as a public witness to her deep belief that the United States should not be involved in training any soldiers in terrorist tactics. As a result, she was arrested on trespassing charges and was convicted and sentenced to serve six months in the federal women's prison in Danbury, Connecticut. Bishop Gomez and all the pastors and people of the Lutheran Church of El Salvador, have thanked Joyce for her courageous stand for an end to U.S. involvement in the repression of the Salvadoran people.

Needless to say, the impact of Cross's simple act of receiving Jorge into sanctuary had an astounding ripple effect on me, on Joyce, and on all the members of Cross Church.

Refugees from Haiti

But the saga of gifts from abroad did not stop with Jorge and Cross's involvement in the sanctuary movement. After Jorge, there came our walk with two Haitian men. It was during the 1980s that the stories of the upheavals and poverty in Haiti and the pictures of desperate boat people fleeing Haiti, were on the nightly news and in the daily papers. Our contact with Lutheran Social Services revealed the need for sponsors for Haitian refugees. Our Bible Class and Social Ministry Committee decided that we should do something about the Haitian crisis. So we received two Haitian refugees: Roger Similien and Ernest Louis.

At the beginning we had a language problem. No one at Cross knew Creole, which was the first language of the two men, so we had to manage with their second language, which was French.

The two men quickly found jobs, worked hard at their English, and developed relationships in the congregation. A retired African American woman in the congregation, Alma Eggert, made a special point of taking them under her wing, and they quickly felt the acceptance of the congregation. They came to the Pastor's Class and had a chance to get to know people in a smaller setting and to practice their English. They soon joined Cross Church and were regular in their worship attendance. Within two years, Ernest married a U.S. woman and began to raise a family. Roger heard about some better-paying jobs in the meat-packing industry and moved to Sioux City, Iowa.

As in the case of all the refugees sponsored by Cross Church, Roger and Ernest enriched us in ways that were both direct and indirect. They made the media stories about Haiti much more significant to us and motivated the Adult Bible Class to do a study of the history of Haiti. As we learned that Haiti is the poorest nation in the Western Hemisphere and that the United States has been involved in their economy and their politics in some domineering ways, Joyce and I decided to join a study mission to Haiti.

Joyce and I returned from our trip to Haiti deeply moved by the poverty of most of the people, but also touched by the determination of some non-governmental organizations and some religious leaders, to do their best to bring about change, to lift the people out of poverty, and to nurture and educate youth.

One unforgettable experience was worship on Palm Sunday in a large Catholic church in Port-au-Prince, where the priest was a charismatic leader for change in the church and in the community. We were impressed by the number of children and young adults attending, perhaps 60 per cent of the congregation of 1,000. Also unforgettable were the lay participation in leading the worship and the 50-voice choir that sang Handel's *Hallelujah Chorus* with amazing fervor and passion.

Upon returning from the study trip to Haiti, I convinced our social ministry committee, along with others in the congregation, to sponsor a "Haitian Gifts" evening. We invited people from the UW-Milwaukee community, from the study mission to Haiti, from the African American community, and the handful of Haitians living in Milwaukee. It was a great evening in which we gathered folks who had any level of interest in the people of Haiti. As a result of the evening, about a dozen people committed themselves to reviving an organization that had been dormant: "Haiti: Mind Body Bread."

We formed a board of Haiti: Mind Body Bread, and began distributing a newsletter, raising funds, and holding annual events, to develop interest in Haiti and to maintain scholarships for elementary and high school students in Haiti who might otherwise not be able to go to school. One student from Cite Soleil, the poorest section of Port au Prince, was named Joseph Nasson Seide. We supported him briefly, and then he came to the U.S. to further his studies. He stayed a few months at Casa de las Rosas, a refugee house sponsored by the Milwaukee Sanctuary Coordinating Committee, and then moved out on his own, working hard at labor-intensive jobs, and going to college. He kept us up to date on what was happening in Haiti, and often spoke to congregations and organizations on behalf of Haiti: Mind Body Bread.

Nasson worshipped at Cross, spoke occasionally at our service and/or Bible Class, and helped us keep the people of Haiti on our congregational and personal prayer list and on our advocacy list, as we kept in touch with our congressional representatives. He was able in 2009 to bring his wife and his daughter to live with him in Milwaukee.

Refugees from Sudan

Still another chapter in Cross's refugee ministry was that of Sudan. It was in the 1990s that the civil war in southern Sudan, and the thousands of refugees fleeing the chaotic conditions, came to our attention. The plight of the southern Sudanese, who were mainly Christian or animist and who were being oppressed by the Islamist central government of Sudan, seldom made the daily papers or the nightly TV newscast. However, religious periodicals kept a steady stream of stories and testimonies in their weekly or monthly issues.

When we inquired of the Lutheran Social Services, we found that there were Sudanese refugees waiting to be placed with sponsors. So it wasn't long before we received a single man, Daniel Makuei, and a woman, Nyankir Bior, and her three small daughters, Aguel, Yar, and Riek.

Daniel had an amazing ability with the English language. When I asked him where he picked up his English, he explained: "When I was in the refugee camp in Kenya, I got an English New Testament, and I began reading it alongside of my New Testament in Dinka, and that's how I learned English." Daniel was a committed Christian when he came to the U.S., so it was a quick, natural decision on his part to become a member of Cross Church. Neither did it take long for him to land a job, keep a job, and put away money in a savings account. Within three or four years, he had purchased a house and is, to this day, making great strides toward acculturating.

When I asked Daniel how he had developed such a self-disciplined way of life and how he had become such a good steward of his earnings, he was quick to reply: "I will never forget where I came from. I will never forget the years in southern Sudan, when we ate leaves and grasshoppers to stay alive. And we kept moving from one place to the next from day to day, to avoid the soldiers and their bullets and their torture and their kidnapping. Here in this country it's paradise, and I want to be able to stay here."

Nyankir found life in the big city of Milwaukee very difficult to adjust to. There was a huge cultural chasm between the Kenyan refugee camp with open tents, and the house in Milwaukee, with locks and gas stoves and refrigerators and thermostats and parental abuse laws. Beyond that, Nyankir had very limited English and only two or three other Sudanese people in Milwaukee with whom she could relax culturally and to whom she could go with her questions and her problems. Consequently, it was with great difficulty that Nyankir began to pick up English, relate to the people around her, and to decide that the U.S. and Milwaukee were good places to be. But after five or six years of testing the culture and laws and the people around her and discovering that she could survive and even thrive in the U.S., she began to make her own decisions, drive her own car, and to feel a part of the community around her.

As in the case of Laotian refugees, the Guatemalan refugee, and the Haitian refugees, Daniel and Nyankir, our Sudanese refugees, helped all of us at Cross Church to catch up on the history of Sudan and to pray and to advocate on behalf of the Sudanese people caught in a devastating, bloody civil war. We let our congressional representatives know that the people in southern Sudan were not to be overlooked or oppressed by U.S. foreign policy, just because the media seldom mentioned them.

Cross Church could have survived without sponsoring any refugees. In fact, we could have convinced ourselves that we could better focus on our mission in the neighborhood and on our own parish's internal growth, if we would have avoided such involvement. However, our experience over the years showed us that in strange and mysterious ways, we were all enriched spiritually by walking with refugees. We added beautiful, committed members to our congregation in the process. We contributed to the forming of the beloved community. And we discovered the joy of the Lord and new dimensions of the Gospel.

CHAPTER 11

TREATMENT WORKS: WALKING WITH PERSONS WHO HAVE ALCOHOL AND OTHER DRUG ABUSE ADDICTIONS

Not that I have already obtained all this, or have already been made perfect, but I press on to take hold of that for which Christ Jesus took hold of me. Brothers, I do not consider myself yet to have taken hold of it. But one thing I do: Forgetting what is behind and straining toward what is ahead, I press on toward the goal to win the prize for which God has called me heavenward in Christ Jesus.
–Philippians 3:12-14

Every Monday evening at 6:00 p.m., the doors of Hephatha Lutheran Church in Milwaukee are open, and three or four members of Hephatha Church will be there to welcome anyone who is struggling with alcohol and other drug abuse (AODA) addictions. They will listen. They will share a piece of their own journey. They will pray. They will not sit in judgment of those persons who come. They will not tell them what they ought to do. But they will tell them where they can find help, if they are ready for it. And they will assure them that with God's help, healing is possible, that treatment works.

All of the three or four persons who discipline themselves to be there every Monday evening for people who are struggling with AODA addiction issues are people who have been there themselves. They know what 10, 15, 20 years of addiction to alcohol or cocaine or crack can do to a person's body, a person's mind, a person's spirit, a person's family, a person's self-esteem, a person's expectations. But they also know what a new life of sobriety and recovery can mean: A sense of self-worth, restored relationships, off the streets, out of the shelters, waking up in the morning with hope for a future, the ability to hold down a job, spiritual and physical wholeness.

And above all, the persons in recovery at Hephatha who invite people to join them every Monday evening in their "Candlelight Recovery Meeting," are saying quietly, but boldly, that recovery is possible and recovery needs nurturing.

Return from the Far Country

Many persons in recovery identify with Jesus' parable of "the lost son" (or "the waiting Father" or the "judgmental brother") in Luke 15. They know the feeling of being "out there," with no connections to anyone who can be trusted, with all their bridges to family and friends and stability and self-respect burned, staring into the abyss of despair and extinction, feeding the pigs as a last resort for survival, and willingness to eat the slop that the pigs eat, because there seems to be no hope for anything better. Such utter despair, with suicidal thoughts, does not usually come early in the journey of addiction to alcohol and other drugs. It often takes 10, 20, or 30 years to arrive at that point of complete despair. At the beginning of the journey, there is the exhilaration of getting high on the drugs, the deceptive sense of community with those engaged in the same risky behavior for the same momentary highs. There is that sense that "I can stop this spiral into the abyss any time I want." And there is that delusion that "this is where true freedom and real life" is to be found.

That is, until one day, the addicted person wakes up to the reality: "I have no real community around me. I am alone. All I have to live for is to feed the pigs and to eat their slop." It is at that point that a person often concludes: "Life isn't worth living. There is no way out."

Or a person concludes, as did the "lost son" in Jesus' parable: "Surely I do not have to live this life with the pigs. I will return to my father, to my family, to a life worth living, even if it means making a 180-degree turn in my life. Even if it means going back to those whom I have hurt along the way and asking their forgiveness. Even if it means owning up to all the hurtful, dishonest, perhaps criminal things I've done along the route of addiction. Even if it means working at some difficult, ordinary tasks of life, like getting and holding an entry-level job, restoring my relationships, living in community with those who value a sober, disciplined life."

In the parable of Luke 15, the son who had decided to return from the far country of his addiction, is ready to take responsibility for his actions, not blaming his wild living on anyone else but himself as he confesses to his father: "I have sinned against you and against heaven and I am no longer worthy to be called your son."

The father, on the other hand, embraces his son, kisses him, places a ring on his finger, sandals on his feet, and orders the fatted calf to be killed so that the whole household can celebrate. "After all," the father says, "my son who was dead, is alive."

Of course, the father's forgiving, affirming embrace is not the typical way in which society, or the Church, has received persons who have come from the far country of substance abuse addiction, asking for help, for treatment, and for a way out of the abyss. Historically, society's response, as well as the church's response, has been more like the older brother's response: "Don't ask me to help. I've lived responsibly. I've worked hard. I've carried my load. He got himself into his own mess. Let him get himself out."

Treatment Does Work

For centuries it was the common understanding that a pattern of drunkenness could be stopped by an act of sheer willpower. Likewise, it has been thought by many that people who regularly get high on other drugs should be able to stop using the drugs if they really want to.

Medical and scientific research has come to the conclusion that there are many physical, mental, and spiritual factors involved in substance abuse addictions, to say nothing of outside factors that can trigger addictive behaviors. As a result, it is accurate to say that alcoholism and other substance abuse addictions are illnesses that need to be treated and can be treated.

Because people often relapse a few months after AODA treatment, some people insist that "treatment doesn't work." That's a little bit like saying that cancer treatments don't work because cancer often reoccurs after treatment.

The truth is that drug treatment does work. Almost everyone has a co-worker, a family member, a friend, or a fellow congregational member who has gone to treatment and has been in recovery for years. Pastors, teachers, truck drivers, counselors, musicians, office workers, people from diverse backgrounds and from all ages, with quality assessment and treatment and with support and affirmation, have become, once again, productive citizens, parents, and family members.

I know that seminary curriculum is different today, but in the 1950s, I learned nothing at the seminary about alcohol and other drug addictions and drug treatment and how congregations might carry out effective ministry with persons/families plagued with substance abuse issues.

AODA at Cross Church

The huge issue of AODA came to our front doorstep at Cross when a fellow Lutheran pastor, who had gone through a nightmarish experience of losing his clergy status and witnessing the breakup of his marriage and family because of alcoholism, started worshiping at Cross. He had gone to treatment, was in recovery, had re-married, and was beginning to feel again the call of the Spirit to pastoral ministry. He found the diversity and the openness at Cross Church a tonic for his parched soul, and he had much to offer in the way of pastoral gifts. He developed a cadre of trained caregivers who systematically began reaching out to people with special needs. Soon Cross Church issued a part-time call to him, asking him to serve as Associate Pastor in charge of caregiving ministry at Cross. This call enabled him to get back on the clergy roll and to be in a position to receive a call to a parish, which happened much more quickly than he had thought it would. His spirits were lifted, and he served parishes creatively and faithfully for over 20 years until his retirement.

Not only did Cross Church experience firsthand the devastating effects of alcoholism, but, above all, we saw firsthand the possibilities of recovery and wholeness and healing. We began to use new language in our worship and in our life together as a congregation. We began to talk about all of us in recovery from various types of addictions and spiritual illness. We learned that it is important to name our addictions, such as shopping, certain kinds of food, watching TV, sexual gratification, and the like, and to seek Christ's help to move into recovery and to grow in our understanding and experience of what it means to continue in recovery.

We began to question some of our practices and programs in the light of our call to reach out to those who are in AODA recovery and our responsibility to support them and to be enriched by them. We questioned, for instance, whether we should use something other than wine in Holy Communion. After considerable discussion among the members of the Board of Elders, we decided we would offer two cups, one with wine and one with grape juice. We discovered later that other congregations had wrestled with the same issue and had come up with other solutions. Reformation Church decided to use non-alcoholic wine. Hephatha Church decided to use grape juice.

Before we switched to using wine and grape juice, we had asked persons in recovery whether the use of wine in Communion was a concern to them. One outspoken man in recovery responded: "No, this is not important as far as I'm concerned. Communion is sacred and different from drinking beer or wine at home or at a social occasion. It doesn't arouse my desire for alcohol. In fact, it gives me strength to continue in recovery."

However, that was one man's opinion, and there were others who said that the use of wine in Communion was a deterrent to their regular participation in the Eucharist.

What we discovered as we began the use of grape juice alongside of wine, is that the vast majority of persons in recovery appreciated our use of grape juice. Not only did it remove that trigger of alcohol from their participation in the sacred meal of Communion. The very fact that we offered grape juice was a signal to everyone in the recovery community that we really cared about them and about their tough day-to-day battle with substance abuse addiction. It also signaled to people who did not have that daily battle that they should be concerned about those who do have that struggle to deal with. I'd like to believe that it nudged people to be more thoughtful about the beverages they offer when they are hosting a social occasion.

Another lesson we learned after we made the change to using grape juice in Communion was the reality that there are many non-addicted persons who really appreciated the grape juice. There was Jessie Andrews, a member of the Board of Elders, who said, "I'm a diabetic, and I never said anything about it before we started using grape juice. But I really had problems with the wine. Usually I would just take the bread and pass up the wine."

We also discovered that parents were grateful there was grape juice for their children. The children and youth themselves had no difficulty accepting the fact that they were expected to partake of the grape juice. In fact, some of them actually said that they preferred the grape juice over the wine. When we later lowered the age of participation in Communion to include baptized children of any age, it was especially appropriate to offer grape juice instead of wine.

Theologically, we had no difficulty in deciding to use the grape juice. Although it was undoubtedly wine that Jesus used when he instituted Holy Communion during the celebration of the Passover, the validity of Communion does not hinge on whether the element used is wine or grape juice. The presence of Christ, the forgiveness of sins, the oneness with Christ and with sisters and brothers in Christ, the power of the Holy spirit to overcome sin and to grow spiritually, are connected with the Word of God and with faith that trusts that Word of God.

We realized, of course, that using grape juice in our weekly celebration of Communion was not the be-all/end-all of our outreach and witness to persons in recovery, and certainly not to those persons caught up in substance abuse addiction and not yet in recovery.

Recovery Sunday

We weren't sure what our next step should be. We finally decided that we needed to walk more intentionally with persons in recovery and addicted persons not yet in recovery. So we decided to schedule a "Recovery Sunday" service during the regular Sunday worship time. We invited someone in recovery to give testimony right before the sermon. The sermon related to walking with persons struggling with substance abuse addiction and persons in recovery, and there was an adult sharing time following the worship that gave people a chance to interact with the person who had given the testimony in worship.

We found "Recovery Sunday" to be an important way to nurture the entire congregation in understanding substance abuse addiction and how to deal sensitively and helpfully as it impacts our family, our congregation, and our community. Probably one of the most significant signs of growth in the congregation, resulting from "Recovery Sunday," was the resulting openness to talking about our addictions of all kinds, our struggles with family members and friends and how best to help, and not to hinder, the path to recovery. We learned the crucial danger of "enabling" someone to continue in his or her addictive habits at the very time we think we are giving the person that needed affirmative boost. In short, "Recovery Sunday," which became an annual event, helped launch an ongoing conversation in the congregation, especially in the Sunday morning Bible Class, that nurtured us and helped us relate to a huge segment of the congregation and community that had been off our radar screen. And we grew theologically and spiritually in ways we would not have predicted.

In this new atmosphere of concern for those struggling with addictions and for people on the "one-day-at-a-time" recovery journey, worshipers, even visitors in worship, would be freed up in the sharing time of the service, to announce a third or a fifth anniversary of sobriety. Such an announcement would always prompt an affirming applause from the congregation and nurtured the development of a small circle of recovering persons in the congregation. They would seek each other out in nurturing conversation from week to week, at worship time and during the week.

Hephatha Church in Milwaukee has developed a more structured circle of nurturing and accountability among the recovering persons in the congregation. The "Candlelight Recovery Meeting," held every Monday evening, requires disciplined leadership on the part of three or four recovering members of Hephatha. It is precisely that kind of weekly structure that translates "good intentions" into actual practice. It creates a rhythm of regular support and accountability among recovering members and, of equal importance, the word is out in the community: "If you want help into recovery or help on your recovery journey, you can find it at Hephatha Church on Monday evenings." What a powerful witness to a God who loves and offers yet another chance, and heals and empowers.

As Cross members began walking more intentionally and more honestly with recovering persons, we were convinced that forgiveness and redemption and healing and unconditional love were important ingredients in recovery for the people with whom we were walking. And that raised the question: How important is drug treatment? Or is treatment unnecessary for people who have faith in God, who forgives and heals and empowers?

There are a few pastors and persons in recovery who claim that treatment is unnecessary, that it is purely a matter of willpower, coupled with faith that God can give a person the power to overcome substance abuse addiction, if we have the faith to believe that God can do it.

There is no doubt that faith and spirituality play a big role in a person's total health and well-being, not just in experiencing and maintaining recovery from substance abuse addiction.

However, the vast majority of clergy and persons in recovery recognize the importance of drug treatment. Substance abuse addiction is recognized as an illness that affects various parts of the brain, as well as other organs of the body. Just as a person needs medical assessment, attention, and treatment for diabetes, cancer, and heart problems, a person also needs medical assessment, attention, and treatment for substance abuse addiction, from clinicians who are trained in the field.

An Effective Treatment Program

I asked Sam Marjonov, former Director of the Matt Talbott Recovery Center in the heart of Milwaukee for over 25 years: "What are the components of an effective treatment program?" He quickly listed the following five points:

1. Comprehensive assessment of a person's history, including physical health, mental health, employment, faith, family, legal issues, and other pertinent factors.
2. Competent, trained service staff, capable of constructing individually based treatment approaches for each person seeking treatment.
3. Focus on addressing non-counseling issues in treatment, such as employment, connection with peer support, and housing placement after treatment.
4. Consistent use of evidence-based approaches to treatment, as they emerge from on-going research in the field.
5. Strong, on-going services of follow-up and intervention to ensure ongoing recovery.

The very fact that comprehensive health insurance policies include AODA treatment, along with physical and mental health treatment, as part of their coverage, is recognition that drug abuse addictions are health problems that need professional treatment, as well as prayer and spiritual discernment.

Every drug counselor recognizes how important it is for the person in recovery to identify with a circle of people who are positive, affirming and supportive of a healthy, sober lifestyle. They also recognize how important it is, to detach themselves from persons who abuse drugs and from groups that hold up drug use as a badge of genuine membership in the group.

Alcoholics Anonymous (AA) groups, as well as Narcotics Anonymous (NA) and Cocaine Anonymous (CA) groups, have played a crucial role in offering men and women in recovery a circle of people who understand the devastating nature of substance abuse addiction and who will help, support, and encourage those who are seeking to lead clean and sober lives.

There are some who think that the 12-step program, originated by Bill Wilson in Akron, Ohio, in 1935, which is is still the basis for AA, CA, and NA groups, is too structured and is not helpful for some people. There are others who say that they have been turned off by such groups because there are people in some groups who are judgmental or who are claiming abstinence, but who are still using. This sounds much like the criticism leveled against the organized Church: "Too many self-righteous hypocrites for me to take it seriously."

Regardless of the presence of "fakers" and "embroiderers" in some support groups, there are always truth tellers in every group, people who tell it like it is, about themselves, about the nature of the illness, and about the possibility and the reality of healing and recovery. It is that truth that every person in recovery needs constantly, as he or she moves from one stage of life and recovery to the next. And it is that truth, as it is experienced by persons in recovery, that needs not only to be received, but also to be shared with others, not arrogantly, but thoughtfully and lovingly and gratefully.

Congregational Responses

It is the recognition of the seriousness of substance abuse addiction and its horrendous impact on individuals, families, children, communities, and congregations, causing an increase in crime and in the growing culture of hopelessness and nothingness, that has moved congregations like Hephatha Church to tackle it on three levels.

There is the weekly inclusion of the issue of substance abuse addiction in the Sunday morning liturgy. The prayers every Sunday include the names of a dozen-or-so individuals/families who have asked to be prayed for as they struggle with this illness and its consequences. The children's sermons and the homilies regularly, almost every Sunday, apply the Gospel and the day's theme to the struggles related to achieving and maintaining a life of recovery. Woven into the fabric of the service at least once every two months, is the testimony of someone who is celebrating an anniversary of being in recovery. The testimonies are regular wake-up calls, not only for those struggling with drug addictions, but for the entire congregation, to realize anew the depth of our struggles with the forces of evil and the depth of God's saving, healing grace.

Dealing in the weekly liturgy with the reality of drug addictions and the struggles connected with that reality, creates a culture that frees people to talk about their own struggles. In the Bible class that follows the Sunday morning liturgy, there are always people who, as we dig into the Word of God for our lives, relate the biblical text to their struggle with drug addiction or to their walk with someone who is struggling. It is that openness and honesty about struggles with drug addiction that help us to be more open and honest about other spiritual struggles and about our walk with God and with others. It helps to save us from intellectualizing Bible study and conversation about spirituality and serves to ground us in real struggles, and open us to the transforming power of the Gospel, of God's grace, and of the Holy Spirit.

There is also the Monday night ministry outreach to people in need of mutual support and truth-telling that has been launched by persons at Hephatha Church, who have themselves been in recovery for five, ten, or fifteen years. They have dedicated themselves to being a weekly recovery prayer circle for each other and for anyone who walks through the door of the church for that support and for that truth-telling.

There is still a third level on which Hephatha Church, and other congregations, address the demonic forces of substance abuse addiction. There is the justice issue of the availability of drug treatment for the uninsured and the issue of the high incarceration rate of non-violent persons who are not a danger to the community, but are saddled with a criminal record and punished for crimes that are driven by their underlying substance abuse issues.

I was transformed in my understanding of the "drug problem" in a slow, incremental, experiential journey. In 1990, Cross Church was discovering new ways to take seriously God's calling to do justice. As part of MICAH, the congregation-based organizing group in Milwaukee, Cross Church was part of an "issues assembly." About 250 people from 15 urban congregations with a variety of denominational backgrounds, came together and in a very democratic process, determined that the three issues we wanted to work on, because they impacted so deeply the lives of our people, were: quality public school education for all children, jobs and economic development, and drugs and crime.

I joined the Drugs and Crime Task Force of MICAH because I felt deeply the impact of drugs and crime on our neighborhood around Cross Church, as well as the impact on the members of our congregation. Grandmothers in our congregation were raising their grandchildren because their sons and daughters were strung out on drugs. Children in the congregation and community were growing up without fathers because their fathers were in prison for drug-related crimes. People in the congregation and community were victims of robbery, theft, check fraud, and break-ins, to a great extent by people who were "feeding their habit" of drug abuse. Cross Church, and Joyce and I, were all victims of this scourge of drug addiction and crime.

So it made good spiritual sense that I, and others on the MICAH Drugs and Crime Task Force, should rise up from our bed of "helpless victim paralysis" and walk by the grace of God, in an effort to find some solutions to the seemingly insoluble aspects of the drugs and crime crisis.

Interdiction or Incarceration

But where should we begin? By this point in U.S. history, our country had two major ways of dealing with the "drug crisis:" Interdiction and incarceration. Hundreds of millions of dollars were being spent to interdict illicit drugs being shipped from such drug-producing countries as Colombia and Afghanistan. It seemed to make good sense to Congressional leaders that if we could stop the flow of illicit drugs into the U.S., we would reduce the abuse of drugs and much of the related crime.

The second approach to solving the drug crisis was incarceration, which also seemed to be a logical way of getting at the flow of drugs and the use of drugs that did get into the U.S. Lock up the people who sell the drugs and the people who buy them, and you can choke off the sale and the use of drugs. It seemed like a simple, logical, sure-fire approach.

Those of us on the MICAH Drugs and Crime Task Force bought into the rationale of the U.S. policy of incarceration. We decided that if we helped the Milwaukee Police locate and arrest the drug sellers in our neighborhoods, we would get rid of the drug houses on our blocks, along with the crime that accompanied the drug selling. In addition we would reduce the flow of drugs and the use of drugs by so many of our family members and community people. It seemed like a win-win situation.

So we proceeded systematically and boldly. We trained members of our congregation on how to spot drug houses, what information to write down and to report to the police, and we encouraged people to take the initiative in reporting drug houses. We encouraged people not to cower in the corners of their fears and their apathy. At a public meeting at Gesu Catholic Church, with about 1,200 members of MICAH congregations present, we got the Milwaukee Chief of Police to promise publicly that he would cooperate with us in our campaign to close down 300 drug houses in the following six months. We had campaign captains in 20 congregations, and we were successful in closing down more than 300 drug houses.

The closing down of a drug house, in some instances, meant that one or more dealers and/or users were arrested and eventually incarcerated. More often than not, the drug house was closed down, no one was arrested, and it simply meant that the drug dealers moved their operation to another location.

After pursuing our campaign for over two years to shut down drug houses and to report drug dealers, we began to evaluate the success of our efforts. We determined that our greatest success was in empowering people to overcome their fears of turning in a drug dealer and to conquer that fatalisitic notion that there was absolutely nothing they could do about a drug house on their block.

I still remember the day that about 30 of us, including several pastors in our clerical collars, marched in the middle of the day in front of a drug house that had plagued the block for months, with people pulling up all hours of the day and night to purchase drugs, and with gunshots piercing the night on several occasions.

We marched back and forth in front of the house for over an hour. In the process of the bold action, people from two or three houses on the block came out and joined us in calling for an end to the drug dealing in the house. At the end of the demonstration, we circled ourselves in front of the house and prayed for an end to the drug dealing in that house and in the City of Milwaukee. We prayed for the safety of the people who lived on the block. And we prayed for all those who were caught up in their drug abuse habits and those who sold the drugs. We prayed that Dr. King's vision of the "beloved community," where we all live for the common good of all, might become a reality on that block and in Milwaukee.

As we left from the prayer circle, the neighbors who joined us thanked us for giving them hope that something could be done about their situation. The following day the drug dealers were gone from the house.

However, it became clear to us that we had not reduced the number of drug dealers. We had not reduced the number of drug houses. We had not reduced the number of persons who were abusing drugs.

When we closed down a drug house, the operation moved to another location. When a seller was arrested, another seller, usually an African American or Hispanic teenaged young man, was hired in their place.

After working hard for nearly three years in the trenches of organized action to reduce drug sales, drug use, and the accompanying crime, we had little to show for it, except the empowerment of people. But we refused to give up.

We started looking elsewhere for a way of cutting the issues connected with drugs and crime. We heard of a book, *The Fix*, written by Michael Massing, a journalist who had researched the very problems that we were dealing with. One of the most revealing points of his book was the basic premise, backed by documented evidence, that there is a third way of reducing drug sales and drug abuse, besides interdiction and incarceration. In fact, the third way is 16 times more cost-effective and outcome-effective than interdiction and seven times more effective than incarceration.

The Third Way: Treatment

It became clear to us, that as long as there is a market for drugs, as long as there are millions of people in the U.S. who are wanting drugs, ready to purchase drugs, or if they don't have the money, they are ready to commit a crime to get the money, there will be people willing to supply the drugs. And the suppliers will make some big money in the process, especially when the drugs are illegal.

So we began to look at treatment and how we could make it more available to people who want it. After all, treatment is the most cost-effective, outcome-effective way to reduce drug sales and drug abuse. Above all, effective treatment doesn't simply reduce drug sales and drug abuse. It helps make individuals and families and communities healthy and whole. The healing, the restoring, the saving of the world, has everything to do with the very purpose of Christ's coming to this earth.

As we did our research, we discovered that the U.S. in the 1970s under President Nixon, was spending more money on treatment than on interdiction and incarceration. One of the big reasons for this was the high numbers of Vietnam veterans who were returning from that hellish war, addicted to drugs, or turning to drugs, upon their return to a nation that was turning more and more to drugs as a way out of stress and dark times.

As we looked at Milwaukee County's expenditures for drug treatment for the uninsured, we saw that the County reached a high point of $14 million for treatment in 1995, and then proceeded each year after that, to reduce the amount by one or two million dollars, until it reached $5 million in 1998.

That was the year, 1998, we decided that as the conscience of the county, we had to call a halt to any further reduction of funding for drug treatment for the uninsured. It was very clear from the long waiting list of persons asking for treatment but unable to get it, that the demand and the need for treatment was greater than ever. But there was a hue and a cry from many middle-income and upper-income people, most of whom had drug treatment coverage in their insurance plans: "Taxes have to be lowered! If that means reducing services to low-income people, so be it!"

The thinking among many taxpayers, including many church people, was: "These drug addicts made their choice to start using drugs. They can quit anytime they want to."

There were other taxpayers who recognized that drug abuse addiction is an illness in need of treatment, but they didn't believe that hard-working taxpayers owed treatment services to people who had no health insurance.

As people of faith, and as members of the MICAH Drugs and Crime Task Force, we decided that drug treatment, like mental health treatment, cancer treatment, heart disease treatment, and treatment for any illness, is a right belonging to all members of the human family, not simply to people who have the wealth or the good fortune of having a health insurance policy that includes drug treatment.

Furthermore, we recognized that not offering treatment to people when they are ready for it and asking for it, is not only locking those persons into additional months and years of substance abuse addiction, but pushing them toward crime and violence to continue to feed their habit. Not providing treatment services for the uninsured, we were convinced, was actually increasing crime and violence in the central city of Milwaukee, the very thing we were struggling to reduce.

So the MICAH Drugs and Crime Task Force was determined to stop the annual reduction in AODA treatment services for the uninsured. We asked for a meeting with County Executive Tom Ament to demand that he replace the amount of AODA treatment funding that he had cut in his proposed budget. For whatever reasons, Ament refused even to talk with us. We decided that we had to make a bold move that would put this issue not only on Ament's radar screen, but on the Board of Supervisors' and the community's.

We gathered key pastors in MICAH, like Joe Games, Louis Sibley, Mick Roschke, Dennis Jacobsen, Mary Rowland, myself, as well as committed lay leaders, about 17 in all, and walked into Ament's office at 4:00 p.m., and announced that we were going to wait and pray there until County Executive Ament came to meet with us.

If Ament didn't meet with us, we were prepared to be arrested, or to stay through the night, holding our own prayer service on the holy ground of Ament's office.

As it turned out, Ament did not meet with us, nor did he have us arrested. Presumably, he thought that we would get a lot of media attention if we were arrested, so he simply had two sheriff's deputies assigned to "guard" us, apparently to make sure we didn't trash his office or the rest of the courthouse. We proceeded to have a five-hour prayer service with personal sharing of testimonies that revealed our frustrations with the lack of drug treatment, the stories of shattered lives of people resulting from the waiting list for treatment, and the grace of God and the resurrection power that transformed the lives of people who moved into treatment and recovery.

By 10:30, it was clear that we were not going to be arrested, so we began looking for a place to curl up and try to sleep. Disagreement persists to this day as to whose snoring was the loudest. But there is unanimous agreement that the floors in the County Executive's office are not conducive to sound sleep.

After a night of fitful sleep, we got word, via cell phone, from the MICAH organizer, Ana Garcia Ashley, that the TV stations would be there at the County Executive's office for a live 7:00 a.m. press conference.

If Ament was hoping to avoid media coverage by not having us arrested, he totally miscalculated. The live coverage we got on all the TV stations and later in the paper, was exactly what we were hoping for. All of Milwaukee County became aware of an issue that directly affected hundreds of lives and indirectly affected every citizen of Milwaukee County, yet was not visible at all to most people, and was at the bottom of the priority list for most politicians, even the central city's elected officials.

Beth Coggs-Jones, a member of Cross Church at the time, and County Supervisor in the district where Cross was located, took up the cause and began to run with it. At the County Board meeting where the supervisors finalized the budget, Supervisor Coggs-Jones introduced a resolution that would freeze county treatment funding for the uninsured at $5 million per year for the next five years. The resolution passed almost unanimously.

We didn't restore the AODA funding at the level that was needed, but we had won three significant victories. We had restored some of the treatment funding. We had raised consciousness among all the elected leaders of Milwaukee County and among most citizens in the county. And we raised hope among people on the street that treatment would be available, and hope among people in MICAH that they do have the power to make changes in the community.

The dramatic actions of 1998 didn't solve the drug treatment problems for years to come. Sad to say, MICAH's AODA Treatment Task Force, as it is called now, has to constantly maintain vigilance on drug treatment funding. Even though more and more people believe that treatment works and more and more people recognize that drug treatment contributes to the safety of the community and to the wellness of families, the scramble for funds at budget time still pushes elected officials to look for places to cut expenditures. And sadly, drug treatment funding for the uninsured is still seen as an expendable service and therefore is a popular budget item to reduce. It just doesn't seem to be high on legislators' priority lists. The people it directly affects are largely non-voting, "invisible" members of the community.

Even though we were slowly winning the battle of minds and consciences, convincing people that treatment works and that investing in treatment for the uninsured saves lives and families and dollars, there were still a lot of addicted people who were not getting treatment and who were winding up in the judicial system and ultimately, in jail and prison. People do all kinds of things to get the money to buy the drugs to feed their craving–shoplifting, prostitution, check forgery, theft, strong-armed robbery, drug selling.

I have been walking with a man who has gone back to prison four times and has spent over 25 years in prison for crimes committed because of his inner craving for "one more hit," one more high. The crimes were determined to be armed robbery and therefore felonies, requiring stiffer sentencing than lesser misdemeanors such as shoplifting or theft. In actuality, he did not have a gun when he attempted to hold up a tavern keeper on two different occasions. He put his hand inside a paper bag and pretended he had a gun. He had no intention of hurting anyone. He was simply desperate for money to feed his habit. In both cases, the tavern keeper called his bluff and had him arrested. He didn't get any money. Instead, he got a 15-year felony conviction for "armed robbery." After all, his pretended holdup had put the tavern keeper and patrons under the duress of a real armed robbery.

The rationale behind the stiff felony conviction for feigned armed robbery is understandable. What is not understandable is that the various persons involved in the process of arresting, charging, and convicting this man (not once, not twice, but four times)–police officers, district attorneys, public defenders, judges–did not see that his underlying problem was not criminality, but substance abuse addiction. Or they saw that, and were convinced that what would turn this man away from the illness of drug addiction would be 15 more years in prison.

The reality of hundreds and thousands of men and woman, driven by an alcohol or cocaine addiction, being convicted and sent to jail or to prison again and again and again, has caught the attention of police, sheriffs, district attorneys, public defenders, and judges. More and more of these authority figures in the law enforcement and judicial systems, are saying publicly: "The system isn't working. Incarceration by itself doesn't cure an illness or terminate an addiction."

James P. Gray, a veteran judge of the Superior Court in Orange County in southern California, former prosecutor in Los Angeles, and criminal defense attorney in the Navy JAG Corps, published a book in 2001 titled *Why Our Drug Laws Have Failed and What We Can Do About It.* The title of the book by itself conveys some of the deep frustration that judges, district attorneys, and others are experiencing as our nation has, until recently, attempted to solve the "drug scourge" by spending billions of dollars to try to stop the flow of drugs into our country and by locking up people in the U.S. who sell or use illicit drugs.

MICAH leaders who were working on AODA issues came to see that hundreds of addicted persons in Milwaukee County were winding up in the judicial and correctional system, either because they were unable to get treatment as uninsured persons, or because they were so caught up in their addiction that they didn't give treatment and recovery a thought. So we struggled with how we could assist these hundreds of persons whom society termed unworthy of assistance.

We read about California and Arizona diverting non-violent persons from the judicial system by offering them drug treatment as an alternative to incarceration. We studied the two programs and discovered that even though the programs were not 100 percent successful in turning out persons who remained in recovery and who stayed out of prison, the success ratio was as high as 50 and 60 percent after two years of tracking.

Then we discovered that our neighboring state of Minnesota, with a very similar set of demographics and population size, had one-third the number of persons in prison (Minnesota with 7,000 in prison compared with Wisconsin's 23,000) and had spent $400 million on prisons, compared with Wisconsin's $1 billion. We researched the reasons behind such a startling difference. We traveled to Winona State University and talked with Glenn Just, retired Minnesota prison superintendent turned college professor. We learned that Minnesota in almost all of its counties is following a policy called "community corrections." This means that persons coming into the judicial system are assessed for underlying issues of mental health and AODA addiction, and if they are not deemed a threat to the safety of the community, they are referred to programs in the community for treatment and assistance as needed, rather than being incarcerated. Studies showed also that even though Minnesota incarcerated fewer offenders because of its diversionary programs, its rate of crime was almost exactly the same as Wisconsin's rate. Diverting persons in the judicial system to treatment did not create more crime in the community, as opponents to diversionary programs often charge.

The more we thought about the high rate of incarceration in Wisconsin, the angrier we got. We discovered that drug treatment costs a third as much as incarceration. Treatment costs $5,000 to $15,000 annually, compared with $30,000 for incarceration. As good stewards of taxpayers' money and as good stewards of people's lives, we saw that treatment alternatives to incarceration made good fiscal sense and good moral sense.

And then, what seemed the final straw, we learned that the incarceration rate of African American males in Wisconsin is higher than in any other state in the U.S., higher than in Texas, Mississippi, or any state in the South.

The MICAH AODA Treatment Committee decided that we would embark on a campaign to change Wisconsin's incarceration policy. We began to meet with DAs, judges, state legislators, and corrections officials, to move them toward a policy that would send non-violent offenders with underlying issues of drug addictions to community-based treatment, rather than to jail or prison. We called our campaign TIP, "Treatment Instead of Prison."

Some seven years later, we have not totally transformed the judicial/correctional system, but we have come a long way. We were a major player in getting the state legislature to pass the Treatment Alternatives and Diversionary (TAD) bill that encouraged counties all over the state, to develop drug treatment courts, mental health courts, and day report centers, all of which offer health-related solutions for health problems instead of the historic incarceration-related solutions for health problems. TAD programs were the major reason why Wisconsin's prison population was reduced by 1,500 in 2010-11, the first reduction in Wisconsin's prison population in 25 years.

There are some who say that treatment alternatives to incarceration are "soft on crime." Actually, a quality treatment program is tougher, in many ways, than incarceration. It calls for accountability and self-discipline. There are some persons facing the likelihood of incarceration, who, given a choice between community-based treatment and incarceration, will choose incarceration, because they know how challenging a quality treatment program can be.

Though the focus of a congregation and of doctors and social workers is likely to be on treatment and on the recovery and healing of individuals and families, it is also essential for thoughtful people of faith and persons concerned about doing justice, to go beyond the availability of treatment for uninsured persons and addicted persons caught in the judicial system, as crucial as that focus on treatment is. As we look at the "War on Drugs" that has been waged since the Nixon presidency in the 1960s that has relied on making the sale of drugs illegal and on an attempt to halt the flow of drugs into the country as the way to solve the drug problems, we have to conclude: "It isn't working!"

Illegal drugs are more accessible now than in the '70s and the '80s, at a slightly lower cost and at a better quality. After spending billions of dollars on trying to halt the flow of drugs into the U.S. and after arresting and incarcerating drug pins, drug dealers, and street-level drug sellers in the U.S., there is a steadier flow of drugs and a more competitive drug market than ever before.

Not only have we failed miserably as a nation in stemming the flow and the sale of hard drugs, we have created monstrous "side" problems in the process. We have tripled incarceration rates, taking billions of dollars away from funding of public education, health care, and basic services necessary for quality of life in our country. We have shattered families by incarcerating fathers and mothers, especially from the African American community. We have contributed to the high dropout rate in urban high schools, where teenagers, especially young men of color, have discovered they can make big money without a high school diploma. We have contributed to the rise in homicide rates, as drug bills and drug turf battles are "settled" by dealers and gangs at the barrel of a gun.

To suggest that we as a society are a causal factor in all of these horrendous side effects of the drug trade and of drug abuse, may seem like a total misunderstanding of the drug scourge that is devastating our country. Most people, including our lawmakers who set our policies, would say: "We are trying to do everything possible to stop the flow of drugs into our country and to punish anyone who sells drugs or uses drugs. That's why we are spending billions on the war on drugs. We are not responsible for these side effects. It's totally the responsibility of the drug users and drug dealers. They are the culprits who are creating the havoc, and we won't solve this dilemma unless we stick with our policy of locking up everyone we can get our hands on who uses drugs, sells drugs, or is in any way connected with the drug trade."

The Failure of the War on Drugs

There are obviously those who believe that we can incarcerate our way out of the drug scourge. That policy has slowly emerged since the Harrison Narcotic Act of 1914, making it extremely difficult and expensive to import or sell opium, cocaine, or any of their derivatives and the Marijuana Tax Act of 1937, making the sale of marijuana illegal. But the policy of really getting tough on drug crimes and allocating billions of dollars toward the interdiction of drug traffic and the incarceration of dealers, sellers, and users, started during the presidency of Richard Nixon, when President Nixon officially declared the "War on Drugs," in 1969. During the '70s, the '80s, and the '90s, right into the 21st century, Congress has gotten tougher and tougher on drug crimes, and as a result, the United States has the highest incarceration rate of any country in the world.

The belief in this policy of trying to incarcerate our way out of the drug scourge is so deeply ingrained in our cultural psyche that people who question the validity of the policy have been laughed at, ridiculed, and considered crazy at best, and subversive and even unpatriotic at worst.

As people of God who are free in Christ, of all people, we should be able to talk freely about any topic, and especially about a topic as urgent as the drug scourge, which affects the lives of millions in some devastating ways and affects the lives of all of us in some crucial, though often hidden, ways.

One of the most helpful ways to enable people to see why our present drug prohibition policy is not working is to look at the alcohol prohibition of the 1920s. The passage of the 18th Amendment made the sale of alcoholic beverages illegal, starting on January 16, 1920. This was a valiant attempt on the part of well-intentioned people, most of them religiously motivated, to bring an end to the scourge of alcoholic addiction and public and private drunkenness, with all its side effects of spouse and child abuse, broken families, and crimes committed while people were intoxicated.

Alcohol prohibition seemed to make sense. Its rationale was simple: If we make the sale of alcohol illegal, it will be very difficult to get alcohol, and the difficulty and illegality of purchasing alcohol will drive most alcoholic drinkers to abandon their habit, and the few who somehow manage to find and/or to sell the illegal beverage will be driven to eventually terminate their drinking/selling habit because of the fines, the incarceration, and the public scorn that they will experience.

We know our history well enough to know that alcohol prohibition did not bring about the desired results. Resourceful entrepreneurs who wanted to make a fast buck discovered that there was big money to be made by brewing illegal beer and whiskey. The mafia, as well as "little dealers" all over the country, cashed in fast on this bonanza that was created overnight by the 18th Amendment. Instead of closing down the sale of alcoholic beverages and converting alcohol drinkers into teetotalling citizens, the 18th Amendment simply drove the alcohol-drinking population to a new source for their beverages, to home distilleries or to black-market distributors of alcoholic beverages of all types and all qualities.

The amazing thing was that within 13 years, the United States saw that alcohol prohibition was not working and in 1933, the 21st Amendment was passed, repealing the 18th Amendment. We discovered as a nation that if there is a demand for a product, there will always be intrepid, enterprising business people who will meet that demand, even if it is illegal and runs the risk of fines, incarceration, turf wars, and violence.

The current drug prohibition policy, initiated in 1916 and enforced in dead earnest by Nixon's declaration of the "War on Drugs" in 1969, is very similar to the alcohol prohibition policy with the same result. Instead of significantly reducing the production, the supply, the sale, and the use of drugs, the drug prohibition policy has shifted the multi-billion-dollar drug industry into the hands of black-market profiteers, whose goal is to hook as many people as possible on the drugs and to sell as much as possible.

So what is the solution, if cranking up enforcement of the drug prohibition policy, is not?

We need to move out of denial and openly admit to each other and to our legislators that the drug prohibition policy is not working and it's time that we talk about it and do something about it.

We need to recognize that the drug abuse problem is a medical, social and spiritual problem, to be solved with medical, social, and spiritual solutions, not with incarceration and punitive measures.

Without a doubt, advocacy for funding for drug treatment for the uninsured would be one of the best approaches for a medical/social/spiritual solution to the drug scourge. The RAND Corporation released a study in 1994 that found that drug treatment is seven times more cost-effective than domestic law enforcement in addressing drug abuse, 11 times more cost-effective than trying to stop the flow of drugs across our borders, and 23 times more cost-effective than crop eradication and substitution programs overseas.

Drug treatment moves people out of addictive behavior and lifestyles, out of a vegetative or bitter state of mind that festers while incarcerated, into recovery and wholeness, into restored family relationships, into productive jobs, into taxpaying, responsible citizenship, into fruitful lives. Good, quality drug treatment is a medical, social, spiritual solution to a medical, social, spiritual problem. Drug treatment works.

After moving out of denial, after openly admitting that the current "War on Drugs" isn't working, after shouting from the rooftops that drug addiction is a medical, social, spiritual problem, not to be solved with judicial/incarceration remedies, after pushing hard for drug treatment as the basic tool for getting at the drug scourge, we need to call on our congressional representatives to launch an objective commission empowered by the President and by Congress to recommend revisions of the drug laws of the United States in order to reduce the harm our current policies are causing. Many organizations and thousands of individuals have been pressing for radical changes in our drug laws for years. We must add our voices to theirs.

Through my experiences and transformation at Cross Church and Hephatha Church, I have come to see how essential it is for the pastor and the congregation to walk with people with AODA issues and to create a culture of openness and honesty in dealing with this issue that touches all of us. The impact of walking sensitively with such persons and grappling with the theological and practical issues involved will cause the whole congregation to be less judgmental, more deeply rooted in the Gospel, more open to all people, and, yes, even to get involved in finding alternative policies to our current "War On Drugs" policies.

CHAPTER 12

WALKING WITH THOSE INCARCERATED AND THOSE RETURNING TO THE COMMUNITY

I was in prison and you came to visit me.
–Matthew 25:36C

Remember those in prison as if you were their fellow prisoners, and those who are mistreated as if you yourselves were suffering.
–Hebrews 13:3

Then (one of the men crucified with Jesus) said: "Jesus, remember me when you come into your Kingdom." Jesus answered him: "I tell you the truth, today you will be with me in paradise."
–Luke 23:42-43

Every Sunday, Pastor Mary Martha Kannass welcomes at the beginning and at the end of worship at Hephatha Lutheran Church, "the visitors in our midst" and "those who have returned to their family at Hephatha." This was a special Sunday, on which she made it a point to welcome back a young man who had been baptized and confirmed, and who had grown up at Hephatha Church. This was the first Sunday after his release from prison, and he was in worship with his mother and most of his siblings.

"We have been praying for you every Sunday during your incarceration," Pastor Mary Martha said, as she welcomed him back at the beginning of the service and asked him to stand. The congregation broke out with spontaneous applause as a sign of positive affirmation and support. "And we will continue to pray for you," she said, "that you will be able to find a job, continue your education, and witness your faith to us at Hephatha."

To seal the positive "welcome home" for the son of the congregation, Pastor Mary Martha asked him to assist her and four others from the congregation in distributing the grape juice during Communion.

Later in the service, at the time of prayer, the assisting minister included a petition, as we do every Sunday at Hephatha, "for those in prison." She went on to carry out our weekly custom of calling out the names of the men and women connected with Hephatha Church who were in prison at the time. On that Sunday, there were 14 names, printed in the bulletin prayer section, for worshipers to ponder and to remember in prayer.

This open, honest, compassionate concern in the Sunday liturgy for persons in prison and for a person returning from incarceration, is not common, regardless of denomination and regardless of the demographics of the community surrounding the church.

Ministry to Prisoners

Persons in jail and prison, and those returning from incarceration, are generally off the radar screen of congregations, not only in the Sunday morning worship, but in their vision of ministry.

When I was pastor at Cross Church, I wrote to a Lutheran pastor and congregation in northwestern Wisconsin, located about three miles from a minimum security prison. I asked the pastor whether he or some persons in his congregation would be willing to visit a young man in the nearby prison, a man who had been incarcerated in a minimum security prison near Cross Church. Some of us at Cross Church had gotten to know this man through our ministry at four minimum security prisons within two miles of the church. Since he was at a minimum security prison, those of us at Cross who were "approved escorts" could pick him up for Sunday worship and adult Bible class, as he had requested. He had been attending Cross Church regularly.

He had really begun to open up in Bible class, sharing his struggles, his faith, his hopes, his dreams. He had even made plans to attend the Pastor's Class and to become a member of Cross Church. But suddenly, he was transferred to the minimum security prison in northwestern Wisconsin. So I promised him I would put him in touch with a Lutheran congregation near his new location.

I explained in my letter to the pastor, that this man, with whom we had been walking at Cross Church, was clearly reflecting deeply on his own life, was responding to the Gospel, was experiencing new life and was eager to be part of a community of believers for his own spiritual growth. I wrote in the letter that if his congregation was already involved in ministry at the nearby prison, they could simply add this man to their list of participants. If they weren't involved in ministry there, I suggested that perhaps this would open the door for them to get started. I assured the pastor that our ministry at Cross with this man was a richly rewarding experience.

When I finally received a letter from the pastor, I was deeply disappointed at first and then I became angry. It was a rather short letter in which the pastor simply indicated that he didn't have time for that ministry. There was no explanation of any special circumstances, such as a conflicted congregation or a personal struggle that the pastor himself was experiencing. It was simply: "I don't have time for it."

I prayed over the situation. I could not understand how a pastor and a congregation didn't have time for prison ministry. For me, it was like saying: "I don't have time to visit the sick or to feed the hungry." So I contacted the area bishop, describing the situation and my concern. I expressed my conviction that the response to my pastoral referral to continue our ministry with someone in prison should have been the same positive response as I hope it would have been if I had sent a transfer of a generous, active, gifted member of our congregation to their congregation. I never heard anything more from the pastor or the bishop.

Ever since that negative response to my request of a pastor to walk with someone who was incarcerated, I have asked myself the question: "Why do so many pastors and congregations fail to include persons in prison and people coming out of prison as part of their vision of ministry?"

A very pragmatic reason for not including persons in prison in the Sunday liturgy and in the congregation's scope of ministry is the fact that many suburban and rural congregations have few, if any, members of the congregation incarcerated. So it is not a fact of congregational reality that is highly visible and constantly calling for some kind of strategy, and plan of involvement.

However, there is no congregation anywhere that has not had some experience with the realities of incarceration. Especially since the launching of the "War on Drugs" in the 1970s and the tripling of incarceration rates in most states since 1980, what congregation has not had a youth or adult in the congregation, in the youth program, in an extended family of the congregation, in the community served by the congregation, who has gotten caught up in the judicial/correctional system? And most congregations, like the congregation in northwestern Wisconsin, are within five or ten miles of a county jail or a state prison, with hundreds of persons serving terms of months or years, with broken lives, soul-searching struggles, shattered relationships, some of them eager for a listening ear.

Why Congregations Are Not Involved

There are all kinds of reasons why every congregation could be engaged in jail/prison ministry at some level. The question still remains: Why are so many congregations not involved at any level?

I believe there are some underlying realities that tend to keep jail/prison ministry off pastors' and congregations' radar screens:

- Our culture tells us that prisoners are criminally-minded and are not likely to change, so why bother to try?
- Our culture also tells us that prisoners are violent people who need to be locked up, and we endanger our lives if we go near them.
- Ministering to people in prison and people coming out of prison will have very little positive effect on the numerical and financial growth of the congregation. It is not a "cost-effective" way of growing the congregation.
- There is such a shame factor connected with incarceration that it is not a reality that is easily discussed in sermons, liturgies, and mission strategies, especially when it is our own members who are incarcerated.
- Seminary courses traditionally have not mentioned prison ministry as part of the walk of every pastor and every congregation. The time factor involved in driving to a jail or prison, going through the process of signing in, placing non-clothing items in a locker, going through the metal detector, waiting for the inmate to be brought to the visiting areas, spending quality time with the inmate, and then going through the checkout hoops and returning home, can take two to four hours. That is

a serious time commitment, for which there may seem to be no room, on the already-full plate.

- Most pastors have grown up in congregations where people in prison and prison ministry were never mentioned, so it's not part of their experienced image of pastoral/congregational ministry.

Given the strong pull of culture and of mainline congregational experience, I am grateful that I have been nudged/pushed/jerked by the Spirit to see that walking with people in prison and with people returning to their communities from prison, is an enriching, fruitful, crucial part of pastoral and congregational ministry. Matthew 25 is profoundly true. As I have visited persons in prison, I have met Christ.

Partly because St. Paul Church, in Birmingham, Alabama, was a small congregation, partly because incarceration rates in the 1960s were less than a third of what they are today, and partly because I was focused on the basics of pastoral ministry, my pastoral involvement with persons in jail and in prison, while I was pastor at St. Paul, was minimal. However, I was nudged into thinking more deeply about the realities of incarceration because of a funeral service I conducted at St. Paul in the early 1960s.

A grandmother who was a member of St. Paul and who had raised two grandsons the best she could on a very limited income, died suddenly. The funeral service was at the Church. I was making last-minute preparations for the services when I saw one of the two grandsons walk into the church dressed in his orange prison coveralls with his hands handcuffed together in front of him and his feet shuffling slowly because of the leg irons fastened by chain at his ankles. Of course, there was a prison guard right next to him, accompanying him into the church. The young man's eyes met mine, and I greeted him with a word of sympathy for him at the loss of his grandmother.

Just seeing the 17-year-old, whom I had confirmed three years before, now labeled as a dangerous criminal, but who was clearly moved to the point of tears at the loss of his grandmother, was an experience that set my mind to thinking.

Why hadn't the grandmother told me more about her grandson, who according to her assessment was "always getting into trouble? Maybe jail will teach him a lesson." Why hadn't I probed more deeply about his situation and offered to visit him? Why hadn't I asked the grandmother whether she needed transportation to see him?

This was the first time I had confronted the harsh realities of standard operating procedures in the world of corrections. I might have expected to see handcuffs and leg irons in the prison or the courtroom, but not at a funeral service. I put myself in the place of the young man, and immediately felt shame in the midst of the family and worshipping community. I sensed potential difficulty for him, and for all of us, in really entering into the worship and into the tender moment of saying farewell to our sister in Christ at the time of the final viewing.

So I mustered the courage to go up to the guard, who was sitting next to his charge, and I spoke softly, but loud enough for both to hear me: "I know this is your decision to make, but I'm asking you whether you wouldn't remove the handcuffs and the leg irons so that he can spend his last moments with his grandmother in some peace and dignity."

The guard looked at me in disbelief that I would even make such a suggestion. After a moment of silence, he blurted out: "Well, I'll do it, if you take the responsibility if he runs off."

I wasn't sure what the guard meant by suggesting that I "take the responsibility if he runs off," but I knew there was a real possibility that he might try to bolt and run. But the Spirit told me: "Take the risk. This is a strong expression of love this young man needs at this moment in his life."

So I responded to the guard: "I understand your concern. But I will guarantee you that he's not going to run, and you can feel good about helping him grieve in this moment of his loss."

Of course, there was no way I could guarantee the young man wouldn't run. I was banking on his accepting this gesture of compassion on my part, and also on the part of the guard, as such a positive, unexpected gift, that he would express his thanks by not running.

The guard did release the handcuffs and the leg irons, and even left his position at the side of his charge, and went to a pew at the back of the church. The service proceeded, and the grandson and I felt a little closer to God, to his grandmother, and to each other, as a result. My Spirit-born instincts were right. He didn't run.

I don't know what lasting impact, if any, that pastoral encounter with a prison guard in a sanctuary before a funeral, had on the grandson. But I know it had an impact on me. It taught me a little bit about the dehumanizing, stigmatizing aspects of incarceration. And it nudged me to be more alert to the church's responsibility to reach out to persons in prison and to their families.

Beginning a Ministry to Prisoners and Ex-Offenders

It was not until the 1970s in Milwaukee that I really began the practice of walking with persons in prison and with returning ex-offenders. I was accompanying members and non-members to their hearings and trials. I was visiting them in jail and in prison. In 1979, our Cross Social Ministry Committee made a study of needs in the neighborhood around the church. They discovered that there were four "pre-release centers" (minimum security prisons) within six to 20 blocks of the church. These were centers, three for men, one for women, designed to give some Milwaukee-area state prisoners who were within six to nine months of their release date, an opportunity to nail down a job and find a place to live before they were released. Obviously, with a job and a residence in place, an ex-offender's chances of making a successful, permanent return to his/her family and community, are much higher than if they are simply turned out on the street with the clothes on their back and a few belongings in a box. This is still the case with ex-offenders who are not fortunate enough to be in the quotas that make it to the pre-release centers before their actual release.

When the Cross Social Ministry Committee investigated the four minimum security prisons, they discovered that hardly any churches were relating to the centers, even though there were opportunities for volunteers, after a relatively simple screening and training process, to escort residents at the centers to job applications, to the library, to church services, to home visits, and even to recreational activities.

The Cross Social Ministry Committee saw the great need. More than 600 men and women were coming to these four pre-release centers every year, needing a leg up with jobs, housing, and restored relationships in the community, as well as spiritual nurture.

The committee saw a great opportunity for congregations not simply to read about rising crime rates and to hire security guards to safeguard people and property. Here was an opportunity for followers of Christ to walk with people who are at a crossroads in their lives, an opportunity to nurture and to be nurtured, to restore individuals, and bring down recidivism rates.

So the committee developed a vision of an agency that would be initiated by Cross Church, but would be open to people of all faiths, an agency that would hire staff and train volunteers, to assist residents at the pre-release centers to find jobs, re-establish relationships with their families, and re-connect with Church and community.

Within a year after the Cross Social Ministry Committee began its study, the agency was named, incorporated, and launched, with a diverse board of persons from various denominations and including ex-offenders.

Project RETURN

The agency was founded in 1980 and named Project RETURN (acronym for Returning Ex-offenders To Urban Realities and Neighborhoods). The mission statement developed later captured the vision of the founders:

> *"Project RETURN exists to help men and women who have experienced incarceration make a positive, permanent return to community, family, and friends." Project RETURN is the embodiment of a great idea that flows out of the vision of the Gospel, living out Good News to persons stigmatized by society as "those incorrigible, bad, dangerous people."*

And it flows out of a common-sense solution to a serious societal problem.

As obviously compelling as the vision of Project RETURN was to its founders, it still was not easy to find congregations, businesses, or foundations to contribute the funds to keep the vision going. For its first 15 years, Project RETURN found it difficult to fund even a half-time director. However, we discovered that we could add a competent, highly-motivated staff person for less than a third of the usual cost of a case management person if we hired a Lutheran Volunteer Corps member, typically a recent college graduate who wanted to give a year of service in a field in which he or she had a special interest, possibly a career interest.

Tough as those early years were, by the time of Project RETURN's 30th Anniversary in 2010, the staff numbered five full-time job counselors and case managers, four of whom were ex-offenders, as well as a director. More important, the agency had grown in its capacity to place ex-offenders in jobs, to the level of 200 to 300 placed on jobs during the course of a year.

Another success measure for the agency is the number of support groups held on a weekly basis. In 2010, there were seven support groups meeting weekly, facilitated by certified alcohol and other drug abuse counselors. The drug counseling is so crucial because 80 percent of persons incarcerated have underlying alcohol or other drug abuse issues and/or mental health issues. Find a job for an ex-offender with a drug abuse problem who is not in recovery, and he or she will likely not hold onto the job beyond the first or second pay check. So the focus of Project RETURN is on three primary goals:

1. Help ex-offenders find a job, preferably a family-supporting job
2. Help ex-offenders deal with drug abuse issues or any other underlying issues that would make positive re-entry into the community unlikely
3. Work to connect them with a positive support group.

Although people from various congregations have been involved with Project RETURN over the years as board members and volunteers, the congregation that has been the most involved is the congregation that was the major impetus for launching the ministry: Cross Church. Consequently, it is Cross Church that has been enriched the most by its ministry.

A very clear dividend that Cross Church has received from its ongoing support of Project RETURN and its concern for persons in prison and those being released, is the gift of people who have joined the community of believers at Cross because of their contact through Project RETURN. The numbers of members at Cross who have come through Project RETURN are not great in quantity. But having just a few such persons in the worship and in the life of the congregation helps to keep prison ministry and re-entry ministry on Cross's radar screen, and it helps Crosss members to de-stigmatize persons in prison and persons who have been in prison and are now back in society.

Teri Woodley is one of those persons who has let her light shine at Cross Church, in her family, and in the community, and she will be the first to tell you that she wouldn't be at Cross Church if it hadn't been for Project RETURN.

Project RETURN staff put in a request at the Women's Center for two of the residents there to do community service at the Cross Adult Center, helping to prepare and serve the meal and to clean up afterward. It turned out that Teri Woodley was one of the two women who were sent by the Women's Center on a given Tuesday to Cross Church to "pull the lunch shift" at the Adult Center program.

Teri felt a warm welcome from Gloria Wright, Director of the Adult Center, as well as from many of the women in the program, as she entered the hall and started her volunteer work. After she had worked in the kitchen, served the food, and helped wash dishes, she was asked to step out of the kitchen into the fellowship hall, where the 40-plus women were still sitting around the tables. Gloria Wright, the Director, introduced Teri by name and thanked her for her help that day. The Adult Center participants gave her a round of applause, and Teri knew for sure that she was welcomed, appreciated, and affirmed for her gifts and for her friendliness. Teri knew that Gloria Wright and the Adult Center participants were aware of the fact that Teri was incarcerated at the time. But she was not put down or held at a distance by anyone. Instead she was affirmed, appreciated, and applauded. She said she wanted to come back as often as possible to help out. And she said she wanted to come to worship on Sundays.

That was the beginning of an interesting journey that brought Teri to worship at Cross. Soon she was released from the Women's Center, and she continued to worship at Cross. She discovered her worth in Christ and joined Cross Church. She brought her teenage son and daughter to Cross. She soon found a place to serve at Cross, helping in the Cross Bread of Healing Food Ministry, filling 50 to 100 bags of food each week for singles and families who came asking for assistance. Then when the Food Ministry Director died, Teri offered to take the demanding responsibility of managing the various aspects of the weekly ministry that kept growing in size from year to year, a job that paid no wages, except the benefit of knowing that you're giving a lift to a brother or sister in need.

In 2006, Teri was hired by Project RETURN to assist with intake and with receptionist responsibilities. Within a year, she was also assisting with case management, helping ex-offenders find jobs.

Teri is a living example of someone whose life has blossomed, thanks to Project RETURN and to the community of believers at Cross. And she is also a living example of someone who has enriched the witness of Cross Church and enhanced the effective outreach and ministry of Project RETURN.

Teri, of course, is not the only ex-offender who joined Cross Church because of the ministry of Project RETURN. There are others. And there are dividends in prison ministry besides adding members to our congregation.

Don Bein, a member of the Project RETURN Board for many years, used to say again and again: "I truly encountered Christ as I escorted men from the Abode Correctional Center to see their families or to apply for a job. Jesus was right when he said, 'When you visit someone in prison, you're visiting me.'"

Just as a person in recovery may refer to their sense of "living by God's grace," ex-offenders often speak about God's love and God's forgiveness as "sheer, unadulterated grace that I don't deserve. Each day, each moment of my life," they say, "is a gift I never thought I'd experience. And I certainly don't deserve God's forgiveness and acceptance that comes with each day and each moment." That's a radical expression of faith that deepens the faith of those who hear such a testimony. That's a part of the spiritual enrichment a congregation receives when it walks with ex-offenders.

There is yet another way in which such ministry feeds us on our journey. Openly reaching out, walking with, listening to, persons in jail and prison and ex-offenders who are out in the community, is the only way most people get in touch with the punitive, overly-harsh incarceration policies followed in the United States and in almost every individual state in the country.

It is possible that people involved in some phase of prison ministry do not see the unnecessary, punitive, counterproductive aspects of the system. There are some people involved in prison ministry who assume that everyone who is incarcerated has gotten a fair shake in the judicial system, is serving a sentence proportionate to the seriousness of his or her crime, and is being treated humanely while in prison, even to the point of being "pampered" with hotel-like conditions and with nothing to do but watch television. They even support politicians who run on the famous line that many candidates for political office are convinced is necessary to get elected: "I promise you I will be tough on crime. I will see that criminals are locked up for a long time. And I will make sure that prisoners are not coddled while they are incarcerated."

However, there are growing numbers of prison ministry people who are becoming aware of the inequities of our judicial/correctional system and the need to assist offenders in getting their lives together when they are released. They are learning about the stone wall of stigma and discriminatory practices that ex-offenders face when they are released, and try to re-integrate into their communities, and start looking for a job. For people seeking to follow the drumbeat of the Gospel, these harsh realities are not simply pieces of demographic statistics; they are pieces of truth and human reality that are essential elements of our understanding, if we are to walk honestly and lovingly with persons incarcerated and with ex-offenders on the outside, and if we are going to work for prison reform long overdue.

Calls for Reform

Books have been written detailing the realities in the judicial and the correctional systems that cry out for reforms on many levels, but here are just a few facts that indicate something is wrong with the system, not just with the people who have carried out a harmful criminal act, made some bad choices, or simply been in the wrong place at the wrong time:

- With more than two million persons incarcerated in the U.S. in 2013, our nation has the highest incarceration rate in the world, surpassing Russia and South Africa, with a rate of 737 for every 100,000 persons. By contrast, Canada and China were at 110 per every 100,000, and Japan was less than 50 for every 100,000. The prison population in the U.S. grew by six times in a little over 30 years from 1973 to 2008 (from 330,000 to over 2,000,000), due to the U.S. "War on Drugs."
- Wisconsin in 2013 had 23,000 persons incarcerated, compared with Minnesota's 10,000. Even though the two states have similar demographics and population size, and similar rates of crime, the two states obviously have different ways of dealing with offenders. Minnesota makes a concerted effort to assess offenders for underlying causes for their criminal activity and looks for community-based treatment programs for low-risk, non-violent offenders. As a result Minnesota spends about one-third as much on the correctional system as Wisconsin. Yet crime rates are very similar in the two states, indicating that Minnesota's community corrections approach does not result in increased crime.
- The racial disparity in the rate of incarceration in the U.S. is striking. Black men are incarcerated at a rate seven times greater than white men, and black women are incarcerated at five times the rate of white

women. One-third of all black men can expect to be incarcerated in their lifetime, if incarceration rates continue at their present level. In looking for an explanation for such disparity, researchers have found that one key lies in the high level of concentrated poverty that exists among blacks. Without high school and/or technical education, and without family-supporting jobs, people are more likely to turn to crime for an income. Even though the use and sale of drugs is proportionately equal in black and white communities, the rate of arrest and conviction of African Americans and Hispanics is much higher than that of whites because of the high concentration of drug enforcement in minority communities.

The higher level of incarceration in the black community has its ripple of negative effects on black families and on black young men growing up in such realities: absence of fathers, lack of positive male role models, and development of a culture among some young black men that sees incarceration as a normal part of life, even a badge of achievement, following in the footsteps of father or big brother. For those who do serve time behind bars, some have a Damascus Road experience and come back to family and community with a deep determination to serve God and others. Others return bewildered at best and embittered at worst. *The New Jim Crow* by Michelle Alexander, is an in-depth study of underlying causes of the high rate of African American incarceration.

- Corrections officials concur that 70 to 80 percent of those who are incarcerated have underlying alcohol and other drug abuse issues and/or mental health issues directly connected with their crime. Most of these persons with underlying issues are low-risk offenders who are not a threat to the community, and who need community-based treatment with incentives and sanctions, rather than incarceration.

Prison-based treatment is usually better than no treatment, but it is not nearly as effective as community-based treatment, partly because of the punitive atmosphere that surrounds any prison-based program. But prison-based treatment is not very effective mainly because it is a program in a bubble, disconnected from family and job and those community factors that are essential for quality holistic treatment and successful recovery. Lois Glover, a member of Cross Church, Milwaukee, and former President of WISDOM, often stated in public meetings: "People with money or good health insurance coverage, who get in trouble with the law because of their drug abuse issues, go to treatment. Poor people go to jail." That is not simply a perception of a well-informed African American woman in Milwaukee. It is a reality all across the U.S. People of faith who become aware of this disparity are called to work for policies that would give the poor the same opportunity as those with money, for treatment instead of incarceration. This is a win-win policy for everyone.

- Hundreds of persons, mainly women, are going to state and federal prisons, some serving terms as long as 15 to 20 years, convicted of "conspiracy to sell illicit drugs." Wives and girlfriends of drug dealers are often sentenced to these long prison terms on evidence that they passed a phone message to their husband/boyfriend regarding a drug deal. The message may simply have been "Call 733-4111." They may not have known that it had anything to do with a drug deal. But if they passed the message, they are legally considered part of the drug selling operation and therefore they were criminals who must serve time for their crime. Often the husband/boyfriend will "turn state's evidence" and submit names of others who are dealing drugs or handling messages, in order to get a lesser sentence. As a result, some of the husbands/boyfriends who were the big dealers, will get off with a three-to-five year sentence, while the wife/girlfriend who was the messenger, knowingly or unknowingly, will be sentenced to ten to twenty years.
- The rate of incarceration has risen at a such a steady rate in many states, between 1988 and 2013, that some counties and states do their five and ten-year planning based on the assumption that the increase will continue to climb at the same rate.

In 2006, the sheriff of Rock County in southern Wisconsin (Janesville/Beloit) went to the County Board of Supervisors to ask for a $25 million jail expansion. He used graphs to show that by 2010, the jail population would increase to a certain level. By 2015 it would be still higher. And by 2020, it would be higher yet. "Based on those projections," the sheriff stated, "we will have to expand the jail capacity to that level, and to prepare for the year 2025, we really need even more bed capacity."

Rock County was not the only county in Wisconsin or the U.S. where law enforcement officials and elected representatives were swept up in the tidal wave of rising incarceration rates and longer sentences that bloated the jail and prison population and convinced them that the rate of increase was inevitable. Many other county sheriffs in Wisconsin and other states were going to their boards and to the voters with the same message: "The jail population will be at a certain level by 2025, so we have to expand our jail."

A small group of congregations in Rock County had come together and founded an organization called JOB (Justice Overcoming Boundaries), part of the statewide network of a justice organization called WISDOM, to work on issues in the Beloit/Janesville area. Representatives of JOB went to the county supervisors and key officials questioning the necessity of jail expansion if they looked at ways of diverting non-violent offenders to treatment programs and other alternatives to incarceration. The county brought in professional consultants to present an account of what other localities, facing a similar potential jail expansion situation, had done. Rock County officials discovered that they had several options, and that they had a great deal of control over what seemed to be an irreversible situation. They decided to initiate some treatment alternatives for low-level offenders with underlying drug addiction and/or mental health issues. The result? They actually reduced their jail population. And they did not have to spend $25 million for a jail expansion.

Restorative Justice

There is a growing movement in the U.S. that's working on radical prison reform. It's called "restorative justice."

The restorative justice movement in the broadest sense includes any initiative that seeks to bring about wholeness and restored relationships where there has been some kind of criminal act that has negatively affected people, communities, and relationships.

"Restoring" people and relationships is what Jesus and the Gospel was all about. When Zacchaeus encountered Jesus' love and forgiveness (Luke 19:1-10), he experienced a change of heart, and instead of continuing to rip off the poor, he decided to give half of his possessions to the poor and to restore four times any amount he had overcharged people in the collecting of taxes. That act of restoring the money and the relationship with the people whom he had hurt is what restorative justice is all about. After Zacchaeus made the promise to restore the stolen money and to restore the relationships with the people he had hurt, Jesus said: "Today salvation has come to this house."

Restorative justice insists that the goal of the judicial/correctional system should be to restore the victim, the perpetrator, and the community to wholeness. As the system usually works in the U.S., restoration of victim, perpetrator and community is not the goal. Determination of guilt, the degree of guilt, and the appropriate punishment of the perpetrator are usually the primary goals and restoration of money losses is a secondary goal. Wholeness for the victim is not usually of primary importance. The victim usually has little role at the trial except to testify as to what happened, to help prove the guilt of the perpetrator, and to indicate the hurt and the damage that was done.

In the case of serious crimes, such as murder, rape, or physical attack, there is concern for the victim's state of mind, and there is concern for the victim's recovery of money or property in the case of theft. Usually a severe sentence is the one thing required by current standards to ease the victim's experience of loss. The perpetrator often has no role at the trial except to admit guilt or to plead not guilty. Attorneys do most of the talking at a trial. The defense attorney is trying to get charges reduced and to get his/her client totally exonerated, if possible. The prosecuting attorney is trying to get a conviction and as severe a sentence as possible. Often a trial is a contest of intellect and legal smarts between two attorneys.

Once the verdict is determined by the jury and/or the judge, the perpetrator, if found guilty, is sentenced to probation with supervision, to community service, or to incarceration. The offender usually has not had a person-to-person conversation with the victim. And never does the perpetrator hear from ordinary members of the community as to how the crime negatively impacts the neighborhood and community where the crime took place.

The main goal of the current judicial system is retribution, not restoration. Punishment, not wholeness. It is assumed that punishment will teach the perpetrator a lesson and thus make him/her whole. And somehow punishing the person who committed the crime should heal the victim and the community. However, that is not the way it works in reality. Long sentences and the threat of parole revocation for a violation of the parole agreement ordinarily do not scare or punish people into wholeness. Instead, such policies and practices tend to drive persons into bitterness. It is no accident that in 2008, with "truth in sentencing" (offender has to serve his/her entire sentence with no reduced time for good behavior or for accomplished education/treatment goals) and with widespread use of solitary confinement as a disciplinary/control tool, Wisconsin had a recidivism rate over 50 percent.

Nor does harsh sentencing, coupled with harsh incarceration practices, heal the victim or the community. The tighter the screws are turned down on offenders, the more people and politicians tend to want still harsher sentencing and treatment of prisoners. And judges and legislators running for election tend to run on the "tough on crime" platform rather than the "smart on crime" platform.

A growing number of community leaders are supporting the "restorative justice" approach, which has as its goal the restoration of the individuals involved, especially the victim and the perpetrator of a crime, as well as the relationships between perpetrator, victim, and the community.

It will take a while before the judicial/incarceration system, which has built up practices and attitudes in our Western culture over the centuries, can be reformed in such a way that restorative justice is a reality. But some significant beginnings have been made.

Treatment alternatives to incarceration are examples of restorative justice. Supporters of the traditional judicial model of punishment find it difficult to support treatment alternatives to incarceration because they insist that there's no punishment in community-based treatment, and there has to be punishment, they say, if the victim of the crime is going to be satisfied that society did something to right the wrong.

Ironically, as mentioned above, a quality drug treatment program is tougher than most incarceration. It requires personal accountability and daily tough decision-making that is so rigorous that some offenders, when they are given the choice of community-based treatment with sanctions (if the treatment is not taken seriously), or the option of incarceration, they choose incarceration.

More importantly, treatment alternatives are designed to restore. First, treatment is aimed, of course, at restoring the perpetrator to wholeness, to that state of body, mind, and spirit that will make it possible for the offender to once again be the parent, the job holder, the church member, the tax-paying, positive contributor to the community, the whole person who can have a sense of personal fulfillment and be an asset to any human community.

Second, treatment alternatives are designed to restore the victims in a very real way. Part of any quality treatment program is the requirement that the person moving into recovery is to go to those persons they have hurt and make personal amends for anything they may have done to hurt a family member, a neighbor, a friend, or a victim of their criminal activity. The victim of a crime may not want the offender to come to the individual personally, and that is the victim's prerogative. However, most victims, many of whom are family members, sisters or brothers in Christ, acquaintances, or neighbors, welcome the opportunity for a personal reconciliation. And certainly they will welcome the restoration of money or goods that may have been stolen from them.

Third, treatment helps to restore the hurt done to the community. Certainly when an absentee father, non-working, criminally-minded offender who has been a threat to the neighborhood, is transformed into a caring parent, a productive worker, and a citizen who is contributing to the welfare of the neighborhood, the community is healed. And as for community safety, an ex-offender with underlying drug addiction issues coming back to the community in recovery and holding down a job makes the community much safer than coming out of prison still addicted and still driven by those urges that caused him/her to offend and to shatter the safety of the community before.

There are many ways to "do" restorative justice besides treatment alternatives. The district attorneys and judges in Milwaukee County are utilizing restorative justice community panels to handle some cases of shoplifting, employee thefts, intra-family crime, and similar non-violent crimes. Rather than send the offender to incarceration, the offender is asked to meet with the victim (if the person agrees to the process) and with two or three community representatives who have been trained to be non-judgmental but to represent the larger community and to describe how the community is hurt by the particular crime in question. They participate with the perpetrator and the victim in coming to a consensus on the restitution that would make the victim and the community whole again and to determine some type of community service that would help the perpetrator learn something about himself or herself and about how to make positive contributions that build the community rather than tear it down.

After some training in restorative justice principles and specifically, how to serve as a community representative on a restorative justice panel, I had the privilege of serving on a panel an assistant district attorney had authorized. It was a serious case of employee theft that could have resulted in a felony conviction because of the value of the stolen item. However, because of the circumstances, the assistant D.A. recommended that a restorative justice panel deal with the case rather than press for the usual felony conviction.

The perpetrator was an 18-year-old Caucasian man living on the south side of Milwaukee (in contrast to the predominately African American north side of Milwaukee). He had managed to remove a piece of electronics equipment from his place of work that was worth about $20,000. When his supervisor discovered that the item was missing, he questioned the young man, as well as others who might have been likely to know something about the whereabouts of the missing equipment.

The young man became aware of the seriousness of his action and the possibility of a felony charge and even some prison time. So he returned the stolen item and confessed to his supervisor.

The assistant D.A. and the company were pleased that the equipment was returned and that there was a confession, but they concurred that it was too serious an offense to just drop the charges. The trust between the employee and the supervisor/company had been broken. It was not certain what the young man or his fellow employees had learned from the incident, if anything.

If punishment was the goal, the young man would have been put through the judicial system, convicted of a felony, and given a prison sentence or at least a certain amount of time on probation, in which he would have to report regularly to his probation officer and abide by the requirements of his probation agreement. If he violated any of the agreement requirements, he would be at risk of going to prison. If he kept all the requirements of the probation agreement, he would still likely have the felony record for the rest of his life. This means that he would always have difficulty getting a job. Most employers will hire a non-offender before they hire an ex-offender, even if the ex-offender is better qualified for the job, and even if the crime had been committed ten years before. Having a felony record means he would not be able to vote in Wisconsin as long as he is on probation, and he would not be able to vote for the rest of his life if he moved to certain states, like Florida or Alabama, or Mississippi, if he had a felony record. And having a felony record means that certain loans and scholarships would not be available to him if he decided to go to college.

If restoration was the goal, then punitive measures that last a lifetime would be avoided, and measures would be aimed at restoring the perpetrator, the victim, and the community. Not that the restorative justice model has no element of punishment. There is an experience of punishment in any measure in which the perpetrator is asked to do something over and above his usual daily schedule. But it is punishment that has a clear goal of growing, learning, and restoring, not punishment for the sake of punishment.

So to the credit of the D.A. and the company, the restorative justice model was chosen, and I happened to be one of the community representatives on the panel.

The young man, his supervisor, and three community representatives made up the panel. We gathered in a meeting room of the city hall of the Milwaukee suburb where the workplace was located. So it was an "official" space, but not a courtroom with a judge, a D.A., an attorney, and possibly some spectators.

The young man was asked to tell his story and how it happened. The community reps asked probing questions, not in a judgmental tone of voice, but more in the tone of a concerned parent. Questions like: "What were you going to do with the piece of equipment that you stole? Why was this piece of equipment so important to you? Can you imagine what would happen to this company, or any company, if employees, including supervisors, were to take items from the plant at will? Was there anything in your upbringing that tells you this action was wrong? What do you think your action has done to your relationship with your supervisors, your fellow employees, and the company? How do you really feel about your actions?"

The young man struggled with his answers because he had not really thought about those root causes and implications of his action. And these were questions that would not have been asked in a typical courtroom process. There would not have been any "ordinary" people from the community present in the courtroom articulating concerns about the common good and the "beloved community." He responded to our questions with a tone of voice and demeanor that indicated he was trying to be honest with his answers and that he recognized the relevance of our questions.

The supervisor was struck by the young man's struggle to be honest with himself, as well as with us. He concurred with us that the young thief was truly sorry for what he had done and that he was trying to get in touch with his own inner core, his values, and the significance of his role in the grand scheme of the community and the economy, of which he was one small, but important part.

After our heart-to-heart conversation, we came to the difficult part of our job: what kind of action in the community could we assign to this young man that would really deepen his awareness and understanding, so that he would not blow off this conversation with his supervisor and with the community reps, as an interesting intellectual exercise, and little more?

We decided that we would ask him to talk to other teenagers about the temptations to steal, the wrongness of stealing, the consequences of breaking the law, the harm done to self and to others in the act of stealing, and the potential lifelong barriers they could face if they are found guilty of a felony charge. The group of youth we asked him to speak to was the Challenges Group, a weekly gathering of about a dozen young men at Cross Church. They came together around pizza and soda and talked regularly with the three men from Cross who had committed themselves to walking with these neighborhood junior and senior high youth, most of whom were not members of Cross. The youth were attracted by the pizza and by the interest that these men showed in their welfare.

I wasn't sure how this white teenager from the south side of Milwaukee, famous for its racial prejudice against blacks, was going to respond to an assignment to meet with a group of African American teenagers on the north side of Milwaukee, on their turf. Definitely the assignment was asking him to step way out of his comfort zone. However, he accepted the assignment without apparent hesitancy, but with a bit of fear about what he would say and how he would be accepted. I talked with him briefly about the main points he was to talk about, introduced him to the three men in charge of the Challenges Group, and then left him to share his story and what he had learned from it.

The following week, I met with the young man to talk with him about the moral and theological aspects of stealing. Since he said he had grown up in the Catholic tradition, I lifted up the Old Testament and New Testament messages about stealing and engaged him in digging a little deeper in his own spirit about the damaging effect of stealing and the life-giving power of giving. Then I asked him how things went in his testimony to the Challenges Group.

"Oh, I was surprised," he said, "at how they listened to me and how they accepted me as one of them. In fact, they invited me to come back and I told them I'd see them this weekend."

I don't know what the young man's journey has been like these years since his experience with the restorative justice community panel and since his out-of-the-comfort-zone testimony and miraculous bonding with his African American peers. However, I am truly grateful that he had the positive experience of being restored in his relationship with his supervisor, the larger community, and hopefully with God and himself. Because of his restorative justice experience, his chances of "staying out of trouble" and maturing and healing are very good.

Getting a Start

Because of my involvement with the statewide campaign in Wisconsin called "Treatment Instead of Prison" (TIP), I was contacted by a young, first-call Lutheran pastor in Fond du Lac, Wisconsin. She said she wanted some advice on how to minister to a man who was in the county jail for a misdemeanor committed because of his addiction to drugs. As I asked her questions about his previous incarceration history, his family, and his church background, she responded: "Unfortunately he is a member of our congregation."

"Quite to the contrary," I countered. "You are fortunate that he is a member of your congregation. This may help you to recruit some caring members of the congregation to take some ownership in the ministry, as they see that it's not just 'those' people, but it's actually someone from their congregational family. This could help you get ministry going, not only for this member of your congregation, but for others as well."

Getting a start in prison ministry is the challenge. If someone from the congregation is incarcerated, or if there is a jail or prison near the church, that can make it easier.

If a congregation or social ministry committee is looking for fuel for the fire to get some form of prison ministry started, there are two types of fuel that are handy for any congregation anywhere.

One good reason for starting a prison ministry is the huge number of men and women from every community who are incarcerated and who need to hear that they are worth something. In fact, they need to hear that they are worth everything to God and to God's people. A study that came out in 2008 revealed that over 2,000,000 people in the U.S. were incarcerated, one in every 150 persons. That same study revealed that one in nine African American men between 20 and 34 were incarcerated. Just the sheer numbers of people incarcerated compel God's people to reach out in love with a message of hope and possibility to those who are locked up, as well as to link arms with community people who have eyes to see that there are some law enforcement and judicial policies that need to be transformed.

But the most compelling reason for Christians to get involved in prison ministry is the call of Jesus. When Jesus, in his dying hour, said to the thief on the cross, "Today you will be with me in paradise," he was making it clear that persons who have committed crimes are redeemable, valuable, and worthy of the time and energy and love of a congregation as its members carry out Christ's mission.

CHAPTER 13

CONGREGATIONAL PARTNERSHIPS: BRIDGING URBAN, SUBURBAN AND RURAL

And now brothers and sisters, we want you to know about the grace that God has given the Macedonian churches. Out of the most severe trial, their overflowing joy and their extreme poverty welled up in rich generosity. For I testify that they gave as much as they were able, and even beyond their ability. Entirely on their own, they urgently pleaded with us for the privilege of sharing in the service of the saints.

–2 Corinthians:8: 1-4

I entered Hephatha Church for worship on a cold Sunday morning in February in 2008. I noticed that two pews midway on the right side of the center aisle of the sanctuary were filled with at least a dozen teenagers and a few adults, all of them white, obvious visitors in the midst of our predominately African American congregation.

I knew without asking that these were visitors from one of Hephatha's 12 partner congregations and that they almost certainly would be serving the meal that follows our Sunday morning worship and Sunday school period. When I sat down in a pew right in front of them, I turned around to the persons immediately behind me and shook their hands, welcoming them to Hephatha Church. Then I looked in the Sunday bulletin and discovered they were from Memorial Lutheran Church in Glendale, a suburb adjoining Milwaukee on the northeast.

Memorial Lutheran had been formed by a merger of two congregations, one of which had sold its central city sanctuary to an African American Baptist congregation in the 1960s. Now 40 years later, the young people and their parents and mentors came to Hephatha Church on a cold February Sunday.

This Sunday morning journey to Hephatha Church was not a "normal" Sunday morning experience. The drive into the heart of the city of Milwaukee was a drive to an area where many suburbanites would never travel unless they absolutely had to for some business purpose. There are some suburbanites who make the journey to N. 18th and Locust to deliver merchandise to neighborhood stores or to purchase marijuana or illegal drugs. But very few who drive in to worship with sisters and brothers.

If you've been to Hephatha before, you know you're going to be welcomed by people who greet you as though they've known you all their lives. You know you're going to experience warmth and hospitality and authenticity. So there's a sense of expectation, rather than fear.

When the time comes for the children's sermon, the pews seem to erupt into streams of children, and yes, teenagers, gravitating to the large chancel area, about 40, from age one to 17. I noticed that the youth from Memorial Lutheran got up and joined their peers in front. I know that journey from the pew to the chancel may not have been easy for the Memorial youth. I know from having led worship at Memorial that the teens there do not go forward for the children's sermon. So this participation in the children's message at Hephatha was a clear sign that the youth from Memorial were willing to learn and to grow and to identify with the youth at Hephatha. They were not just checking out an exotic cultural experience.

The youth and the adults from Memorial heard Pastor Mary Martha follow her usual pattern of the children's sermon, starting with her traditional opening: "All of you are special, we are thankful that you are here, aren't we, Church?" To which responses come from all sections of the sanctuary: "That's right!" and "Absolutely!" and "Amen!"

Pastor Mary Martha continues her introduction to the children's sermon: "You help keep our faith alive. You give us hope. In fact, you are the hope for our community and for our city." Then she asked three boys, ages 10 to 12, to stand. "I want the whole church this morning to know that these three young men were the first persons here this morning. On this cold morning, they came early to God's house on their own, to help with anything that needed to be done. What a witness to all of us." And the congregation gave the three young men a sturdy applause.

That wasn't the end of the affirmations. Pastor Mary Martha then asked two girls to step forward. She asked them for the report cards they had showed her earlier as they arrived for worship. With slightly embarrassed smiles, they handed the cards to their pastor, who proceeded to read the data on the cards to the congregation: "Days absent: 0. Times tardy: 0. Reading: A. Math: A. Art: A." Both cards were almost identical. And, of course, each girl received a hearty ovation from the congregation.

The contingent from Memorial was catching a glimpse of the central city that didn't match the stereotypes rampant in the suburbs and reinforced by the media. Yes, there is a high truancy rate in the central city. And yes, there is a high dropout rate. And yes, there is violence. But during these moments in worship at 18th and Locust, it became clear that there are some youth who put adults to shame in getting to worship on a cold morning–ahead of time! And there are some students who attend classes as though their life depended on it and who obviously pour themselves into their daily assignments with extra determination. And the message was getting through to the youth of Hephatha: "Against all odds, you can do it, with God's help."

As they sat there in the midst of these young people growing up in a difficult world, just four or five miles from their world, the young people from Memorial began to get a glimpse, even a feel, for the challenging journey that the Hephatha youth faced. And they got a clearer picture of the mission of the Church, which should include walking with people at the edges, especially with young people facing harsh odds and alluring temptations to give up on the meaning of life.

The children's sermon was not the end of the nurturing experience for the cadre form Memorial Church. The whole service was a broadening experience of Christian worship and urban realities. The choir's Gospel-style song, *The Lord will See You Through* was an experience of the expressive Gospel beat in worship music and a testimony to the real life struggle that is persistent and deep. The pastor's sermon addressed the daily challenges for Hephatha worshipers, to stay the course of the road to recovery from addiction, to stay dedicated to non-violence in a culture of violence, to believe that you can make it through high school and into college when no one else in your family has reached those goals, to trust that God loves you no matter what. The prayer time lifted up by name 48 persons with health struggles, 11 persons in prison, 12 individuals at various stages of recovery from drug addiction, eight individuals and families with special concerns, seven agencies in the community working for uplift and empowerment, including the local Hopkins St. public school, Hephatha's partner congregations, as well as the two partner church bodies in El Salvador and Tanzania, the work of MICAH, the congregation-based justice organization that Hephatha is part of, for an end to "this time of war," and finally, thanksgiving for Jesus and all blessings.

There was a visible sign of community that folded Hephatha and Memorial people together, as participants took the hands of the persons to the right and to the left and across the center aisle during the praying of the Lord's Prayer. And then we got in line to receive the body and blood of Christ, signs of his love, his forgiveness, his presence and his power to live the new life in him. The morning worship was a rich tapestry in which members of Hephatha and members of their partner congregation intertwined their lives and their realities in a way that enriched us all. We saw one another in new ways, shattering some stereotypes and discovering amazing unity and common ground.

Yet the worship that Sunday morning was not the end of the bridging experience between urban and suburban. The Sunday school/Bible class experience and the meal were yet to come. The dozen youth from Memorial joined the 20 youth from Hephatha in a Bible study/sharing/prayer time, led by Pastor Mary Martha and Karen Perry, an adult member of Hephatha who is also one of the leaders of the Monday night recovery circle at Hephatha. One adult from Memorial joined the adult Bible class, and the other Memorial adults proceeded to the kitchen to work with two Hephatha adults to get the meal ready to be served in another 45 minutes. The folks from Memorial had brought the food. Preparing, serving, and eating the food with the sisters and brothers at Hephatha, half of them children and youth, helped to transform a potential "do-gooder act of charity" into a unique experience of fellowship and mutual learning and growing.

Just how radically the life and the witness of members of Memorial and Hephatha are affected by the common experience of worship, Bible study, and table fellowship is impossible to measure. But the spontaneous responses of friendships and service from both sides of the urban/suburban gap are signs that the partnership is more than a meaningless ritual.

Partner Congregations

The reality at Hephatha Church is that eight of the 12 partner congregations are engaged to some degree of regularity in the Sunday morning shared worship, Bible study, and fellowship meal. The development of partner congregations may have started originally as primarily a way of giving financial support to urban congregations and "saving" them from going under. Over time, the practice of partnership has evolved into a mutually shared experience and a recognition that such partnerships, if they are forged prayerfully and creatively, actually "save" the suburban congregations from a sterile disconnect from the urban realities of concentrated poverty, racial separation, cultural isolation, and rigid stereotypes that suburban folks are partially responsible for, whether they realize it or not, and with which they are intrinsically and inescapably connected. Likewise, the shared experiences with suburban congregations "save" members of Hephatha from that common view of urbanites that all suburban folks want to avoid authentic contact with folks in the central city, at best, or they are arrogant, hateful, prejudiced and racist, at worst.

Many are the ways in which urban and suburban/small town congregations can interact and in some small ways begin to close the racial gap and the economic gap that separate people in the United States on a daily basis.

Christ the Victor Lutheran Church in New Berlin, Wisconsin, about 30 minutes from Hephatha Church in Milwaukee, for several years, conducted a joint evening vacation Bible school with Hephatha. They sent a bus to Hephatha and picked up about 40 children, along with four or five adults every evening for a week. The result was a thoroughly integrated staff and set of classes that shared a meal, worship, Bible study, and recreation time. The shared experience resulted in relationships that lasted longer than the week of classes, relationships that were deepened when people from Christ the Victor Church came periodically on Sundays to worship and serve a meal afterward.

One of the more radical partnership developments was forged by Bay Shore Lutheran, on the northeast side of Milwaukee about 25 minutes from Hephatha. Not only have they sent representatives to Sunday worship and supplied and served the meal following Sunday school. They decided that if they were going to be serious about walking with the people of Hephatha, they needed to work with Hephatha in tussling with some of the underlying causes of poverty. So they joined MICAH, the congregation-based justice organizing group of which Hephatha is a part.

But Bay Shore Church didn't stop there. One of its members, Tim Nelson, decided that its MICAH core team needed to know the issues that Hephatha's MICAH core team was wrestling with and to get some pointers from Hephatha's leaders on how to launch Bay Shore's own core team. So he appointed himself as Bay Shore's representative to Hephatha's core team. He was there at the table every month, sitting alongside the 15 people who regularly gathered from the congregation, the neighborhood, the local school, and the district police station, to talk about the nitty-gritty challenges in the neighborhood. He mainly listened, but he was not afraid to act when the Hephatha core team planned a neighborhood cleanup or an action at City Hall. Tim Nelson would take the word back to Bay Shore Church and put out a call for people who care, to join him and the people of Hephatha, to do what was needed to be done in the cause of justice.

Then there's Kingo Lutheran, on the east side of Milwaukee. Not more than 15 minutes form Hephatha, Kingo's partnership with Hephatha goes back to 1981, and has continued at some level over the 30 intervening years. The one constant over the years has been the practice of Kingo's choir, and a few additional members of Kingo, traveling to Hephatha Church for a shared Thanksgiving Day worship. In addition, Hephatha's choir, plus a few members, has traveled most of those 30 years, to Kingo on the evening of the festival of the Epiphany for a shared worship.

But Kingo has engaged at a deeper level of partnership, especially since 2001. Kingo has supported a full-time parish nurse, Louise Meyer, and designated that she spend half of her time with the people and community of Hephatha.

"Most Hephatha members don't fully realize what a blessing Nurse Louise is to our ministry here," Hephatha's Pastor Mary Martha Kannass has stated. "She has walked with dozens of Hephatha's folks through their medical traumas, and has even made emergency house calls at 2:00 a.m."

In addition to supporting a half-time parish nurse at Hephatha, the Kingo congregation offers a weekly tutoring session for Hephatha students, along with transportation. Of course, Kingo members come regularly to Sunday worship and provide the meal after worship. One of Kingo's members, Gail Povey, became known as "the salad woman." Whenever Kingo served a meal, Gail Povey brought ingredients of a "make-your-own-salad." Besides two or three kinds of lettuce, she brought 10 to 12 exotic toppings, including slices of boiled eggs, bacon bits, mushrooms, two or three varieties of olives, croutons, cherry tomatoes, carrot slices, and you name it. The amazing thing is that the children and youth of Hephatha rushed to the table to make their salads. They even went for seconds.

It is not surprising that Gail Povey became an associate member of Hephatha and worships there regularly. She knows most of the members of Hephatha by name and interacts with them as a regular member. But she still hangs on to her membership at Kingo, determined to keep the connections as ongoing and deep as possible.

As part of my work as an organizer with WISDOM, I stopped by Gloria Dei Lutheran Church, in Neenah, Wisconsin, 90 miles north of Milwaukee in the Fox River Valley, to see whether I might talk with one or both of the pastors, Tabitha and Jon Gallatin. I found Pastor Tabitha at the church and began talking with her, in the hope of demonstrating the value of engaging their congregation in justice work and possibly linking their congregation with ESTHER, the congregation-based organizing group in the Fox Valley linked with MICAH in Milwaukee.

I apologized to Pastor Tabitha for not participating in their installation service the week before, especially since I knew that Gloria Dei is a partner congregation with Hephatha Church. As soon as I mentioned Hephatha Church, she became very animated and exclaimed: "I can't tell you how much it meant to the whole congregation for the praise dancers from Hephatha to be here for the service. They did such a beautiful job of adding praise to the service. And they were so friendly and talkative with the people after the service. I can assure you that we will be strengthening our partnership with Hephatha."

Pastor Tabitha and I proceeded to talk for about 15 minutes about the value of a small-town congregation maintaining a lively relationship with an urban congregation 90 miles away. She realized how vital it was for their congregation, and especially for their youth, to know first-hand, how enriching it is to share experiences with racially and culturally diverse sisters and brothers in Christ. Thanks to the partnership between Hephatha and Gloria Dei Church, Neenah, my relationship with the clergy couple at Gloria Dei is especially positive and real. I had no difficulty talking with Pastor Tabitha about the connection between their working on justice issues such as "treatment instead of prison" and their support of a strong witness to the Gospel at Hephatha Church.

Beginning in Birmingham and Milwaukee

My appreciation for partnerships between urban and suburban congregations grew over time. In Birmingham, Alabama, in the 1960s, living out an urban-suburban partnership would have meant a living, pulsating relationship between a black urban congregation and a white suburban congregation.

The demographics were clearcut. It would have meant that the white congregation would have to welcome black sisters and brothers to their church, and they would have to be willing to reverse the journey and travel into the black community and to the black church. Given the segregation laws and the cultural taboos that reinforced the harsh realities of racial segregation, and given the fear of retaliation from the KKK, it is not surprising that urban/suburban partnerships did not exist. The white Church in the South and the North is just beginning to come to grips with the 350-year history of white congregations accepting the racially segregated way of life within the Church, as well as in society, and not openly and courageously living out the Gospel vision of equality and mutual support of one another in the Body of Christ.

There were always those wonderful exceptions to the rule, even in Birmingham, Alabama, in the 1960s. There was the Hrbek family, members of Trinity Lutheran in Birmingham, who gave financial and spiritual support to St. Paul Church, the African American parish I pastored, and who worshiped with us on many occasions. However, they were unable to get congregational support to make it a mutual partnership between our two congregations.

As is the case with most authentic changes and growth experiences in our life as Christians and as a Church, the reality of urban-suburban congregational partnership emerged in a spontaneous, Spirit-led manner. During my pastorate at Cross Church, 1967-2001, six partnerships developed, as pastors and congregations were led by the Spirit to explore ways to cross racial, cultural, and class barriers to live into a Gospel vision of unity and mutual support.

When Cross Church left the Lutheran Church–Missouri Synod (LCMS) to join the Association of Evangelical Lutheran Churches (AELC) in 1976, there was a mutual, spontaneous sense of need on the part of all the LCMS congregations in Wisconsin (all six of them) that joined the AELC, to find ways of expressing our oneness in mission and in living out the Gospel of Christ. We began doing things together that we had not done together before.

Of the six LCMS congregations that joined the AELC, Cross Church was in the central city, made up predominately of persons of color, and in need of financial assistance. As the partnerships began to develop, these were largely one-way in terms of going to another congregation to share our faith and our gifts. It was the Cross Youth Choir going to Faith Church on the Southside of Milwaukee, or the Cross Adult Choir going to Ascension Church in Waukesha (a suburban city 30 minutes west of Milwaukee), or to Capitol Drive Church on the northwest side of Milwaukee.

Those beginning partnerships for Cross Church in the 1970s were rather typical of the few partnerships that did exist between urban and suburban congregations at the time. The suburban congregations sent an annual or semi-annual mission offering, and the urban congregation responded with a choral offering of gratitude for the financial support. Usually a member of Cross would give a short report in the worship, along with a testimony of faith. Sometimes I went along with the choir and gave the sermon in the worship, lifting up not simply the realities of Cross Church's journey of faith, but also the realities of life in the central city and the challenges of living out the Gospel as a congregation in the midst of those realities.

One of the original three AELC congregations that started out on the partnership journey with Cross Church, Ascension Church, Waukesha, has remained in partnership and has been part of the transformation of the partnership model over those 30-plus years of walking together.

From the very beginning of the partnerships, Cross Church did not view the inter-congregational relationships as a way of securing additional funds for our ministries. As a matter of fact, there were years that we did not receive any contributions from some of our partner congregations. We saw the sharing of Spirit-filled Gospel songs by our choirs and testimonies by pastor and lay leaders in suburban congregations as an opportunity to bridge the deep chasm between urban and suburban realities, to combat racism, and to celebrate the power, the joy, and the love of the Gospel.

Cross choirs and leaders who participated with me in the shared events with partner congregations found meaning and purpose in the shared services. But we came to recognize that the activities and sharing needed to go in both directions if the partnership was to be really mutual. And the conversation needed to be on a deeper level and involve more people, if we really wanted to bridge the chasms and combat racism and transform lives.

Church of the Wilderness

Cross Church developed a new understanding and experience of partnership when the Lutheran Church of the Wilderness in Bowler, Wisconsin, left the LCMS, joined the AELC, and expressed its desire for a partnership with Cross Church. The partnership didn't require any convincing of Cross folks. Members of Cross and especially African American members welcomed the opportunity to walk with members of the predominately Native American congregation, even though it was three hours north of Milwaukee in central Wisconsin. Native Americans and African Americans have felt the oppression and the systemic discrimination by white America in slightly different ways, but the harsh injustices and the results of poverty and marginalization impacting both African Americans and Native Americans have helped to bind the two communities together ever since the forced arrival of blacks in the American colonies in the 1600s.

The yearly expression of the partnership between Cross and Church of the Wilderness was one Sunday, usually in October, when some Wilderness members would worship at Cross, and another Sunday, usually in August, when some members of Cross would travel to Church of the Wilderness for worship, followed by a meal. The two Native American staples always offered at the meal were fry bread and venison. Usually a member of Wilderness would give a witness talk at the service at Cross, and the reverse would happen at the service at Wilderness. On occasion, the Cross Praise Choir or Youth Choir would travel to Church of the Wilderness for their annual "Friends of Wilderness" service.

On at least two occasions, the Cross Youth Choir sang a concert at Church of the Wilderness as a stop on one of their concert tours. This gave Cross youth and accompanying adults an opportunity to stay overnight in the homes of members of Wilderness.

At one of the Youth Choir concerts, during the second half of the concert, one by one the people began to leave the church until only a handful were left. What was happening? We thought perhaps the music was boring. But before the end of the concert, people returned one by one. The last of the returning members were accompanied by the congregational president. He had been in the hospital for a lengthy recuperation following an automobile accident and had just been released from the hospital. He had come by the church when he learned of the concert. So word had filtered into the church that he was outside, and each of the church family had felt compelled to go out to greet him, welcome him home, and express thanks for his recovery. When he entered the church, we paused in the concert, and we all joined in prayer, led by an elder of the congregation, giving thanks for the recovery and return of their brother in Christ.

Members of Cross learned in a vivid manner the deep sense of solidarity that members of Church of the Wilderness felt for each other. Members of Cross also discovered why the congregation calls themselves "Church of the Wilderness" when, following the concert, the singers and their chaperones went with their hosts to their respective homes in the "wilderness" of the deep woods on the reservation. The rustic homes nestled in the forest were a far cry from the duplexes built side by side in the City of Milwaukee.

Each group from Cross took the guided tour through the small, but well-kept, museum in the heart of the reservation, just a few hundred yards from the church. There we saw pictures and proof of the tribe's trek all the way from Massachusetts back in the 1800s, when the Stockbridge Indians traveled first to Michigan and finally to central Wisconsin to try to find a safe place away from the seemingly inevitable conflicts with European settlers. The museum also chronicled the horrendous story of the boarding schools in the 1900s for Native American children in elementary grades, where Native American children were forbidden to use their native language or to practice their native religion and were forced to learn to read and write English and to adopt the white man's culture.

Unlike most Native American tribes, the Stockbridge Indians had begun to use English already in the 1700s, when they were in Massachusetts, and many of them had become Christians, aligning themselves with the Congregational Church. As the tribe moved westward across Pennsylvania, Ohio, settling briefly in Michigan, and finally moving to Wisconsin, the faithful band of Christians aligned themselves denominationally on the basis of clergy availability. As a result, they were connected with the Methodist Church and finally with the Lutheran Church–Missouri Synod (LCMS) in the mid-1900s. They were attracted to the LCMS because of the Synod's willingness to establish an elementary school for their children.

After the split in the LCMS in 1976, the walkout of almost all the professors and students at Concordia Seminary, St. Louis, and the formation of the "breakaway" Association of Evangelical Lutheran Churches (AELC), Church of the Wilderness found itself with a pastor, Jonathan Schedler, who was a graduate of Seminex, the seminary founded by the professors who had walked out of Concordia Seminary, St. Louis, over issues of Biblical interpretation and the role of women in the Church. Church of the Wilderness had no problems with the theology of Pastor Schedler or with his graduation from Seminex. In fact, they loved Pastor Schedler, who walked with the people of the congregation, with people on the reservation, and in the larger community with genuine empathy and pastoral concern.

However, the LCMS made it clear to Church of the Wilderness that if it wanted to belong to the LCMS, either Pastor Schedler would have to comply with the doctrinal position and constitutional requirements of the LCMS, or the Church of the Wilderness would have to terminate its call to Pastor Schedler.

Church of the Wilderness took the ultimatum from LCMS seriously. They prayed over it, and then got in touch with the AELC and with me, since I was Dean of the Wisconsin Region of the English Synod of the AELC.

Even though there was financial risk in leaving the LCMS, Church of the Wilderness and Pastor Schedler decided to cast their lot with the AELC. It meant that they would be dependent on offerings of individual congregations willing to help support their ministry, rather than on the more solid subsidy of the North Wisconsin District of the LCMS.

Church of the Wilderness and Pastor Schedler came to the prayerful conclusion that the Gospel of Jesus Christ called them to be part of a church that recognized and used the gifts of women on an equal basis with men, was genuinely open to work with Christians of other denominations, and where church rules were less likely to trump Gospel values and truths.

That decision on the part of Church of the Wilderness put it in a close relationship with Cross Church and with the other congregations in Wisconsin that had left the LCMS and joined the AELC. It was as we walked together and met together as part of the Wisconsin Region of the English Synod of the AELC that the partnership between Cross and Church of the Wilderness took shape, and it has ebbed and flowed ever since.

African American members of Cross met members of Church of the Wilderness, and they began to tell their stories about blood relationships and cultural bonding with Native Americans. Alma Eggert, an African American member of Cross said: "I don't know the names of the Native Americans in my family tree, but I know that my grandfather talked about his Indian father and about living with his tribe for a short time."

Johnson Hunter, African American member of Cross, had a similar story to tell. It's no accident that Alma Eggert and Johnson Hunter were among the first to volunteer to participate in joint services and activities between Cross Church and Church of the Wilderness.

One of the unforgettable moments in the partnership between Cross Church and Church of the Wilderness was the service that took place at Church of the Wilderness in 1982, when Joel Schlachtenhaufen was ordained into the ministry of Jesus Christ and became the pastor of Church of the Wilderness, succeeding Pastor Jonathan Schedler.

I had the honor of performing the rite of ordination. I was asked by English Synod Bishop Harold Hecht to take his place because of a schedule conflict for him. Reverend Will Herzfeld, an African American pastor who had been a pastor in Alabama and fellow traveler with me in the civil rights movement, serving at that time as the Assistant to the Bishop of the AELC, was the preacher for the occasion. Several members of Cross, as well as the Cross Praise Choir, traveled three and a half hours to add their gifts to the special occasion.

Making history as the first African American Lutheran pastor to preach at Church of the Wilderness, Will Herzfeld made it a point in his sermon to connect with the journey of native Americans: "As an African American pastor in the Lutheran tradition, I can say that we know a good deal of your journey. We, too, have been treated as second-class citizens in a country for which we have bled and died. We, too, have sometimes been treated as stepchildren in the Body of Christ. But we know whose we are and whom we serve. And freedom is coming."

Seldom do partner congregations have such defining moments as that day of Pastor Joel Schlachtenhaufen's ordination. The fact that they do occur is a reminder of why partner congregation relationships are worth nurturing.

There is always a struggle, as congregations seek to walk together, to make that walk more effective for more people. As Cross Church moved into the 1990s, with two partnerships going fairly well and two more just starting, leaders at Cross and in the partner congregations came to realize that if the partnerships were going to impact congregational life more significantly, and if these bonds were to last, and to grow, then all of us had to be more intentional and more reflective in the planning of events.

Yes, another meeting. We decided to spawn a Partnership Planning Committee that would be composed of two or more representatives from each congregation and we would meet every three or four months. It was determined by this committee that there would be a "Praise Fest" once a year, in which choirs of all the congregations would come together to produce a joyful noise of music and worship, to be followed by a meal and informal conversation across congregational lines. Sometimes this conversation would be guided by pre-planned questions, and sometimes it would be free flowing.

Part of the agenda of the joint planning meetings was designed to schedule plans for a joint activity with Cross. Such joint activities have included: joint weekend youth confirmation sleepovers, small-group discussions in homes, and regular volunteer activities in Cross's weekly Bread of Healing meal program. At times, families from partner congregations worship at Cross and stay for Sunday school/Bible class, sometimes with a meal and activity added.

Pres Hoffman was a member of First United Lutheran, Sheboygan, one hour north of Milwaukee, and a partner congregation with Cross Church. He began attending Cross Sunday worship on a monthly basis. He helped plan two Lenten series of shared discussions between members of Cross and members of First United. Partly because of his experience of the Gospel in new ways at Cross Church, Pres pursued seminary studies, became an ordained ELCA pastor, and began serving a first-ring congregation in greater Milwaukee.

Partner congregations began to form collaborative relationships in the 1970s and 1980s, largely because there was a real need for urban congregations to receive the funding necessary to survive or to carry out the ministries needed in economically depressed areas and in racially transitioning areas.

However, it has become clear, since the 1980s, that urban/suburban/rural congregational partnerships are essential if the Church is going to work at bridging the racial and income-level gulfs that exist in society and in the Church, if the Church is going to help nurture the "beloved community," and if the Church is going to build the power necessary for shaping a just society. There is no cookie-cutter formula for developing congregational partnerships. And it does take energy and time to creatively structure such partnerships and constantly work at making them more relevant and more effective.

When congregations creatively, prayerfully, and lovingly set about walking and working together to cross those "artificial," but persistently real, lines that separate black and white, low-income and middle-upper-income, urban and suburban, then we know this is God's work. It is good. It is incarnational Gospel in the 21st century. It is the Body of Christ transcending racism and fear and apathy. It is far more than we ever dared to ask or imagine.

CHAPTER 14

BEYOND DENOMINATION: ECUMENICAL AND INTERFAITH WORK AND WORSHIP

My prayer is not for them alone. I pray for those who will believe in me through their message, that all of them may be one, Father, just as you are in me and I am in you. May they also be in us so that the world may believe that you sent me.
–John 17:21-22

It was 9:00 a.m. on a Sunday morning in 2007, time for worship at Hephatha Church to begin, and I noticed that there were five or six well-dressed African American men sitting in the back pew. I introduced myself to them and discovered that they were deacons from Bethesda Missionary Baptist Church, two short blocks from Hephatha.

As Pastor Mary Martha introduced the service that morning, she invited all of us to follow her and the deacons from Bethesda Church, as they were about to exit the sanctuary and walk two blocks to the corner of 16th Street and Locust. She announced that a twelve-year-old girl had been killed the previous week by a fast-moving car on Locust Street, as she left the corner grocery store and attempted to cross the street. "As the people of God, the people of Hephatha and Bethesda," she announced, "will proceed to the corner where the tragedy happened so that we can rightly remember this child of God and pray for the family and the community so deeply affected by this loss."

We got up from our pews, close to a hundred of us, and proceeded outside on a sunny Sunday morning to gather on the sidewalks intersecting at the corner of N. 16th street and Locust street. We were joined there by Reverend Robert L. Sims, Pastor of Bethesda Baptist Church, and by some family members, some community people, and some friends and classmates of the girl who tragically lost her life.

It was a very moving public witness to the Good News of God's love for all people and to the value of a 12-year-old child from the community as she was remembered and honored by two Christian congregations in the neighborhood. It was also a visible witness to the oneness of the Church across denominational lines. Unfortunately, Lutherans and Baptists and other Christian denominations do not come together very often in prayer and in worship and in common work, to bring healing and wholeness and justice to a broken world.

That Baptist/Lutheran prayer vigil on the corner where a neighborhood girl had been killed by a speeding motorist, was a vigil not likely to happen in very many places.

Barriers to Interdenominational Ministry

Even though it was 2007, in the era of more and more interdenominational and interfaith activities, there were still three reasons why it was an unusual happening.

First, the local congregation still thinks of its reason for existence primarily as an internal mission proclaiming the Gospel to the faithful and the seekers who gather on Sunday morning or during the week for worship and for spiritual nurture. Moving out into the neighborhood to publicly identify with the hurts and the fears and the loss of the people of the community, is not part of the common practice of most congregations, regardless of denominational or faith background.

Secondly, if a congregation does think of moving out into the neighborhood to make a public testimony, it is likely to think of doing it alone, not inviting a nearby congregation to join them. It's just the nature of congregations, even within the same denomination, to think unilaterally, not mutually.

But there is still a third reason why congregations don't act interdenominationally. There are denominations that see such activity, especially joint prayer and worship, as a negative witness to the Gospel and to the faith that they profess. Two such denominations are the Lutheran Church–Missouri Synod and the Wisconsin Evangelical Lutheran Synod.

As a former member and pastor of the Lutheran Church–Missouri Synod, I know the struggle of wanting to lead a congregation to live out its oneness in Christ across denominational lines and bucking up against the strong position of my former church body that says such action is "contrary to our basic belief system" and a church body that threatens congregations practicing such unity with removal from membership. Clergy who would lead such action would be threatened with removal from the clergy roll.

Many clergy and lay leaders of mainline Christian congregations and of most independent and non-denominational congregations would probably suggest that crossing the denominational divide and working ecumenically is a non-issue. "We worked through all that throughout the 1900s," they would say, "and there really isn't much to say about it in the 21st century."

I beg to differ. There are still major church bodies that take a strong stand against inter-denominational worship and grassroots inter-congregational cooperation. And the many denominations that permit it have varying degrees of involvement on the congregational level. In the 21st century, the Church is still struggling with what it means to be a congregation or a denomination with a certain history, a certain set of beliefs and traditions that are important for their identity and integrity, yet at the same time, they are part of the one, holy, catholic, apostolic Church of Jesus Christ.

At Concordia Seminary, St. Louis, in the 1950s, I was taught that there was the one Body of Christ and there was the Lutheran Church–Missouri Synod, with certain distinct teachings based on Scripture. We were taught that we were part of both entities, and that we should pray and work for the unity of the Church. However, the only way that the unity of the Church could be actualized and visibly expressed here on earth was to get the leaders of the various denominations together and to hammer out agreement on all the major doctrines of the Church. Realistically that meant that other denominations would have to agree with the doctrines and Scriptural interpretations of the Lutheran Church–Missouri Synod. Then there would be visible unity, and then we could worship, pray, and work together across denominational lines. But to worship and work together before that doctrinal agreement was officially attained was to be guilty of "unionism."

It was against the grain of that LCMS teaching, that I managed to forge over the years, a vibrant, deeply-rooted belief that crossing the denominational divide at the grassroots, personal, and congregational level was not

The four girls killed in the bombing of the 16th St. Baptist Church were like martyrs for the cause of racial justice. Certainly they would not have been killed if it had not been for their faith that drew them to church to participate in the Youth Sunday worship scheduled for that day. Their innocent deaths were a strong catalyst in moving Congress to pass the Civil Rights Act of 1964.

simply a privilege I have as a Lutheran Christian pastor. It is an action that the Gospel calls me to undertake as an essential part of my witness to the love of Christ for all people and as a witness to the "one body, one Spirit, one hope, one Lord, one faith, one Baptism, and one Father, who is over all, through all, and in all." (Ephesians 4: 4-6)

Breakthroughs in Ecumenism

I really began to wrestle with this issue of inter-denominational prayer and worship in 1963, when I was in my fifth year of ministry in Birmingham. The Sixteenth Street Baptist Church had been bombed on September 15, killing four girls who had come to their church that morning for their youth Sunday service. Chris McNair, the father of one of the four girls, was a member of St. Paul Lutheran, the congregation I pastored. Chris McNair and his wife Maxine, along with the parents of two of the other three girls, decided that they would have a joint funeral service, with the pastor of the Sixteenth Street Baptist Church officiating. They invited Martin Luther King to preach the homily, and Chris and Maxine McNair invited me to read the Scripture lesson in the service, as well as to do the committal service for Denise at the cemetery.

Word got out quickly to Edgar Homrighausen, President of the Southern District of LCMS and, in effect, my "bishop," that I was slated to participate in this high-profile funeral service in a Baptist church with Baptist

Worshipers pack the sanctuary of the Sixth Avenue Baptist Church for the funeral of three of the four girls killed in the bombing of the 16th Street Baptist Church. Dr. Martin Luther King is in the pulpit. The author, who read the Scripture lesson, is seated between two other pastors to the right of the pulpit.

pastors officiating. I received a phone call from President Homrighausen in which he asked me not to participate in this service. "If you join with these Baptist pastors in this service," he stated in very clear terms, "you will be guilty of unionism. And this is not an ordinary service," he added. "This service will be televised all across the country."

I had already prayed over it, and I responded in a tone of voice that hopefully reflected to him the struggle I had in coming to a decision to participate in the service, but also reflecting the certainty of my conclusion. "I don't see how I can say no to the member of my congregation who has asked me to walk with him and his wife at this crushing moment in their lives, when they have lost their precious daughter. I believe that a negative response to their invitation would be a negative witness to the Gospel of Jesus Christ."

I did not articulate to President Homrighausen, as perhaps I should have, a compelling factor in my decision. The African American community was not only deeply, deeply hurt over this incident, but there also was rising anger

Worshipers leave St. Paul Lutheran Church, Birmingham, following Sunday morning worship. St. Paul Church, where the author was pastor (1958 to 1967), is situated about 25 blocks from the 16th Street Baptist Church, which was dynamited on a Sunday morning, September 15, 1963. Chris McNair, father of Denise McNair, one of the four girls killed in the bombing, was teaching Sunday school at St. Paul the day of the bombing. (Photo by Chris McNair)

targeted at the white community. The racial atmosphere was highly charged. Here was an opportunity to communicate to the black community and the white community, in the midst of the raw feelings of the moment, that black and white can come together and should come together, rather than explode in further violence. The very fact that the McNairs invited a white pastor to participate in this service at this super-sensitive time in Birmingham history, is a testimony to the faith of the McNairs in the vision of the Gospel and their belief in forgiveness and reconciliation. It was such a dramatic moment that helped me to see that in a world that is broken with racial, ethnic, and classist divisions, we dare not let denominational divisions keep us from a bold witness to the unifying, reconciling power of the Gospel.

Yet another experience connected with the bombing of the 16th St. Baptist Church moved me to think more deeply and more positively about ecumenism and interfaith relationships.

It was on the afternoon of September 15, the day of the bombing, that two women whom I had gotten to know through my activity in the racially integrated Birmingham Council on Human Relations, came to me and asked me what I thought about the three of us going together to visit the families of the four girls who were killed in the bombing. Both women were white. One was Jewish and one was a member of the Unitarian Universalist Fellowship. Both of the women were deeply moved by the pathos of the event. "We feel the horrible loss felt by the parents," they said. "But we also know the deep anger felt by the whole black community over this act of racist hatred and venom carried out by white KKK extremists. We believe that some representatives from the white community need to go to these families and express our profound sadness over their loss and to assure them that there are white folks in Birmingham who share their grief and their anger."

I was surprised and impressed by the empathy and the courage of these women. I was humbled that they trusted my judgment and that they saw me as a bridge to the black community. I concurred with their reasons for wanting to personally express sympathy to the families and to reach across the racial divide. My one reluctance was whether this was the best time to do it. After all, this was the day of the families' tragic loss, and they needed privacy at such a time. But on the other hand, I thought, no time in the next few days would be a perfect time for carrying out such a mission.

So the three of us went that afternoon on a difficult mission of expressing sympathy and remorse. It was such an emotional moment for persons of conscience in Birmingham, and for me personally, that I don't remember specific conversations, as we went to the four homes. This was not a time for cliches or for conversations of any duration. All we could do was say: "You have our deepest sympathy. We cannot find words to express our sadness over your loss and our outrage over this act of hatred and revenge. Our prayers are with you. May God give you strength for these difficult days."

What I do remember from the visits is the amazing openness and love and appreciation with which we were received. Not one sign of hostility or questioning of sincerity, which might rightly be expected on such a day as this.

Reflecting later on these unusual Sunday afternoon visits, on a most devastating day in Birmingham history, I realize how the whole experience nudged me forward on my journey of positive ecumenism and interfaith connections. I have not lost sight of the fact that my companions on that existential mission, in fact, the very persons who proposed the visits, were from very non-Lutheran traditions: Jewish and Unitarian. There was a closeness and a unity that we felt that day that would be hard to match. Each of us acting out of our faith and our experience of God's love and God's call to share that love with all. It was an experience that opened my eyes to the value of people of faith coming together, over against the alternative of staying apart.

Then there was another unforgettable aspect to the Sunday afternoon visits: The profound, authentic love with which we were received by the grieving families. As I thought later, these were sisters and brothers in Christ, of the Baptist tradition. There is no doubt that the clerical collar that I wore that afternoon conveyed my faith in Christ, and my presence conveyed my love and concern for them. They responded with faith and love that was very apparent. The labels of Lutheran and Baptist were insignificant. Our oneness in Christ was of great significance. I was learning that ecumenism did not hinge first of all, on doctrinal agreements between Lutheran and Baptist theologians, as meaningful as such agreements would be, but on the open and honest recognition of one another's faith in Jesus Christ and the open and honest expression of the love of Christ.

As I moved more and more into the planning meetings and actions of the demonstrations in Birmingham in 1963 and in Selma in 1965, I was thrust into a movement that was led by African American pastors, mainly Baptist and Methodist. I attended several of the nightly meetings at the 16th St. Baptist Church, during the demonstrations in Birmingham in the spring of 1963. Even though they were called "meetings," they were also worship gatherings which included choirs, and prayer, and singing by the audience, and messages that were as much sermons as they were speeches.

So my experience in the movement challenged me to see sisters and brothers and colleagues in other denominations in a new light. No longer were they those "separated brethren" to be avoided because they do not have "correct doctrine." Now they were sisters and brothers who were taking the lead in working for justice and for long-overdue change in a segregated church and a

Rev. C. Herbert Oliver, with his wife to his right, accepts an award for "bold contributions to racial justice and unity" on May 25, 1965, from the author, who made the presentation as President of the Birmingham Council on Human Relations. At great risk to his personal safety, Rev. Oliver, a Presbyterian minister, formed the Inter-Citizens Committee and collected stories of African Americans who suffered abuse at the hands of the KKK and the police. He sent these stories to members of Congress and other public officials, asking for remedies for such egregious torture and intimidation.

segregated society. The praying and singing and working together was not, for me, a negative witness to the Gospel, as I had been taught, but a positive witness to the unifying, transforming, empowering love of Jesus Christ. Slowly I was beginning to live into a new way of "doing Church."

Still another experience in Birmingham nudged me to see the issue of ecumenism in a different light from that of the denomination I was part of.

Reverend C. Herbert Oliver, an African American Presbyterian pastor in Birmingham during the 1950s and 1960s, approached me with a deep concern of his. He had gotten to know me through his involvement with the racially integrated Birmingham Council on Human Relations. He took great pains to share his bold plan with me to try to do something about police brutality in Birmingham, specifically their practice of attacking and/or falsely accusing black citizens. Every adult African American in Birmingham knew of such practices by the city police, county sheriffs, and state patrolmen, and many had personally experienced some level of verbal abuse, if not physical abuse, by law enforcement officers.

However, the common attitude among blacks toward such abusive practices was an attitude of helplessness. After all, what avenues of redress did they have? To file a complaint with the authorities at the city, county, or state level would never achieve anything because it would be the officer's word versus the citizen's word. And everyone knew whose word would be believed. The only likely result of such an attempt to file a complaint against the police, would be a determined effort on the part of the police officer to exact some type of revenge against the citizen for even thinking of reporting him.

So Reverend Oliver's plan was to go to persons in the community who had experienced physical abuse from the police and/or had been falsely charged, and Reverend Oliver would write up their story. He would double-check details and credibility with family members, witnesses, and friends. Then he would bring the story to the Inter-Citizens Committee he formed, to give the stories credibility and to provide some power behind his personal advocacy on the Congressional level.

This is where my story intersects with Herb Oliver's and the Inter-Citizen's Committee. Reverend Oliver asked me to serve on the Inter-Citizens Committee, along with several African American pastors. Reverend J. L. Ware, a prominent Baptist pastor, was President of the Inter-Citizen's Committee. I was Vice-President, and Reverend Oliver was Secretary.

Reverend Oliver did the time-consuming job of interviewing the victim of the abuse and others involved in the story. He took personal risk in corroborating details with the police or sheriff's department. And all of us officers of the Inter-Citizens Committee took some risk in having our names at the end of each story that the Committee approved for release.

The stories were sent to certain U.S. senators and representatives on key committees, as well as to print media and civil rights organizations. Most of the stories never were picked up by the media because the media were fearful of threats and lawsuits. However, two or three stories were published by black newspapers, and the stories, along with the name of the Inter-Citizens Committee, were circulated among civil rights groups in the South. The efforts definitely lifted police abuse to a higher level of consciousness among several sections of the community in Birmingham, in the South and in Congress.

I have learned many things from the experience with the Inter-Citizens Committee. I will never question the reality of the long history of police abuse in the African American community right up to the present, and the impact it has left on the psyches of most African Americans.

I learned from Reverend Oliver and others on the committee a little more about taking risk for the sake of the Gospel and for the sake of justice. And here again, I was nudged and nurtured by a non-Lutheran pastor, Reverend Oliver, who happened to be Presbyterian, to learn something very important about being the body of Christ and a witness to the Gospel at a crisis time in the history of Birmingham and of our nation. It was a lesson I did not learn from my Lutheran sisters and brothers. I would never have learned it if I had worked and walked only with LCMS colleagues.

Reaching Out in Milwaukee

When I accepted the call to be pastor of Cross Church, Milwaukee, I purposely reached out to churches and agencies in a four-block radius of Cross Church, to find out what I could about the neighborhood and to develop relationships with people who shared the same vision of mission. I discovered that exactly three blocks from Cross Church was Christ Presbyterian Church, a racially integrated congregation with a white pastor and a black pastor. It was a congregation that was seeking to make a transition similar to the one going on at Cross Church, from a former all-white congregation to a racially-mixed congregation.

The white pastor at Christ Presbyterian left soon after I arrived at Cross Church, and Ernest Glenn, the African American pastor, remained the only pastor at Christ Church. So when I stopped by Christ Church, to get acquainted with the pastor, it was Reverend Glenn who was there to respond to my unannounced visit. "Ernie," as I soon came to know him, was a friendly, outgoing pastor, almost exactly my age.

I soon found out that Reverend Glenn, even though he was my age, was just beginning his pastoral journey, having spent some time in military service before he went to seminary and became ordained. I discovered that Christ Church was the remnant of the former Perseverance Presbyterian Church. Most of the white members of Perseverance Church had moved in the late 1950s from the central city location at N. 18th street and Walnut to a new location, still in the city of Milwaukee, but about seven miles west and north of its old location. The move came right at the time that African Americans were moving into the area around the 18th and Walnut site in large numbers. The congregation had begun to reach out to their new neighbors and had called Reverend Glenn to assist in the outreach. However, the majority of the members decided that they needed to move to a new location, closer to where most of the white members now lived.

The move left the new African American members, a few white members who were committed to the racially integrated congregation, and Reverend Glenn, to forge ahead with a witness to the Gospel at 18th and Walnut.

As I talked with Reverend Glenn, I discovered how similar our congregations were. Cross Church had not experienced the phenomenon of a huge number of white members establishing a new congregation at a site away from the expanding black community. However, huge numbers of white members at Cross had transferred their membership, one family at a time, to various congregations at the edges of the city and in the suburbs. The membership had peaked at 2,500 in 1954, and had shrunk to about 900 in 1967, the year that I arrived as pastor, and white members were continuing to transfer out, or "drop out," at the net rate of about 100 per year until 1972.

The challenge for Reverend Glenn and Christ Church and for me and Cross Church, was the challenge of reaching out to our new neighbors, almost all African American, drawing them in, to become part of the community of believers, empowering them to become leaders in the congregation, and forging them into a racially diverse parish that still had a dominant European background of liturgy, music, and congregational structure and culture.

As we swapped stories of disappointments, challenges, and surprising moments of grace, Ernie and I began to develop a relationship of trust and to share visions that led us to look for ways that our congregations might come together in a shared walk.

Reverend Glenn and I decided as a first step in this shared walk that we would plan a joint Thanksgiving Day service. We each took the proposal to our respective boards and got a favorable response from both congregations. Ernie and I were especially happy that several people in each congregation were really excited about the plan.

In the 21st century, an interdenominational Thanksgiving service is seen as a token of ecumenical activity, not that deep or significant. But in 1969, for a Lutheran Church–Missouri Synod congregation in the heartland of conservative Lutheranism, to be worshiping with a Presbyterian congregation, was more than tokenism. It was a witness to the members of the community that our faith in Jesus Christ and our determination to forge interracial congregations in the midst of the poverty and the changing neighborhood, was something we should celebrate.

At the first shared Thanksgiving service, Cross Church traveled to Christ Church. The Cross Youth Choir sang and I preached. We didn't set an attendance record, but both congregations turned out in about equal numbers. We used the Presbyterian hymnal. We followed the liturgy of Christ Church. We split the offerings of food and money for use in the emergency food ministries of each of our churches. We got to know a few members of each other's congregation during the fellowship hour following the service. The result of the joint worship was a growing sense between our two congregations of connection and relationships and common mission. It was now more than a relationship between Pastor Joe and Reverend Glenn.

That first joint worship went so smoothly and positively that we almost forgot we had just transgressed the accepted LCMS policy on joint worship with Christians of other denominations.

However, the smoothness was not to be the following year. We began making plans for the second joint Thanksgiving worship already in September of the following year. The basic plan for the service seemed rather easy. Cross would host the worship. We would simply reverse the preacher role with Reverend Glenn doing the homily. We would invite a choir from each of the two churches, and Cross Church would plan the liturgy.

The worship committee at Cross reported its plans to the Church Council, and we began announcing the service in the monthly newsletter and in the Sunday bulletin.

About ten days before Thanksgiving Day, I received a phone call from Karl Barth, President (the equivalent of Bishop) of the South Wisconsin District of the LCMS: “Joe, I understand you’re planning a joint Thanksgiving Day service with a Presbyterian church. Is that correct?”

“Yes, it is,” I responded. “We had a joint service last year and found that it was such a positive experience and that we had so much in common as two neighboring Christian congregations with similar challenges and opportunities, that we should encourage one another in our faith and in our witness to the Gospel and do it again.”

“Well, Joe, I think you know Missouri Synod policy on joint worship with other denominations,” President Barth responded in a friendly, but slightly condescending tone. “You can invite the members of a church to your worship, but you can’t have their pastor preach.”

“I know that is the stated policy,” I answered. “However, I know there are exceptions to almost every rule. We are not doing this to try to go public against the position of the LCMS, even though we disagree with it. This joint service has emerged out of a real relationship of trust with Reverend Glenn and with the congregation. They proclaim the Gospel in exactly the same neighborhood we are struggling to proclaim the Gospel. It seems like something that would be God-pleasing for us to do, to express the unity that we have with our fellow Christians.”

“Well, I’m sorry,” Barth retorted, “but it is simply not acceptable for you to have a Presbyterian preacher in a Lutheran pulpit. The LCMS does not have pulpit and altar fellowship with the Presbyterian Church. You and the congregation are in danger of being dropped from membership in the LCMS, if you persist in this.”

I promised that I would take the matter to the Board of Elders and that I would convey President Barth’s warning to them. I did not ask how he found out about our plans, though we were quite sure that one of the long-time white members of Cross had undoubtedly reported the matter to him. The fact that a member of Cross felt compelled to report to the “bishop” a proposed ecumenical worship, is a testimony to the depth of the impact of denominational separation over the years.

When I took the matter to the Board of Elders, they were deeply disappointed in President Barth's position and his threat. "I could maybe understand his position," one of the Elders stated in the meeting, "if this was not a Christian congregation. If they believe in Christ and are trying to spread Christ's Word, like us, why can't we sing and worship and pray with them? It seems almost to be contrary to the Gospel and to Jesus' command to love one another, to say we won't pray with you because you don't belong to our denomination and don't have exactly the same teaching on every single doctrine."

The Elders saw President Barth's main concern was that we had invited Reverend Glenn to preach. We felt badly about "uninviting" him to preach, so we decided that we wouldn't have either preacher do the homily. Instead, we would have a lay person from each of our congregations make a witness to his or her faith, and we would do the rest of the service as we had planned, with a choir from each church singing and with Holy Communion celebrated as a public sign of our oneness in Christ.

I don't know whether the person who had reported our planned breach of LCMS policy was there for the worship. And if he or she were there, I don't know whether they reported what happened to President Barth. At any rate, we didn't hear anything more from President Barth.

The tension caused by President Barth's threat forced us to decide whether this expression of oneness in Christ across denominational lines was just a frill to our mission, or whether it was really an integral part of it. In evaluating our foray into public expression of ecumenical unity, we decided it was important for us to practice oneness in Christ, not just talk about it. The joint worship with Christ Church has not only continued every year since those first two services, the tradition expanded over the years to include Wauwatosa Presbyterian and Clement Memorial AMEZ (African Methodist Episcopal Zion), a congregation about six blocks away from Cross Church.

Of course, if an interdenominational relationship between congregations is real, then much more is going to happen between the congregations than an annual joint Thanksgiving worship. Invitations began to go back and forth among the congregations to special events, like choir concerts, Gospel fests, vacation Bible school, revivals, anniversary events, and the like.

Not long after the second joint Thanksgiving service, Ernie and I, in evaluating our shared worship, asked the question of ourselves: "Is there something we could be doing together as congregations that would meet some of the needs in the community?" We saw the glaring needs of many in the neighborhood. There was the need for affordable housing, family-supporting jobs, positive activities for youth, accessible drug treatment, and more parent involvement in local schools.

As we thought about the scope of the challenges in a poverty community, where 85 percent of the residents were low income, we decided that our two congregations working together could make small dents in the problems, but that we needed to call more area congregations together, if we were going to make a significant impact.

Ernie and I talked to members of our congregations to get their feedback on such a plan. One member of Cross, Cardell Willis, responded very positively. Cardell, the new custodian at Cross had a heart for youth, and became Scoutmaster as a way of relating to the boys in the congregation and neighborhood. He joined Ernie and me on a cold winter day to talk about the possibility of organizing congregations on the near northside of Milwaukee, around our two churches, to work on issues faced by people, especially low-income persons and families.

The three of us, Ernie, Cardell, and I, gathered at Christ Church in the furnace room because the rest of the building that morning was downright chilly. The furnace must have warmed not only our bodies, but also our spirits and our minds. We determined on that cold morning that we would try to launch an organization made up of any congregations that would be willing to walk the challenging journey of togetherness and a serious search for solutions to needs in the community,.

We were serious enough that cold morning that we decided we needed a name that would communicate our vision to pastors and congregations. It was Cardell who said: "We need a name that makes it very clear that we are church people working on these problems because of our faith, not politicians or academics or economists. Why don't we call this organization 'CHURCH Inc,' and figure out a name that fits the letters of the word 'church'?"

CHURCH Inc.

That very morning, in the glow of the coal furnace, we figured out the name: "Churches Helping Uniting Reviving Community Here." The name may have been a little lengthy, but it accurately described who we were and what we wanted to accomplish.

The organization we called "CHURCH" was launched within weeks of our "high-level conference." We reached out to pastors and churches Ernie Glenn and I had relationships with. There was House of Peace, a Catholic social service outreach agency run by the Capuchins and situated within two blocks of Christ Church. There was New Light Baptist and Northminster Presbyterian and Fellowship Congregational UCC Church, and Hephatha Lutheran and Incarnation Lutheran and Gospel Lutheran and St. James U. Methodist. It really was an ecumenical variety of congregations whose pastors and lay leaders agreed with the vision of "churches helping, uniting, and reviving community." We were determined to really do something together that we couldn't do by ourselves, something that would nurture community among our own members, as well as revive the social and economic roots of the larger community around us. We began visioning and planning and came up with the idea of establishing a printing and office supply business, with the goal of creating a few jobs and a source of funding for the running of CHURCH Inc. We figured that we could get our own congregations, and a few others, to purchase such things as paper, envelopes, mimeograph stencils, and ink. That would give us a minimal amount of business for a startup, and we would have to take a risk, as every business does, to attract sufficient customers to make a go of it.

We called our office supply company "Benu Ltd." Dennis Hawk, one of the more creative young pastors in our group, had discovered that *benu* was a phoenix-like bird. And so we used the story of the phoenix rising from the ashes as the story to describe what we were trying to accomplish with our business–to lift people out of the ashes of poverty.

We were successful in landing a significant grant that enabled us to hire a part-time executive director to launch Benu Ltd., and CHURCH Inc. found a few dedicated pastors and lay leaders who had caught the vision of ecumenical grassroots community building and economic development. But we never reached the critical mass necessary for a viable organization capable of supporting a paid executive director and for a sustainable business that generated enough sales to cover the minimal costs of the business.

Scholarship Coalition

Consequently, Benu Ltd. went out of business less than two years after its inception and CHURCH Inc. lost its part-time executive director after three years. However, CHURCH Inc. continued to carry out its mission, on a limited scale, for another 15 years. In fact, one of the programs it launched in 1980 expanded and is still flourishing: the Martin Luther King Scholarship Coalition.

Reverend James Lyles, a deployed African American United Methodist minister in Milwaukee in the late '70s, met with Ernie Glenn and me over lunch one day and unloaded his thoughts: "You know, I've had something on my mind for some time. I think we need to have some kind of program in Milwaukee that keeps Martin Luther King's legacy alive in the minds of young people. As new generations of young people emerge, they will have little knowledge of all that he stood for and accomplished. We need to create a program that will help interpret in a relevant way, the meaning of King's message and vision for the Church and for the human family."

The three of us batted ideas back and forth and finally came up with a plan that all three of us supported: The Martin Luther King Scholarship Program. We decided to announce a celebration to be held on King's birthday the following year, 1979, for the purpose of lifting up King's prophetic word applied to the current scene, and to raise funds for the MLK Scholarships, to be awarded the following year.

The first MLK Scholarship Celebration, sponsored by CHURCH Inc. was not a howling success, but neither was it a failure. About 150 people gathered for the occasion, and we raised over $700. The following year, we set the celebration again for King's birthday and awarded our first Martin Luther King Scholarship. The amount of each scholarship was only $250, but we were determined to get started with the program. Applicants for the scholarship could be any full-time post-high-school student from one of the 10 congregations in CHURCH Inc. The two recipients of the first scholarships were Danny Murphy, a member of Christ Presbyterian, and Connie Lindsey from Cross Lutheran.

Danny Murphy was a student who was counseled in high school not even to consider going to college. But he went on to finish college and seminary and to pastor a Presbyterian congregation in South Carolina. Connie Lindsey, who grew up in a single-parent household in a federal housing project in Milwaukee, went on to become a vice-president of a major bank in Chicago and President of the Girl Scouts of America.

We knew we were on the right track. We were disciplining ourselves to relate King's message to our own lives with the annual celebration. And we were inspiring a few young people to think college.

However, awarding two $250 scholarships each year, as we did for three years, was reaching a very small number of youth, with a very small scholarship.

It was Ernie Glenn who came up with the idea of the MLK All-a-thon, a fundraising strategy aimed at getting people to complete a five-mile route by walking, running, biking, skateboarding, skating, or by driving (for senior citizens). In other words, you could choose a method of completing the route out of all the possible methods. Hence the name "All-a-thon." Of course, everyone who completed the route was asked to collect money from friends, fellow congregants, co-workers, relatives, to be remitted to the MLK Scholarship Fund.

The MLK All-a-thon was a resounding success. Already after the first All-a-thon, we were able to award ten $500 scholarships, and we continued to increase the number of scholarships and the size of the scholarships year by year until we reached a plateau of about 25 scholarships ranging from $500 to $1,000.

To get young people to think about King in deeper ways, we require each applicant to write a 500-word essay on some aspect of King's teachings. For example, the question one year was: "Dr. King took a definite position against U.S. military involvement in the Vietnam War. What position do you think he would take in regard to the U.S. military action in Iraq and why?"

Even though CHURCH Inc. is no longer functioning as an ecumenical organization, one of the programs launched by CHURCH Inc. continues to carry out an important mission embraced by over a dozen congregations from a variety of denominations.

The MLK Scholarship Program is a good example of a grassroots effort that accomplishes great things, which simply would not be achieved if it weren't for the variety of gifts pooled by members of congregations from several denominations.

Such a joint effort also nurtured positive attitudes toward other denominations. The various committees, and the annual celebration and annual All-a-thon, afford opportunities for lasting relationships, for meaningful conversations, and for shared prayer and faithfilled stories. The awarding of 25 or more scholarships each year to some of "our own young adults" gives members of each congregation a sense of common identity, common faith, common mission, and common destiny. What a contrast to the former pattern of suspicions, faultfinding, and non-cooperation.

The sad reality is that there are still Christian denominations that discourage their members from expressing the oneness that is theirs in Christ if it means crossing denominational lines. Some denominations would even label such ecumenical activities as sinful and thereby lay guilt on people's consciences.

Equally sad is the reality of a huge proportion of Christians and congregations whose denomination places no roadblocks in the way of interdenominational worship and action. Yet they fail to seize the opportunities for such positive, nurturing relationships.

As I look back on my journey, I see a wide variety of ecumenical experiences, from the funeral service for three little girls in a Baptist church in Birmingham, Alabama, to the annual ecumenical celebrations in Milwaukee, when we praise God together for 25 to 30 young adults who have overcome diverse obstacles to be on the road of a college education. The experiences include struggle and a lot of hard work. But above all, there is deep joy. Joy that we accomplished much good in the lives of many people. Joy that we made tangible contributions toward building the beloved community. Joy that I, and many others, experienced the presence of Christ and oneness in Him, that oneness for which Jesus so earnestly prayed the night before his crucifixion.

CHAPTER 15

DOING JUSTICE IN THE PUBLIC SQUARE: CONGREGATION-BASED ORGANIZING

Away with the noise of your songs! I will not listen to the music of your harps. But let justice roll on like a river, righteousness like a never-failing stream!

–Amos 5:23-24

He has showed you, O man, what is good. And what does the Lord require of you? To act justly and to love mercy and to walk humbly with your God.

–Micah 6:6-8

Woe to you, teachers of the law and Pharisees, you hypocrites! You give a tenth of your spices—mint, dill, and cumin. But you have neglected the more important matters of the law—justice, mercy, and faithfulness.

–Matthew 23:23

"I want you to know that it isn't easy for me to stand here before you tonight and tell you my story. I've never given a speech before a lot of people like this. And besides, I have to wonder whether telling my story is going to make much difference."

Yvonne Modisett, a member of Hephatha Lutheran, was speaking at a MICAH public meeting in 2006, before more than a thousand people gathered for the MICAH annual public meeting at Our Savior Lutheran Church in Milwaukee.

Clergy and leaders from MICAH (Milwaukee Inner-city Congregations Allied for Hope) gather at a press conference in front of the Milwaukee Secure Detention Facility in February, 2011, to launch the statewide "11X15 Campaign." The goal of the campaign was to cut the prison population in half—to 11,000 by 2015—for safer and healthier communities.

"But I think I have to speak, for the sake of my children and for the sake of the community. Just three weeks ago at about 7:00 in the evening, I heard some loud popping noise. I knew immediately it was gunfire. So I told my four girls, who were doing their homework in the front room, to get down on the floor. We all stayed down on the floor for about a half hour, until the shooting stopped. Something like this happened again last week. I don't think my children, your children, or anyone's children should have to live like this, do you? I trust God for protection. But I think God expects us to do what we can, to make our community safe. That's why I'm inviting each congregation here tonight to join in the MICAH Holy Ground Campaign. You'll be hearing more about it from others, but it's a campaign where each congregation is asked to work with its local school, the neighbors around its church, the community liaison from its district police station, neighborhood businesses, and other nearby congregations, to work out ways to keep children safe and to curb violence."

The scary episodes of shooting were unforgettable experiences for Yvonne Modisett. In a more profound way, the testimony she gave before a thousand people from 30 congregations was life-changing and empowering. Instead of being frozen in fear and with a sense of victimhood, Yvonne was empowered by congregation-based organizing and the Holy Spirit to believe that there was something she could do about a seemingly hopeless situation.

This small vignette from a public meeting of a congregation-based organizing group provides some insight into the value of such organizing, for a congregation, for an individual, and for a community.

Organizing for Justice

For a congregation, such organizing for justice gives it clout to speak powerfully to a city council, to a county board, and to state legislators about issues that affect the lives of its members. And it brings about change for the common good of all. It provides an authentic channel for the congregation to live out its call to express oneness in Christ across congregational and denominational lines. It provides an effective way to minister to its own members, helping to free them from fear and leading them to hope and a strategy for action. It encourages and empowers congregations to demonstrate to their members that love of neighbor calls us not only to feed the hungry and to house the homeless, but to work at changing the systems and the policies that cause or abet hunger, homelessness, and poverty.

For an individual, it offers an opportunity to rise above a sense of helplessness, to become part of a larger faith community with a vision and plan of action. It offers leadership training that can move a ritual observer to become a leader in the congregation and in the community.

For a neighborhood or a community, it offers a clear antidote to the demonic forces that can paralyze and destroy the fabric of a community. Part of what gave Yvonne Modisett a sense of power and basis of support that night, was the presence of 35 members of her own congregation at the MICAH public meeting, each of them congratulating her for her courageous testimony. Then there were a thousand others there that night from the other 34 congregations in MICAH, who gave her several rounds of applause during her story and then spontaneously stood to affirm her at the end of her witness and her challenge to join the "Holy Ground Campaign of MICAH."

Reverend Willie Brisco, president of MICAH, at the extreme right, the author at the extreme left, Father Bill Brennan, center foreground, and other MICAH leaders, stand in solidarity with low-wage workers in a press conference in the summer of 2012, demanding that the minimum wage be raised.

But there has to be something that lasts beyond the inspiration of a mass meeting, well planned and well led by leaders. That's where the discipline and the support of a strong core team is important for people like Yvonne Modisett and for congregations like hers (Hephatha Lutheran), and a campaign like the MICAH Holy Ground campaign.

Fortunately for Yvonne Modisett and for Hephatha Church, there is a strong core team of trained MICAH leaders, concerned congregational and community members, and representatives of community businesses and agencies, who meet every month, to report on crime and violence in the neighborhood, but, above all, to plan ways of combating that violence and the threats to the safety of children.

Key persons on that MICAH core team at Hephatha Church are:

- Pastor Mary Martha Kannass, who, in spite of all that is on her pastoral plate, makes it a point to be there at the monthly meeting. She opens with a reflection that ties together the Scriptural message of the previous Sunday's lessons, an important current dynamic in the life of the congregation/community, possibly an example of leadership in the congregation/community and the purpose of the Hephatha MICAH Core Team.
- Ruby Harden, Chair of the core team, faithful member of Hephatha, who grew up at Hephatha, and on the block of the church, now lives with her husband and family across the street from the church. She works full-time as Parent Coordinator at the local public school, Hopkins Lloyd School, just three blocks from the church.
- Joyce Ellwanger, adult Bible class teacher at Hephatha, trained leader in congregation-based organizing, secretary of the core team, sees to it that the notice of the monthly meeting goes out to the 20 persons on the core team, with a detailed meeting agenda, honed by pastor and chairperson. The importance of sending out that meeting notice and detailed agenda cannot be overestimated in analyzing the success of the core team meetings.
- Jessie Peters, is a dedicated teacher at Hopkins Lloyd School, three blocks from the church.
- Sister Patricia Rogers, is Director of the Dominican Center, a Catholic neighborhood center six blocks west of Hephatha Church, that offers GED training, literacy and art classes, and home buyer/repair clinics.
- Five neighborhood people, including the Sikh manager of a corner store two blocks from the church. They are not members of the congregation, but they find the core team meetings to be problem-solving, informational, and empowering.
- The police community liaison updates the core team on neighborhood crime trends and responds to requests from the core team to check out trouble spots.
- A member of Bethesda Baptist Church (two blocks from Hephatha), a member congregation in MICAH, lives in the neighborhood and brings to the table neighborhood and congregational concerns.
- Clarence Royston, representative on the Hephatha Church Council and representative on the MICAH Board, along with four other members of Hephatha, serve as a connecting link between the core team, the congregation, and MICAH.

The Hephatha Core Team is consistently carrying out actions that are beneficial to the neighborhood. It regularly sponsors neighborhood walks with city officials and residents to target troublesome properties and discover residents with special needs that should be addressed.

One of the accomplishments of the core team, noticed and appreciated by the whole neighborhood, after five years of hard work, is the installation of a traffic light at an intersection one block from the church, making the street safer for the scores of children who walk that route every day to school and to the neighborhood store. Hephatha's MICAH core team worked with city alderpersons, city engineers, and city committees for more than four years to finally make it happen. After numerous accidents and two deaths along the three-block stretch of the busy street, the core team refused to give up. This change surely would not have happened without the hard work and persistence of the core team leaders and the backing of a strong congregation-based organization like MICAH.

Besides the actions in the neighborhood, the core team connects Hephatha Church with bigger actions that bring about systemic policy changes to benefit people in the entire city and state. Thanks to Hephatha's core team leadership, Hephatha members helped other MICAH leaders get the MORE Ordinance passed, which requires any contractor doing a project with more than $1 million of city money to hire at least 40 per cent of its workforce from the unemployed and underemployed of the city.

But beyond the more visible action-oriented aspects of the core team's productivity, are the less visible fruits of its work, such as empowering people to develop a vision of what can be, and to believe that we can bring about change. And then there are the fruits of relationship building and community nurturing that are so much a vital part of the Church's mission and so crucial to forging hope in the midst of seeming hopelessness.

Origins of Congregation-based Organizing

But what are the origins of congregation-based organizing? And how was I transformed to see it as an integral part of the mission of the Church?

Certainly I did not grow up in a congregation that made congregation-based organizing a part of its life. In fact, I never heard the term, nor even the slightest reference to it when I was at Concordia Seminary, St. Louis, from 1952 to 1958. Most seminaries do mention it today. A few even have a course on it. However, most current seminary graduates have not been part of a congregation that was actively involved in congregation-based organizing. That factor, I believe, is a major reason why it is difficult for some pastors/priests to envision and implement congregation-based organizing as part of their pastoral ministry and their congregation's mission.

Without realizing it, I was being introduced to congregation-based organizing in the 1960s, when I was pastoring in Birmingham. In February of 1963, Martin Luther King came to Birmingham to meet with the pastors of black congregations. Invitations went out to all the pastors, including myself. The invitation was rather direct: "I would like to talk with the spiritual leaders of Birmingham to test your reaction and hopefully gather your support for a proposed movement for justice in Birmingham some time this spring."

I had heard that the Alabama Christian Movement for Human Rights, the Birmingham affiliate of the Southern Christian Leadership Conference, headed by Fred L. Shuttlesworth, had asked Dr. Martin Luther King Jr. and his staff to come to Birmingham to lead a major series of demonstrations in the spring of 1963, to call for the elimination of racial discrimination in public places, like theaters, restaurants and hotels, and in key jobs, such as the police department, fire department, and cashier positions in downtown department stores. The goal would be to break the back of segregation in Birmingham and in the process, get the attention of Congress to create a national civil rights law that would outlaw racial discrimination in public places and in hiring practices throughout the nation. It was obviously a bold initiative.

I was simultaneously excited and scared by the invitation. I was excited that King and his staff might be coming to Birmingham. I knew that the focus of the nation would be on us. But I was scared because I would have to make a decision as to whether I would participate, and if so, to what degree.

I was very sure about the rightness and the oughtness of the goal of the proposed demonstrations. I thought about the members of my congregation and about African Americans throughout the U.S. Why should they be second-class citizens, when the Constitution of the U.S. guarantees these rights and my Christian faith tells me such rights are a matter of God's justice and love for all people?

But then some pragmatic questions started bubbling up inside me. Does this mean going to jail? Am I ready for jail and the Birmingham Police Department? How would my involvement affect my pastoral work? What impact would this involvement have on my relations with fellow Lutheran pastors, including my own father, all of whom took a position of opposing non-violent, direct-action demonstrations. Almost unanimously, they said: "The goals of desegregation and integration are God-pleasing goals, but the method of non-violent demonstrations is wrong. You can't force people to do the right thing. You have to go slow and change people's hearts with the Gospel."

Above all the practical questions running through my mind was the overarching question: "What is God's will for my life and for my ministry?"

Well, I went to the meeting called by Dr. King. There were pastors from the main black denominations: Baptist, United Methodist, African Methodist Episcopal, Christian Methodist Episcopal, Church of God in Christ. And there I was–one lone white Lutheran pastor–among probably 35 African American pastors all told. It was a lively discussion, with Dr. King and Fred Shuttlesworth fielding questions. There was no question about the need to bring about radical change in Birmingham and in the nation. There was little discussion about the method of non-violent direct action. The main discussion revolved around the question: Is this the right time? There were spring elections for mayor coming up, and one of the mayoral candidates who had a chance of winning was Albert Boutwell, a self-styled moderate who promised to bring about change.

Even though there were a lot of questions that day, King and his staff, along with Shuttlesworth, decided to go ahead with the demonstrations in the spring of 1963. As King often said when he was criticized for bad timing: "The time is always right to do the right thing." I didn't want to rush into the demonstrations, but neither did I want to sit them out. I had a sense of being called to do something about the dehumanizing system of racial segregation. I decided the place to start was to participate in some of the nightly mass meetings that were held each evening at the 16th Street Baptist Church in downtown Birmingham, once the demonstrations had started in early April.

The nightly mass meetings were a vital part of the movement. Reports would be given about how many participated in the demonstration that day, how many were arrested, the behavior of the police, and usually there was a testimony from someone. People told their stories. It might be the story of someone who was fired from his job because his employer heard he was attending the mass meetings. Or it might be the story of someone who had gotten up the courage to march the next day.

There were usually two or three speakers, perhaps a local preacher, and a lay leader who would warm up the crowd as it began gathering at 6:30. It was an important time to show the broad multi-congregational, multi-denominational support for the demonstrations, and a time to lay out the reality of the injustice that was being confronted, as well as the biblical underpinning of why we were working to transform Birmingham and the nation. Quite often the message was a call to spiritual renewal and personal growth, a call to become like Christ, a call to give up selfish goals and to live for Christ and for others. There was always a strong emphasis on non-violence, on loving the enemy, and on commitment to Christ and to a higher cause. Jim Bevel, one of the SCLC staff, would often go through the Ten Commandments of Non-violence and remind people that they would have to sign a commitment to strive to follow the way of non-violence if they were planning to march the next day.

There was always some humor in the mass meeting. Reverend Ralph Abernathy, a close friend of Dr. King's, was accustomed to lightening up the crowd with some humor. One of his oft-repeated jokes communicated truth as well as humor: "You know, Dr. King and I and the SCLC staff are often accused of being 'outside agitators,' when we come to a place like Birmingham to work alongside of our sisters and our brothers to make the city a better place. Folks who say things like that make it sound like an agitator is a terrible person to have around. Well, I want you to know that when I was growing up, my mother had an old, round washing machine. I asked my mother one day what that paddle in the middle of the round tub was for. And she told me, 'Son, that's an agitator. That's what gets the clothes clean. It knocks the dirt out of them.' Well, I want you to know that that's what we're trying to do here in Birmingham. We're trying to knock the dirt of segregation and the filth of discrimination out of this city so that it can be the beautiful, sparkling, clean city that God wants it to be."

Toward the end of the meetings, plans were laid out for the next day's demonstration. Sometimes they were a bit mysterious about the plans because Governor Wallace and Police Commissioner "Bull" Connor always had a couple of detectives in the crowd for the purpose of taking down names of leaders who were identifying with the movement and to get leads on actions being planned. There was the call for marchers the next day. There was sacrifice and commitment and accountability in the movement, or little would happen the next day. Nor would people get excited about the mission of doing justice.

Each mass meeting climaxed with a ringing call to act, to take risks, to build community, to grow in love, to transform society. Quite often, the ringing call was given by Dr. King. Sometimes an outstanding leader would travel some distance to lend his or her support and to make it clear that the future of the nation was at stake, not just Birmingham. One such outstanding leader who came was Ralph Bunche, a Nobel Peace Prize winner and peacemaker of great stature.

The closing word of hope and expression of unity that tied together the visions and the goals of the movement at every mass meeting was the moving song *We Shall Overcome.* It wasn't a "let's-hurry-up-and-do-it-and-get-it-over-with" song. We stood. We clasped hands by crossing our arms in front of us and reaching the hands of our neighbors who crossed their arms and grabbed ours. A Gospel singer from one of the churches would lead, belting out verse by verse: "*We shall overcome... The Lord will see us through... We're on to victory...Black and White together... The truth shall set us free... We shall live in peace.*"

In the midst of a struggle, when 2,000 children were in jail and three people announced that they just lost their jobs because of their involvement in the movement, *We Shall Overcome* was not a ditty or perfunctory closing song. It was a cry of hope deep from within. It injected strength for the never-ending struggle. It was courage for the march tomorrow. A thousand people physically holding one another up with firm handclasps, from dozens of different congregations, singing with the fervor of folks in a life-or-death struggle, surrounded by people who were risking their jobs, risking incarceration, risking dogs and firehoses. All for the sake of justice, for the common good, for the beloved community. None of us by ourselves could have accomplished much. But together, and with God's help, we knew that all things were possible. All of this pulling at my heartstrings, rushing through the folds of my mind, tugging at my soul as I crescendo at the end of the mass meeting, with a thousand others, the affirmation, the hope, the cry for help: "*We shall overcome. . . The Lord will see us through.*"

I soon was asked to serve on the Committee of 20, the central committee , made up of SCLC staff and local leaders that met twice a week at the Gaston Motel, to assess the progress of the movement and to lay plans for the next step. We met with the SCLC staff, including Dr. King, Andrew Young, Jim Bevel, Fred Shuttlesworth, and others. I was deeply humbled to be asked to serve on this committee. I knew the leaders. We had a mutual trust. I was slowly immersing myself in the movement. But I hadn't put myself on the marching line yet. I was gaining the courage and clearing the deck of my pastoral calendar. And "suddenly" the demonstrations in Birmingham were over.

I didn't know it at the time, but I was preparing myself to participate in the Selma demonstrations in 1965. And I was preparing myself for congregation-based organizing in Milwaukee 25 years later.

Learning from the Civil Rights Movement

Looking back, I see how much I learned about congregation-based organizing through the lens of the civil rights movement in Birmingham and Selma:

- Congregations coming together around justice issues can achieve more together than they can separately.
- Congregations doing the research, cutting an issue, taking risks, getting organized, can achieve more than they even dared ask or imagine.
- People need to hold each other accountable, if they are going to achieve their goals.
- Congregations organizing together across denominational lines and faith lines can find shared values and can develop the beloved community.
- Congregations going public with the truth are not abandoning their faith, but, in fact, are expressing love, speaking truth to power, and forging justice, all of which are integral to our Christian faith and to Christian discipleship.
- Carrying out a public non-violent demonstration to call attention to an injustice and to call for a just solution, is not creating tension so much as revealing tension and hurt, and calling for healing.

That great period in American history when the United States officially abolished legal racial segregation and discrimination is commonly referred to as the "Civil Rights Movement." One major segment of that movement, that part of the movement led by the Southern Christian Leadership Conference, could be described as "congregation-based organizing." Or more accurately, we could call it "black congregation-based organizing." It was African American congregations that came together across Baptist/Methodist/Pentecostal differences and systematically organized themselves to advocate for change.

And change did occur. Deep, radical change in the way we live together as a nation. The effects of 100 years of racial segregation and discrimination following the Civil War, reinforced by culture-sanctioned forms of intimidation and lynching, will be felt by whites and blacks for generations to come. But blacks and whites now work together and eat together at the restaurants and public places all across this country. And blacks vote and hold public office, even in Wilcox and Lowndes counties in Alabama, where, in 1965, there were zero black voters, even though they comprised 80 per cent of the population.

There were many individuals and organizations that participated in these massive changes, from different motivations and with different methods of operating. But no one can question the outstanding leadership of the SCLC and the black churches in these historic changes. They left their imprint not only on U.S. history but also on the way more and more congregations are coming to live out their faith, a faith that calls them to speak truth to power and to work for change.

Sometimes today, when we're working for change on a huge, complex issue like "treatment instead of prison" or prison reform, it seems like we're getting nowhere and that we'll never be able to accomplish our goals. It's then that I recall my roots and my learning from the 1960s.

C.T. Vivian, one of the SCLC veterans and a key leader in the 1965 Selma demonstrations, once helped me get in touch with lessons learned from that amazing era. It was March, 2005, and he and I were in Selma for the 40th anniversary of Bloody Sunday, the Selma-to-Montgomery march, and the whole series of demonstrations in early 1965, calling for a voting rights act. In a desegregated restaurant on the Alabama River, one block from the Edmund Pettus Brridge, C. T. Vivian came to my table and stated emphatically and emotionally: "You know, Joe," he began, "When I think of the massive changes that we brought about in Selma and throughout this country by our humble efforts here in 1965, there's nothing that we can't accomplish with God's help, if we are truly committed, if we stay organized, and if we don't give up."

The amazing humanizing changes that have taken place in the South and in the entire nation since 1965 as a direct or indirect result of the Civil Rights Law of 1964 and the Voting Rights Act of 1965, were in large part the result of the courageous, non-violent actions of the civil rights movement of the 1960s, led especially (but not only) by black religious leaders, clergy and lay.

As we organize people of faith today to work on justice issues, large and small, we would do well to remember the power of such people to bring about change. It is easy to become discouraged when success does not come quickly, or does not come at all. It is then that the sweeping results of organizing in the 1960s should be remembered, along with the persistent, unrelenting commitment that was poured into the effort.

There are some who would say that the 1960s were so different from this part of the 21st century, that we should not liken organizing then with organizing now. There are those who say that the issues are not as clear-cut today. There are even those who would suggest that the big issues like fighting Communism and ending racial segregation are behind us now, so we should let the system work out the kinks that are left.

If the issues seem to be more complex and more subtle, that means that we need to summon more research skills to analyze them and more creativity to figure out solutions. And if people think that the system will work out the "kinks" of injustice and thwart the persistent attempts to sabotage the progress that has been achieved, they have not studied history. As Martin Luther King wrote, "Human progress never rolls in on the wheels of inevitability. It comes through the tireless efforts and persistent work of people willing to be co-workers with God, and without this work, time itself becomes an ally of the forces of social stagnation."

Accomplishments of MICAH

Perhaps a short list of some of the accomplishments of MICAH (Milwaukee Inner-city Congregations Allied for Hope), a congregation-based organizing group of 30-plus congregations in Milwaukee, will indicate concretely how some people of faith creatively figured out ways to get at the humongous problem of poverty and persistently worked to bring about change in a city with one of the highest levels of poverty in the country:

- Won passage of a city ordinance requiring that at least 14 percent of jobs in the Department of Public Works contracts be set aside for unemployed residents of the city of Milwaukee. That requirement was later increased to 25 percent and then to 40 per cent. This ordinance has created hundreds of jobs for central city workers and for low-income/no-income people.
- Won passage of a city ordinance mandating that at least 50 abandoned houses be rehabbed annually for low-income housing. This initiative not only created jobs to carry out the rehabbing efforts, but it provided affordable housing for people who otherwise would have to pay a higher percentage of their income for housing, or would have been unable to secure housing at all.
- Implemented the Banking Campaign of MICAH, which successfully engaged 17 mainline banks and lending institutions to set aside over $500 million for loans to first-time homebuyers in an area of the city that had been red-lined by many of the banks. In cooperation with MICAH, the lending institutions developed new marketing strategies, hired more minority loan officers, and changed their credit and debt ratio criteria for securing a loan. Some of the banks opened branches in the central city as a result of the expanded business. The banks discovered that the mortgage holders in the central city had a better record of on-time mortgage payments than their counterparts in the suburbs.
- Launched a successful campaign at the state level that brought 51 additional SAGE schools to Milwaukee, thus increasing by 500 percent the number of Milwaukee Public Schools with a 15:1 student-teacher ratio for children in kindergarten through third grade. Research shows that the one factor that consistently improves student achievement levels, especially in schools with a high percentage of students from neighborhoods with concentrated poverty (more than 40 percent of families below the poverty line), is lowering the student-teacher ratio to 15:1 or less.
- Has doggedly and successfully worked at increasing funding for uninsured persons seeking alcohol and other drug addiction treatment in Milwaukee County. After many other efforts failed, an all-night pray-in at the office of the Milwaukee County Executive, followed by a press conference, resulted in the restoration of proposed cuts in drug treatment funding for the uninsured and an agreement not to go below

this level of funding in subsequent budgets. An effort at the state level secured an additional $5 million annually in TANF (Temporary Aid for Needy Families) money for drug treatment for custodial parents. MICAH collaborated with other groups to secure significant federal Access To Recovery(ATR) funding for AODA treatment in Milwaukee County for six consecutive years.

- Spearheaded a successful campaign to empower counties in Wisconsin to implement treatment alternatives and diversionary programs that send non-violent offenders with underlying drug-abuse issues to treatment rather than to incarceration. The campaign was called Treatment Instead of Prison (TIP). The state legislation that resulted from MICAH's TIP campaign was passed in 2005, and was called Treament Alternatives and Diversion (TAD). TAD programming continues to expand around the state from year to year, sending hundreds of persons into treatment and recovery in the community instead of to prison.
- Won a community benefits agreement with Milwaukee County that commits the county to develop valuable downtown brownfields (cleared land) with an assurance of 25 percent of the construction jobs going to workers from the surrounding neighborhoods and the inclusion of mixed housing in the overall planning.
- Won passage of a city ordinance stiffening the penalties for negligent landlords, providing for ongoing monitoring of problem landlords and increasing communication of tenant rights.
- Successfully pressured the Immigration and Naturalization Service (INS) office in Milwaukee to expand its hours of operation, hire bilingual staff, and create easier access to information for immigrants seeking citizenship.
- Starting with a prayer vigil on October 14, 1993, at the site of the drive-by shooting of 12-year-old Monte Fuller, MICAH has conducted prayer vigils at the site of every homicide, to hold up the value of every human life, to stand in solidarity with family, friends and loved ones mourning their loss, and to continually raise consciousness in the larger community that 100-plus homicides in Milwaukee per year are intolerable and that all of us need to work creatively and tirelessly to get at the root causes of violence of all types.

None of these accomplishments, plus others that have not been listed, would have occurred, if people of faith had not come together, built a community of trust, sharpened a vision of justice, and worked courageously for change in the larger community. That is what congregation-based organizing can accomplish. When we doubt the value of the hard work of starting and maintaining such an organization, we need to remember those flesh-and-blood, real-life, visible changes that have come about as a result of the organizing.

There are even more than these quantifiable, concrete accomplishments that can be listed. There are the less visible, seldom-heralded results of congregation-based organizing in the development of leadership, the growing of congregations, and the shaping of the cultural air that everyone breathes.

Leadership Development

Yvonne Modisett, whose story of addressing the MICAH public meeting of 1,000 people is reported at the beginning of this chapter, is an example of someone who had never dreamed of speaking before a crowd of 50 persons, much less a thousand. Her leadership in various roles in her congregation, her assessments of her gifts and abilities, and her self-confidence as a leader were deepened immeasurably as a result of doing her part in a powerful public meeting calling people to work for justice and calling officials to be accountable to the people.

Lois Glover, a retired Milwaukee County Welfare worker and member of Cross Lutheran, became active in the Cross MICAH Core Team because, she said, "I wanted to bring about change. I saw in my work in the County Welfare Department what poverty does to people. I thought if I could help lift some people out of poverty, I would be expressing Christian love in a way that would really make a difference in people's lives."

Lois Glover's amazing story of leadership development is told in Chapter Six. She moved from her experience as MICAH Core Team leader at Cross Church, to leader on the MICAH AODA Treatment Task Force, to Chair of the Cross Board of Elders, to President of WISDOM (statewide network of congregation-based organizing groups). She developed leadership skills that included the chairing of meetings large and small, public speaking before groups as large as 4,000, and the nitty-gritty recruiting necessary to turn out 100 people from her congregation to a MICAH public meeting.

Loyd Hubbard had been raised up as a member of the African American New Hope Baptist Church from childhood through his teen years. As an adult, married and father of five children, he brought up his family in the Church and nurtured in them a love for God, a strong work ethic, and a deep sense of the value of education. When one of his sons, after graduating from college and starting a career, began to abuse alcohol, then marijuana, then cocaine, he got caught in the net of incarceration, not once, but again, and again. Loyd Hubbard's love for his son and anger toward a drug policy and an incarceration policy that he believed to be unjust, set him to thinking and to action.

Loyd Hubbard, as a member of a congregation that was active in MICAH, heard about MICAH's Treatment Instead of Prison campaign, and attended a meeting of the task force. He became convinced that this is where he might be able to bring about change in a system that was simply arresting young men like his son for possession of an illicit drug, warehousing them in prison for three or four years, and then releasing them, still ravaged by their addiction to cocaine.

The very title of the MICAH TIP task force captured Loyd Hubbard's imagination and his deep passion to do something about addicted young men in his community who were being sucked into the judicial/correctional system. As he became more active in the task force, he became even more convinced that men and women who were committing non-violent crimes to secure the money to feed their insatiable habit of abusing drugs, needed treatment, not simply incarceration. He found some people of similar conviction and passion on the task force. And he discovered the power of 35 congregations bonded together in MICAH, and the power of 130 congregations joined together in WISDOM, the statewide network

So Loyd Hubbard engaged his work ethic and his passion and his faith in the sometimes tedious but vital meetings of the task force. He saw to it that the MICAH core team in his congregation was maintained and strengthened. He came to see his leadership gifts and his need to grow in his leadership skills. He attended MICAH trainings in doing one-on-one conversations and in strengthening core teams in the congregations. He participated in the more demanding week-long training offered by Gamaliel, the national organizing network with which MICAH and WISDOM are affiliated. (There are three other national congregation-based organizing networks besides Gamaliel: IAF, PICO, and DART.)

As Loyd Hubbard became a dedicated, contributing member of the MICAH TIP Task Force, his leadership skills were recognized by his peers. He soon became Co-Chair of the WISDOM TIP Committee. He participated in state legislative committee hearings with WISDOM TIP advocates. He told the gripping story of his son's need for treatment, but only experiencing incarceration. He helped move the state of Wisconsin in 2005 to pass TAD (Treatment Alternatives and Diversion) legislation. He helped MICAH nudge the state legislature to secure $5 million per year in AODA treatment funding for TANF (Temporary Assistance for Needy Families) eligible adults with children in Milwaukee County.

For all the significant victories Loyd Hubbard helped bring about and for the many persons who were able to secure drug treatment and move into recovery and productive lives, unfortunately his son was one of many persons in Wisconsin who fell through the cracks and did not receive the appropriate treatment when needed, and who continued to battle his addiction. Through it all, Loyd Hubbard did not give up on his vision of treatment alternatives for all the non-violent offenders in Wisconsin who have underlying mental health and/or drug addiction issues. He did not give up on the power of congregation-based organizing to bring about change. Above all, he did not give up on his own leadership skills and ability, and he did not give up on his son's ability to lead a drug-free productive life. His growth as a leader through congregation-based organizing has had significant impact on himself, his congregation, and on the state of Wisconsin.

Training leaders to be able to chair committees, facilitate hearings and press conferences, conduct one-on-ones, speak truth to elected officials, recruit others for vital roles in their congregation and in their organizing group, build and maintain a strong congregational core team and demonstrate other leadership skills, is a significant contribution of congregation-based organizing to the development of individuals, congregations, and organizing groups.

The Growing of Congregations

"Growing congregations" brings to mind for most people adding members to a congregation. That certainly would be a part of growing a congregation. But also included in that concept is the growing of the spiritual and theological culture of a congregation. Both aspects of growing a congregation are positively impacted by congregation-based organizing.

There are members of Cross Church who were attracted to Cross and who became members, precisely because of Cross's involvement in MICAH. A young man who had experienced incarceration because of his drug addiction, but who was in recovery, came to a MICAH TIP Committee meeting. His mother soon followed him to MICAH meetings, some of which were held at Cross Church. They both saw my involvement on the committee, as well as the involvement of two members of Cross. They began attending Cross, and discovered a racially-diverse, justice-oriented congregation, and they soon joined.

It would be an exaggeration to suggest that a congregation involved in organizing for justice will add scores of new members through their involvement. But it can be verified that new members are attracted when congregations engage in organizing in more than a peripheral way. If members of a congregation are visible and active on task forces, if they are visible in leadership positions when the organization holds a public event, then some people may be drawn to check out the congregation's worship and activities. If they find that the congregation's worship and programs reflect their concern for fairness and justice in the larger community, they may take that giant leap from cynicism and distance from organized religion to become part of a congregation struggling to be authentic in its witness to the world.

Any congregation or clergy who join in congregation-based organizing for the main purpose of adding members to their congregation will be deeply disappointed. A congregation's witness to a God of justice and love has to demonstrate a genuine love for people, an authentic concern for the entire community, and a willingness to take some risk for the sake of justice and for the sake of the Gospel, simply because the Gospel requires that kind of genuine discipleship.

For the sake of honesty, it must be stated that a few congregations have encountered tension within the congregation when it aligned itself with a congregation-based organizing group. When an organizing group takes a public position on an issue on which the public does not agree, there will possibly be some kind of pushback from within the congregation. Usually, members who disagree with the position of the organizing group will either keep an open mind and will be open to change. Or they will agree to disagree, recognizing that there is no congregation anywhere where there is a unanimous agreement on all issues affecting people's lives.

It is important for congregations to recognize that a strong reason for a congregation to become part of a congregation-based organizing group that works intentionally on doing justice in the public square and on addressing justice issues openly and powerfully, is to grow a congregational culture in which children growing up in the congregation will hear and learn from the liturgy and from the programs of the congregation, that justice work is a normal and important part of the life of a congregation.

Perhaps looking back to the Jim Crow era will help put this concern for a congregational social justice culture in perspective. During the 100 years following the Civil War and the abolition of slavery, the faith community was largely silent about legal segregation and racial discrimination in the South and about de facto segregation and racial discrimination in the North. Most white faith communities never addressed race relations, racial discrimination, the segregation of the races, or the Jim Crow laws that enforced segregation throughout the South and in many cities and towns in the North. Not only did faith communities not talk about the racial prejudice and stereotypes that pervaded the American culture, but faith communities, with few exceptions, practiced segregation themselves. To this very day, Sunday morning worship time is one of the most segregated times of the week.

Without a doubt, the hundred years following the Civil War is one of the darkest periods in the history of the Christian Church, and of the religious enterprise in the United States.

There were some major efforts on the part of Christian church bodies, following the Civil War, to assist African Americans in their transition from slavery and from total disenfranchisement to their rightful, productive place in American society.

Congregational churches in the North helped establish some very successful grade schools, academies, and colleges throughout the South. Some of the historic black colleges, still vital and productive to this day, like Fisk University in Nashville and Talladega College in Talladega, Alabama, give testimony to the value of their worthy efforts. Other denominations, such as Roman Catholic, Lutheran, Presbyterian, Methodist, Baptist, and Episcopal, likewise started elementary schools, academies, colleges and congregations, some of which still exist to this day with a high degree of vitality.

The establishment of schools to serve African Americans is a clear sign of the church's recognition of the capabilities and the worth of African Americans and their potential for participation in American society at every level, preparing doctors, teachers, pastors, technicians, craftsmen, artisans, and the like, to play their role in the American enterprise. There was even some sense of equality, especially at the college level, where often black and white professors taught side by side, although there was often a pay differential between blacks and whites serving at the same level of degree attainment. And often, the president of the college was white, with an all-white board of control.

However, at the congregational level, there were white congregations and there were black congregations in the North, as well as in the South. With few exceptions, racially integrated congregations, even in the North, did not emerge until the 1950s. Without a doubt, the struggle of the United States to treat African Americans as full citizens, equal to everyone else, has been one of the most crucial, agonizing struggles in the history of our nation. Gunnar Myrdal, the Swedish sociologist, in his classic book about the struggle, titled the book *The American Dilemma*. This dilemma was a moral dilemma, a dilemma permeated with justice issues and theological issues. The U.S. Constitution states unequivocally that "all men are created equal." The Hebrew/Christian Scriptures state unequivocally that God created humans "in the image of God." Our national and religious dilemma was that we acknowledged in our Scriptures and in our Constitution that all human beings are of equal worth. But the white majority, and the white power structure in the South, and in most places in the U. S., were unwilling to make the changes necessary to live into the meaning of those creeds and truths.

If any segment of U.S. society should have been addressing the racial inequalities and the racism rampant in the nation and organized religion, it should have been people of faith, whose Scriptures affirm the value and dignity of every human being, and Christian congregations, whose Scriptures state clearly that "there is neither Jew nor Greek, slave nor free, male nor female, for we are all one in Christ."

How did it happen that the Church did not take the lead in demonstrating the equality of the races? How did it happen that congregations went along with the Jim Crow segregation laws and all the daily indignities heaped upon African Americans because of the system of segregation? How did it happen that bishops and church leaders and clergy denounced Martin Luther King and non-violent demonstrations in the 1960s, when they called for an end to Jim Crow? Or if they didn't denounce the prophetic actions of the 1960s, why were so many congregations totally silent about the injustice of segregation and the justice of bringing about change?

If there is agreement that organized religion, and Christian congregations in particular, failed tragically during the 100 years following the Civil War, to lead our nation to live out our creed of equality, we need to analyze the reasons for this huge moral and spiritual breakdown, if we are going to avoid a perpetuation of such quietism and silence in the future.

Certainly in the South, the fear of the KKK was a very real factor, especially in places like Tuscaloosa and Birmingham, Alabama, where the KKK was extremely active. However, the call to take risks for the sake of justice and peace and for the Gospel has always been central in the witness of the spiritual community, from Jesus though Bishop Polycarp, Martin Luther, Gandhi, Bonhoeffer, and Martin Luther King. It is precisely when people of faith take risks because of their faith and their values that the world takes notice. One of the oft-quoted truths at the mass meetings during the struggle for justice in the 1960s was: "If you don't have anything worth dying for, you don't have anything worth living for."

I know that for some congregations and pastors, the quietism and silence came from a failure to empathize with African Americans, a failure to see how deep and profound a hurt it truly was for an African American man, doctor, pastor, truck driver, factory worker, to be called "boy" with all the other daily indignities, and to face daily the possibility of vicious attacks and lynching that accompanied the "separate but equal" system of segregation.

There were eight leading white clergy in Birmingham, Alabama, including the Episcopal Bishop, who placed a full-page ad in the Sunday *Birmingham News* in the spring of 1963. Dr. King was leading non-violent demonstrations, calling for some minimal changes in the hiring practices of downtown stores in Birmingham. The ad called on Dr. King to stop the demonstrations and let the issues of hiring practices and segregation be settled by the courts. The ad called on the black community to have patience. There was not one word in the ad indicating that the eight clergy recognized the injustice of Jim Crow practices and the deep pain that African Americans had suffered during 250 years of dehumanizing slavery and 100 years of debilitating segregation and disenfranchisement.

Right up to the present, a major reason why congregations do not feel compelled to speak out against injustices, such as the high rate of incarceration, or the lack of affordable housing, or the absence of jobs for ex-offenders, is because many clergy and congregations do not empathize with the people and the families who are feeling the pain. When congregations are not simply conducting ministries "for" people at the edge, but actually "walking with" such people as equals and who are receiving as much as they are giving, then clergy and congregation will perceive the injustices, and they will feel the need to work for justice because they are feeling the pain of the injustice.

Mixed in with the lack of empathy for the oppressed is a huge element of racism, along with racism's cousins: classism, arrogance, paternalism, and self-righteousness. These are traits difficult to recognize in ourselves and even more difficult to admit, to talk about, and to overcome. Anti-racism training can help white people get in touch with the racism and the "person of privilege" reality in the cultural air that white folks breathe in the United States.

Still another reason for the silence and the quietism of congregations and clergy of the 1960s was the fear of dissension and disagreement in the congregation, with the possibility of splitting the congregation, losing members, or ousting the clergy. The obvious challenge is to develop a congregational culture that learns how to talk about all issues of injustice, including the controversial issues, in an atmosphere of acceptance, in which no one is belittled because of his or her position. The congregational culture, at the same time, must be open to the witness of Scripture, to the testimony of the larger spiritual community. It must lead toward a position of not only satisfying spiritual hunger and intellectual curiosity, but to ultimately standing with the poor and the oppressed and with the God of justice and compassion, working to bring about a greater degree of unity and solidarity among people of faith and a greater degree of justice in society.

Given all the factors that pulled clergy and congregations into a shell of silence and quietism in the 1960s, when some blacks and a few whites were laying their lives on the line to bring about change to an evil system, what have we learned about living out our faith in the years since? What can we do differently to avoid the silence that reinforces the evil of the status quo? How can we avoid building a congregational culture that teaches our children to turn a blind eye toward the glaring injustices of the world?

If we want to be sure, as the faith community, that we do not get pulled into the quietism that characterized most of the religious communities of the 1960s, each congregation of believers must develop a culture that encourages and models walking with people who are experiencing injustices, grappling with the issues interlaced with those injustices, and joining with people of faith to call for justice and to build the power that can bring about change in unjust systems.

Congregation-based organizing, for all of its weaknesses that might be cited in a particular organization or in a particular campaign, offers congregations the opportunity to build a culture of thinking justice, visioning justice, talking justice, and doing justice in powerful, creative ways. And at the same time, it pushes congregations to intentionally build–across congregational and denominational and faith and racial and class lines–that beloved community, which, with God's help, is possible.

Congregation-based organizing cannot be an add-on to the congregation's list of meetings. It cannot be done by just one or two activist members of the congregation. It has to be seen as a way the congregation carries out part of its mission. It has to inform the congregation's liturgies and prayers and sermons. It has to impact the congregation's studies and conversations. It has to be an initiative into which the congregation invests money and people and time. It has to become an important part of the warp and the woof of the congregation's self-image and history.

When congregation-based organizing is truly part of the culture of a congregation, it will be more ready to recognize, to study, and to resist the demonic forces of our culture. It will break the silence. It will take some risks. It will discover more of the truth. And the truth will set it free.

CHAPTER 16

NON-VIOLENCE IN A CULTURE OF GUNS, GANGS, AND MILITARISM

Put your sword back in its place, Jesus said to him, for all who draw the sword will die by the sword.
–Matthew 26:52

He will judge between the nations and will settle disputes for many peoples. They will beat their swords into plowshares and their spears into pruning hooks. Nation will not take up sword against nation, nor will they train for war anymore.
–Isaiah 2:4

It was a rainy Tuesday morning in June. About 40 youth and adult supervisors from Hephatha Lutheran's work program were crowded on the sidewalk in front of the house just two blocks from the church, at 18th St. and Locust. Five or six persons from MICAH congregations were there. A few neighbors joined the group, upon learning that this would be a prayer vigil in memory of a young man who was gunned down as he was getting out of a car in front of the house where he was living. I managed to find a spot on the curb toward the center of the group that spread 20 feet in each direction.

Not even the police or the newspaper reporters had been able to find out the story behind the shooting. All that we knew was that the young man, an African American in his twenties, had just been released from jail. He had been unusually fortunate in having a job waiting for him. He had just finished his second shift trick and was shot between the car and the house. It was not clear whether it was a case of mistaken identity, or evening a long-standing score, or simply gang horseplay. But the ripple effect of the mysterious shooting of a 20-something African American male was clearly seen on the faces of the young people gathered on the sidewalk.

One of the Hephatha youth led in a prayer for the family of the victim and for the community. Mary Martha Kannass, Pastor of Hephatha, had printed out copies of the *Prayer of St. Francis*, which were distributed among the people gathered there. We all prayed it together: "Lord, make me an instrument of your peace…" I prayed that God would pour down the Holy Spirit and teach us how to be peacemakers in our families, in the community, at school, at work, in the world. We held hands, as a sign of our connectedness, and prayed together the *Lord's Prayer.*

Prayer Vigils

There may be only four or five members of MICAH congregations gathered in a circle on a Milwaukee sidewalk. Or it may be 75 people from the neighborhood and from all parts of Milwaukee. It may be raining or it may be snowing. It may be a rare Milwaukee temperature in the 90s, or it may be 5°F above. Whatever the weather, however many people come together, you can count on one of these prayer circles happening once or twice a week, nearly every week of the year in Milwaukee, with Sister Rose Stietz leading and most of the four or five faithful from MICAH congregations offering up their own prayers.

The prayer vigils are in memory of an infant who died as a result of child abuse, or a 13-year-old girl killed in a drive-by shooting while she was sitting on her front porch with two of her friends, or a 23-year-old African American young man who was shot in a turf war over drug sales, or a 40-year-old woman who was stabbed to death in the heat of a domestic dispute.

Ever since 1993, a prayer vigil has been sponsored by MICAH congregations at the site of every homicide in Milwaukee. Sister Rose schedules the vigils, and Joyce, my wife, brings a "MICAH Holy Ground" banner, with the name and age of the homicide victim printed by hand on the banner, which is planted in the ground at the site before the prayers begin, so that passersby know what is happening and may stop to join the prayer circle, if the Spirit moves them. And they sometimes do.

The prayer vigils are MICAH's way of saying to the families of the victims, to the neighborhoods where the tragedy happened, and to the City of Milwaukee: "Every human life is precious. There are no throw-away people in this city. We commend this person who is no longer with us into God's hands. We praise God for their gifts. We ask God to comfort friends and loved ones. We pray for safety and peace for the families and children of the neighborhoods. We pray for justice, cleansing, and transformation for the perpetrators. And we pray for MICAH congregations, all clergy and congregations, and elected/organizational/business leaders of Milwaukee, to not give up in working for safety, peace, and an end to violence.

There are those who would suggest that these prayer vigils are futile exercises in wishful thinking and pious platitudes. For people of faith who pray for peace in the whole world almost every time they gather together, the vigils are a reality check. They are a reminder that we live in a violent world, and if we pray for peace in the stillness of a beautiful sanctuary, we had better work for peace in the midst of a violent world, or our prayers are pious platitudes, signifying simply our hope for a peaceful world and, God, it's all up to you.

As someone has written: "We should pray as if it is all up to God. And we should work, as if it is all up to us." The two statements are not contradictory. They are profoundly complementary. If we pray for peace, and do nothing to work for peace, we are shirking our personal and corporate responsibility. If we work for peace, without praying for peace, we will miss the visioning power and the source of strength that every peacemaker needs if he or she is to stay the course and never give up.

Blessed Peacemakers

When Jesus said, "Blessed are the peacemakers, for they shall be called children of God," he was not suggesting that two or three people in a community were called to be peacemakers. He was clearly calling us all to be peacemakers. And what is really involved in being a peacemaker in

Martin Luther King and the author participating in a Southern Christian Leadership Conference dinner event in Birmingham in 1965, following the passage of the Civil Rights Act of 1964 and the Voting Rights Act of 1965. King's insistence on non-violence as a method of resisting oppression and as a way of life was his great prophetic contribution to the peace and justice movement of the 20th century. (Photo by Chris McNair)

Milwaukee, or in Mexico, or in Zimbabwe, or in Afghanistan, or in Israel, or in Palestine, in the 21st century? Obviously, Jesus did not lay out a blueprint for every child of God in every place in every time. But he did make it clear that the struggle to be a peacemaker is the struggle in which we are all called to engage. And his charge to "turn the other cheek" and to "love our enemies" and his warning to Peter that "those who take up the sword will perish by the sword," and his refusal to use violence to defend himself and his disciples and instead gave up his life to the violence of the Jewish and the Roman authorities, and in the process, overcame the powers of darkness, must all be taken into consideration as signs of Jesus' own vision of peacemaking.

The very night before the world's violence nailed him to a cross, at a time when Jesus was talking openly about being betrayed and about dying a violent death, Jesus said to his disciples: "Peace I leave with you. My peace I give you. I do not give to you as the world gives. Do not let your hearts be troubled and do not be afraid." (John 17:27)

There is a profound peace that Jesus gives to his followers, the peace of knowing we are forgiven, the peace of knowing we are loved by God and that we are right with God, the peace that comes from knowing that God is bringing in God's Kingdom of justice and peace and healing and wholeness and love and forgiveness, the peace that comes from laying down one's life rather than taking a life.

But Jesus did not give his disciples this profound inner peace simply to fortify them for the visible separation from Jesus that they would soon experience and to give them strength for their transition back to fishing and tax collecting. He was granting them peace to fortify them for a life of peacemaking that would pit them against the violence of the world. In fact, part of the peace Jesus gives his disciples in every age is the peace that comes from being in tension with the world's way of violence and at one with Jesus and his non-violent way of radical love and justice.

Children and Peacemaking

The call to non-violence and to peacemaking means that parents, teachers, clergy, and youth workers are all called to nurture children in ways that do not verbally, emotionally, physically, or sexually abuse them. Almost every religious leader would agree that parents must demonstrate non-violence while they are nurturing their children and youth, if they expect youth to grow into peacemaking adults. However, there are still religious leaders who deeply believe that physical punishment is the only way a child learns right from wrong, and it is the only way that some adults think they can get a child's attention. It is the same line of thinking that is often used to justify spousal abuse. Usually it is the woman who is the victim of verbal/physical/ sexual abuse, though occasionally it is the reverse.

It is crucial that children grow up in an atmosphere where parents, teachers, and religious leaders hold children accountable for their actions, not by using threats and abusive tactics, but by strong, affirming, unconditional love, tough love when necessary, but never abusive actions that hurt and scar for life. Using verbal and physical violence against children and teens—to get them to "shape up," or to "show who's boss"–is teaching them that "if you want to accomplish a particular goal with someone, use abusive, violent tactics. That is a sure way to accomplish your goal."

We need to demonstrate that there are ways to accomplish good goals without using violent means. Families where fathers and mothers treat each other and their children with kindness and thoughtfulness and where there is no tolerance for violent words or actions, children are growing up in a culture of active non-violence and positive love that nurtures the fruits of the Spirit: love, joy, peace, patience, kindness, goodness, faithfulness, humility, and self-control.

In a context of non-violence and unconditional love, it is still a challenge for parents and children to control passions and refrain from violent words and actions. But it is much easier than when children and adults are living in an atmosphere of "might makes right" and in a culture where savage words and physical abuse are daily occurrences and where guns are packed for use "when necessary."

Whether the family culture is one of non-violent, unconditional love or one of chaotic outbursts of violent words and actions, the role of the religious community is to teach and nurture non-violence and peacemaking as a way of life.

Mary Martha Kannass, Pastor of Hephatha Lutheran Church, in the heart of Milwaukee, where violent and non-violent households live side by side, and where the gangs and the drug dealers attempt to "control" the neighborhood by violent means, has worked creatively with Hephatha leaders to develop a culture of peacemaking.

The "Friends of Jesus Work Ministry" is designed, among other things, to nurture the 40 to 50 youth, ages 10 to 17, in the spiritual art of peacemaking. Besides beginning and ending each work session with reflection and prayer, a very common exercise that everyone is asked to participate in, is the creation of an artistic note, with a personal message, directed to someone in the congregational family or the surrounding community. It may be a congratulatory, thank-you card to a congregational member who is turning 70 or 80 or 85. It may be a prayer for healing blessings for someone in the hospital or someone who has experienced the death of a loved one. It may be a "thinking of you" note to the principal of the local school who experienced family trauma in a kitchen fire in their home.

Week after week, Pastor Mary Martha is nurturing the children in the work program, along with their adult mentors, in the art and the posture of peacemaking. Writing messages of congratulations and "get-well-soon" and thank you, to real people in the congregation and in the community is at the very heart of peacemaking. It is living into the vision and the reality of love and interdependence and connectedness and peace that is the opposite of violence. It is also a vision and practice that overcomes violence and snuffs out those inner urges of retaliation and anger and disconnection and self-righteousness and "each man for himself" that so often lead to violence.

In yet another effort to nurture a vision and practice of peacemaking, Pastor Mary Martha asks the summer work program participants to select the "Peacemaker of the Week" from their own midst. And that young person then has his or her name and title ("Peacemaker of the Week") printed on the front of the Sunday worship bulletin. In addition, the Peacemaker of the Week is presented with a certificate during the children's sermon, and the specific acts of peacemaking enacted by the recipient of the honor are mentioned by the Pastor. The whole congregation, in the process, is vividly reminded and inspired, by one of its own children, to take seriously its own calling to be peacemakers.

The Church and Peacemaking

Of course, there are countless parts of the liturgy, and many Sunday School Bible class lessons, and various congregational activities that directly or indirectly nurture a theology and practice of non-violence and peacemaking and that help people overcome attitudes and practices of violence.

However, it is essential that congregations and religious leaders recognize how readily and openly the Church has countenanced and even supported violence as acceptable means to an end. Recognizing and confessing the violence of the Church can hopefully lead us to see the importance and the constant challenge of nurturing the non-violent way of life and peacemaking as a daily calling.

During the first three centuries of the life of the Church, Christians were not often in positions of power and were widely persecuted because they called Jesus "Lord of all," rather than the Roman emperor. They were often put to death because they refused to bear arms in the Roman army because of their faith in a Christ who refused to fight violence with violence, but who, instead fought violence with sacrificial love and forgiveness.

However, the theology and practice of the Church changed after the conversion of Constantine and the Christian faith became the accepted religion of the Roman Empire. Soon military force and violence became not only permissible for Christians to participate in, but they became tools the Church itself would come to use, to bring people and territories under its control and to try to maintain doctrinal correctness.

To the shame of the Church, the Middle Ages are replete with Church-sponsored wars and violence. The pogroms against Jews, the burning-at-the-stake of persons perceived to be guilty of false doctrine, the Crusades to take back the "Holy Land," the violent persecution of any religious group that veered from strict adherence to the teachings and the sway of the Pope, were horrendous actions done in the name of the Church, yet diametrically opposed to the Gospel of love and forgiveness proclaimed by the Church.

The Church has come a long way in repenting of Church-sponsored war and violence and is no longer carrying out war and physical violence itself. However, the Church, and individual Christians, still have a long way to go in coming to terms with the appropriate use of military force and in embracing non-violent resistance as a way of life.

War and Peace

Our nation's going to war, as we did in Vietnam, in Afghanistan, and in Iraq, seems not to have any thing to do with an individual's accountability, with congregational life, with sermons, with liturgies, with prayer vigils at the site of a homicide in Milwaukee. There are those who would say that going to war is a decision we should leave to the military experts and to our governmental leaders. After all, so the argument goes, it's naïve, at best, and arrogant and unpatriotic, at worst, to question our governmental and military leaders.

It was soon after my arrival as pastor of Cross Church in 1967 that the social ministry committee, brought to the Church Council for its approval, a resolution to be sent to the South Wisconsin District (LCMS) convention, that would call upon congregations to prayerfully discern God's will regarding U.S. military involvement in Vietnam. The resolution encouraged congregations to study Scripture, especially the New Testament, in regard to the use of violent military force, and to study the history of the people of Vietnam and the rationale for U.S. military involvement in Vietnam, to help them in their discernment.

The proposed resolution did not take a position for or against U.S. military involvement in Vietnam. It simply encouraged congregations to prayerfully struggle with the question. I will not forget the drama of the Church Council meeting. The moment that the Council voted in favor of the recommendation, the president of the Council stood up, called to his wife, and stormed out of the meeting, never to return to the congregation. He told a member later that the resolution was unpatriotic and had nothing to do with the real mission of the Church.

Unfortunately, the view of the president of Cross Church in 1969 is similar to the view of many people of faith through the centuries, right up to the 21st century. Even discussing the use of military force and its rightness or wrongness, is totally inappropriate and uncalled for, according to many.

Franz Jaegerstaetter, a husband and father of three young daughters, living in Austria during World War II, received a call to serve in the German army in 1943. His conscience and his Roman Catholic upbringing told him that he could not participate in the Nazi army, in a war of aggression and in a war that was engaged in the brutal elimination of Jews, gypsies, homosexuals, and persons with certain disabilities. He talked about his conscience struggle with his wife and with his priest. They all urged him to report for duty because the alternative would result in his loss of life by beheading. He struggled and he prayed over the matter. When the day to report for duty came, he walked to the town and reported to the authorities. However, he told them that in good conscience he could not participate in the Nazi cause. On August 9, 1943, Jaegerstaetter was executed.

In the 21st century, most wars are not as clearly wars of aggression and of genocide, as was World War II. And in the U.S. no one is currently being drafted, and there are certain rights guaranteed to conscientious objectors. However, individual people of faith, and congregations, are still called upon to struggle with the questions of when and how to use military force. Struggling with issues of war and the use of military power in our nation's foreign policy is not unpatriotic nor outside the mission of the Church. It has everything to do with standing up for our nation and witnessing to the Gospel and to the God who loves and saves and heals.

Martin Luther King often said that three of the most demonic forces at work in our culture are racism, materialism, and militarism (the belief that our nation's safety, its greatness, and the achievement of its goals, hinge on its military power and the use of it). Dr. King also stated that the United States, with its nuclear warheads, its establishment of over 140 military bases around the world, its frequent wars (Vietnam, Iraq I, Afghanistan, Iraq II), its military engagements in Nicaragua, El Salvador, Colombia, Haiti, and its CIA-supported coups and assassinations in Guatemala, Chile, and Panama, is one of the "greatest purveyors of violence in the world."

Urban Churches and Peacemaking

And why should Cross Lutheran or Hephatha Lutheran, in the heart of the central city of Milwaukee, struggling with spiritual and economic poverty, struggling with gang wars and drug dealing, struggling with teen pregnancy and climbing high school dropout rates, struggling with drug addiction and homelessness, why should such urban congregations talk about militarism and foreign policy matters, much less try to do something about them?

First, the assumption that use of military force to achieve our nation's goals is acceptable and appropriate, whether it is retribution against a perceived enemy or to preserve preeminence in the world, is not lost on children and youth in the central city of Milwaukee, or anywhere. The waging of preemptive wars and the constant deployment of service personnel to theaters of war, communicates to children, youth, and young adults that a very effective, acceptable way to achieve power and preeminence and to accomplish your goals is to pack a weapon and to use it freely. Some of the weapons used and uniforms worn by gangs are military surplus or military facsimile. Just how much causal effect U.S. military action abroad has on violence in the central cities of our country is impossible to determine. But clearly the television news coverage of military action, the TV ads and programs affirming military engagement, the consistent efforts by the military to recruit high school students, upon graduation, to join the armed forces, and family members and friends telling their stories of military involvement, all contribute to a culture that not only accepts the use of violent force to achieve one's ends, but at times, glorifies it.

Secondly, a budget that allocates more than half a trillion dollars to military expenditures creates an economic situation that simply does not contain the dollars needed for quality public school education, for job training, for alcohol and other drug addiction treatment, for mental health treatment, for job creation, and the like. Yet these are the very things that are needed to bring down levels of violence in the cities, and to create peaceful communities.

Overseas Partners and Peace

Christian congregations, whether in the heart of the city or in the suburbs, small towns, or rural areas, have another connection with the militaristic culture of the United States. This is especially true for Evangelical Lutheran Church in America (ELCA) congregations, as well as Roman Catholic congregations. All of the ELCA geographical synods (districts) have a partner relationship with a church counterpart abroad, and many ELCA and Roman Catholic congregations have partner relationships with congregations abroad. These relationships put congregational members from such urban congregations as Cross Lutheran and Hephatha Lutheran in Milwaukee, in direct contact with pastors and people abroad, who tell their story of how U.S. military policies have affected them.

I was with a delegation of people from the United States visiting in El Salvador, out in the countryside near Chalatenango. In the free-flowing conversation, I asked of the Salvadorans: "As we go back to the U.S., what is it that we could do that would really benefit you in your struggles?"

Back came the first reply: "Well, if you could close down the School of the Americas, where so many of the Salvadoran army officers are trained, it would help tremendously."

I was stunned. I was amazed that an ordinary Salvadoran peasant farmer would know about the School of the Americas (now called Western Hemisphere Institute for Security Cooperation), that has functioned at Fort Benning at the edge of Columbus, Georgia, since the 1970s, and that he would consider the impact of this seemingly insignificant piece of U.S. military policy to be so harmful to the welfare of the people of El Salvador.

As we talked further with Salvadorans, it became apparent why they were so set against the School of the Americas (SOA). They knew that the assassinations of Archbishop Oscar Romero, of the four U.S. churchwomen, of the six Jesuits and their housekeeper at the University of Central America, and the massacre of the entire village of El Mozote, as well as countless other acts of intimidation and terror, had been carried out by graduates of the SOA.

We learned in El Salvador that our country's supply of weapons to El Salvador and our methodical teaching at the SOA of "low-intensity warfare" and of the use of torture and intimidation, as a way to control the people and as a means to maintain an outward climate of peace for the operation of U.S. business interests, was having a horrendous impact on our Salvadoran brothers and sisters.

The Way of Non-Violence

We are a schizophrenic nation and a schizophrenic Church. We want a calm and peaceful world, but we spend more money on arms and military power per capita than any other nation in the world. We preach peace and healing in the Church, yet we are reluctant to even talk in our congregations about the rightness or the wrongness of our nation's military policies and war efforts. We decry the violence in our urban areas and in our small towns and rural areas, yet we do little to fund adequate alcohol and drug addiction treatment or to provide jobs for everybody, two efforts that would reduce violence.

As the Church, we are called to teach, preach, pray, and live out more radically, the way of non-violence.

Most people of faith have no problem embracing the concept of non-violence, especially on the level of person-to-person relations. However, honesty requires us to admit that every one of us has to struggle throughout our lives to recognize and overcome tendencies toward emotional violence, verbal violence, and attitudinal violence.

There are two areas where people of faith are deeply divided when it comes to living out the principle of non-violence: non-violent resistance against injustice, and non-violence in international relations and foreign policy.

Martin Luther King and the Southern Christian Leadership Conference in the 1960s were criticized vehemently by white moderate Christians, by some black Christians, and by political and business leaders for their non-violent direct action resistance against the injustices of Jim Crow segregation. And at the same time, they were verbally attacked by black radicals for their insistence on non-violence.

The white and black moderates charged King and the SCLC with fomenting violence by their non-violent demonstrations. They pointed to the tensions created every time there was a mass meeting, a march, or a public demonstration, calling for an end to the evil of racial segregation and calling for the justice and equality of an integrated society with equal opportunity for everyone. They pointed to the resurgence of the Ku Klux Klan and the threats and actual violent activities carried out by the Klan.

One of Dr. King's repeated replies to this criticism of non-violent resistance was: "True peace is not the absence of tension, but the presence of justice."

In his *Letter from Birmingham City Jail,* King stated that, "non-violent direct action seeks to create such a crisis and establish such creative tension that a community that has constantly refused to negotiate is forced to confront the issue."

Non-violent direct action is aimed at what can rightly be described as "systemic violence." The system of racial segregation that had been in place, especially in the South, but also in the North, through 250 years of slavery and 100 years of racial segregation following the Civil War, was an unjust system that did violence to every person subjected to its demeaning rules and requirements. The hundreds of lynchings were only the tip of the iceberg of violence perpetrated by the system of racial segregation.

And so non-violent direct action, in any decade, when it is aimed at transforming a system or policy that is doing violence to people, is a way of refusing to be complicit with an evil system. It is a way of living out what Paul in Romans 12:9 calls on followers of Christ to do: "Hate what is evil, cling to what is good."

Of course, if people of faith are seeking to do justice and to do away with systemic violence and injustice, it is absolutely essential that while we are seeking to remove violence, we ourselves remain non-violent.

The temptation to resort to violence in the 1960s was always present for King and the participants in the movement. This was the source of real tension between Malcolm X and King. And it was the inevitable urge within every participant in a march or demonstration. When the rocks come at you, to hurl them back is the immediate urge.

Because the leaders of the movement were keenly aware of this natural urge to return violence for violence, they required participants in a demonstration to take some training in non-violence. Here is the pledge that even the youth who participated in the marches in Birmingham in the spring of 1963, were required to study and to sign:

I hereby pledge myself, my person and body, to the non-violent movement. Therefore I will keep the following 10 commandments:

- *MEDITATE daily on the teaching and life of Jesus.*
- *REMEMBER always that the non-violent movement in Birmingham seeks justice and reconciliation, not victory.*
- *WALK and TALK in the manner of love, for God is love.*
- *PRAY daily to be used by God in order that all men might be free.*
- *SACRIFICE personal wishes in order that all men might be free.*
- *OBSERVE with both friend and foe the ordinary rules of courtesy.*
- *SEEK to perform regular service for others and for the world.*
- *REFRAIN from the violence of fist, tongue, or heart.*
- *STRIVE to be in good spiritual and bodily health.*
- *FOLLOW the directions of the movement and of the captain of a demonstration.*

I sign this pledge, having seriously considered what I do, and with the determination and will to persevere.

If the movement of the 1960s had not been a non-violent movement, it is certain that it would not have achieved its goal of dismantling racial segregation and removing the many barriers to full enfranchisement of African Americans.

Bloody Sunday, March 7, 1965, is a striking example of the power of non-violent resistance. About 500 men, women, and children marched over the Edmund Pettus Bridge in Selma the afternoon of that historic Sunday in March. It was a march that Dr. King and other SCLC leaders who were in Atlanta on that day had instructed them not to undertake. There would be more time to prepare for the march, counseled the SCLC leaders, and leaders like King and Abernathy would be able to be with them if they would wait until the following Sunday.

But the people who had gathered at the Brown Chapel AME Church thought differently. Many of them had traveled some 40 miles from Marion, Alabama, to march in memory of Jimmie Lee Jackson, who had been killed just days before by a state trooper while he was trying to protect his grandfather during a demonstration. Angered by the unprovoked brutality of the state trooper, the people from Marion were determined to demonstrate to the powers-that-be that they were not going to be deterred, not even by the brute force of the Alabama state troopers, from marching for their freedom. And after such a vicious, undeserved attack by a law enforcement officer, the resolute demonstrators undoubtedly were tempted to bring along some weapons to defend themselves, in case they were to meet up with such an attack again.

But the 500 marchers, in keeping with their commitment to non-violence, carried no weapons as they walked two abreast across the bridge. As John Lewis and Hosea Williams led the column to the other side of the bridge, they were stopped by a formidable mix of law enforcement officers. There were Dallas County sheriff's deputies and state troopers, some on horses, some equipped with cattle prods, some with billy clubs, some with tear gas, some with shotguns.

The marchers were told: "You have two minutes to turn around and return to the church."

In just a few seconds, the whole group of law enforcement officers moved forward at a fast pace, as if they were in attack mode, and forced to the ground the first 50 or so marchers, as they used tear gas, cattle prods, and the formidable force of the advancing horses, to turn around a long column of marchers. It was John Lewis and those at the head of the line of marchers who experienced the brunt of the vicious attack.

After the column of demonstrators had been turned around and the cloud of tear gas had lifted, the dozen or so who lay on the ground were taken by ambulance to the hospital. John Lewis, with a severe brain concussion, remained hospitalized for several days.

The name given to March 7, 1965, "Bloody Sunday," is an apt name. And the scenario is a classic example of violent suppression of non-violent cries for justice and for correcting deeply embedded wrongs of society. At first observation of the drama of Bloody Sunday, it seems obvious that the law enforcement officers of Governor George Wallace and of Dallas County Sheriff Jim Clark won the battle on that day. And it would seem that after viewing the outcome of that afternoon's contest, there is no question about winners and losers. It is precisely such an event where violent force is pitted against the force of non-violent commitment to justice that seems to demonstrate unequivocally the winning power of violent force.

After Bloody Sunday

However, the subsequent story of what happened after Bloody Sunday would say otherwise. It so happened that the media were there on March 7, to chronicle exactly what happened on that fateful afternoon. The story was told, with graphic pictures that showed the truth, on the Sunday evening news broadcasts across the nation. Soon the story and the pictures were seen on television newscasts and in newspaper accounts around the world.

People of all faiths in the United States, ordinary people of conscience, lawmakers in Washington D.C., and leaders and citizens around the world saw the pictures and knew that something was radically wrong in Selma and in Alabama and in the United States. The vast majority of people who learned of the story were ready to stand on the side of those who had been bloodied by the blows of mean, oppressive violence.

On the Tuesday following Bloody Sunday, hundreds of pastors, priests, nuns, rabbis, and regular people of faith poured into Selma to march in solidarity with the veterans of Bloody Sunday. The undeserved suffering of a band of non-violent protesters marching to attain voting rights for themselves and others, galvanized hundreds of people, with 12-hours' notice, to come from all parts of the country to carry on the freedom journey where it had been stopped two days before.

Intro

The Commission on Religion and Race of the National Council of Churches arranged to send a diverse group of religious leaders, on the Friday following Bloody Sunday, to meet with President Lyndon Johnson about the passage of the Voting Rights Act. I was honored to be the Lutheran representative among the interfaith group of 17 clergy. Inspired by the courageous stand of the non-violent freedom marchers who were bloodied by the violent purveyors of hate, we told President Johnson from our individual perspectives: "We need a strong Voting Rights Act now."

President Johnson, on March 15, just a week after Bloody Sunday, addressed Congress and came on national television in his southern Texas drawl, saying: "The time has come for our nation to guarantee every U.S. citizen their constitutional right to vote… and we shall overcome."

After some diehard tactics on the part of some Southern congressmen to kill the Voting Rights Act, and after some equally determined pressure from President Johnson and some civil rights advocates in Congress, the voting Rights Act became law in August, 1965. Gradually over the ensuing decades, African Americans in the South and the North began voting in large numbers and took part in the democratic process, helping to elect African American sheriffs, district attorneys, judges, city council members, county supervisors, mayors, state legislators, Congressional representatives, and in 2008, helping to elect an African American President. The enfranchisement of millions of African American voters, and the recognition on the part of anyone running for any office that the concerns of African American voters must now be taken seriously, resulted finally in the demise of legal racial segregation and the enforcement, even in the deep South, of equal access to public places and employment opportunities.

If the marchers on Bloody Sunday had not been deeply committed to non-violence and had not been willing to risk their lives in the living out of that principle, the subsequent chain of events would have been quite different.

Non-violent resistance on Bloody Sunday appeared to be a failure, the philosophy of a band of naïve dreamers. History shows it, instead, to be amazingly powerful because it was born of commitment to truth, love of fellow human beings, and exercised by a well-organized community of people who were authentic in their struggle for justice.

Non-violence and non-violent resistance, some would say, may be effective as a way to bring about change, if it is exercised in a country like the U.S., where there are legal and judicial safeguards for the physical protection of citizens. But in countries where there are no such safeguards, and in situations like Nazi Germany, non-violent resistance is futile and foolhardy.

Gandhi and the Cross

One of the most famous exponents of non-violent resistance as a way of bringing about change for the good of all was India's Mahatma Gandhi. Even Martin Luther King testified to Gandhi's influence on his understanding of non-violent resistance and his commitment to its power to bring about change. History bears out the power of Gandhi's non-violent force of resistance as the most potent factor in freeing the nation of India from the colonial tentacles of the British Empire.

There are those who point to the humongous proportions of evil perpetrated by Hitler's maniacal drive to conquer all of Europe, if not the world, and his barbaric attempts to exterminate the Jews, the gypsies, the homosexuals, the Communists, the developmentally disabled and all those he considered impurities in the human race, as the perfect proof that non-violence and non-violent resistance doesn't work. There were those who resisted non-violently, like Franz Jaegerstaetter, who were simply mowed down by Hitler's violent machine. The only way to oppose Hitler, it seemed, was to pit a violent force against him, a violent force greater than his, which is what the allied forces did in World War II.

There were those, such as Dietrich Bonhoeffer, who saw the monster of Hitler's ruthless use of violence and concluded that the way to stop the Nazi juggernaut was to eliminate its driver. And there was Martin Niemoeller and the Confessing Church, non-violently trying to stop the juggernaut. I must praise God for these persons of faith, who wrestled and struggled and prayed and risked their lives, in an effort to stop the juggernaut of evil. Their non-violent witness is powerful to this very day.

As we look back on this critical period of human history, we can glean from the Confessing Church lessons all of us should strive to learn. Should not people of faith in every age be alert to what is happening around them? Should they not free themselves from the false patriotism that can so easily grab hold of every citizen of every nation? And should they not thoughtfully, prayerfully, struggle with such questions as: "What is best for all the people of our country, especially those at the edges? What part of official policy in our country is diametrically opposed to the teachings and example of Christ? What is the best way for us to come together as people of faith, across congregational/denominational/cultural lines of separation, to work together for the common good of all? And should not every community of faith have deep, profound relationships with those at the edges in their congregation and in their community, with gypsies, with homosexuals, with Jews, with people in prison, with developmentally disabled, with political mavericks?

Strangely, it was Gandhi who spoke of a vision of Christ crucified that called even him to profound commitment to a life of radical commitment to non-violence at every level of life. This is Gandhi's own description of his deep, spiritual experience upon seeing a rough-hewn crucifix at the Vatican, on his way back from the Roundtable Conference in London in 1931:

> *"What would not I have given to bow my head before the living image, at the Vatican, of the Christ crucified. It was not without a wrench that I could tear myself away from that scene of living tragedy. I saw there at once that nations, like individuals, could only be made free through the agony of the cross and in no other way. Joy comes not out of infliction of pain on others, but out of pain voluntarily borne by oneself."*

Christian theologians through the ages have studied and written about the meaning of the cross. Even the writers of Scripture have described the meaning of Christ's life and death on the cross in various ways: "God was in Christ reconciling the world unto Himself." "God so loved the world that he gave his only begotten Son, that whoever believes in him should not die, but have everlasting life." "He was the sacrifice once and for all, for the sins of the world." "I, when I am lifted up, will draw all people unto myself."

The authorities hated Jesus and feared Jesus enough that they wanted desperately to get rid of him. And why? Because he actively walked with all sorts of people–lepers, women, children, tax collectors, prostitutes, soldiers, politicians, wealthy people, poor people, people with mental health issues, Gentiles, Samaritans, ritually clean, ritually unclean, theologians, fishermen–as though they all had equal value before God. He was establishing a community based on God's love and forgiveness, not on human perfection or observance of rituals or on society's scale of worth.

And when Jesus' life was under threat of torture and crucifixion, he did not try to escape, as he could have. He did not return violence with violence, as he could have. He did not compromise his teaching, as he could have. Instead, he non-violently let them torture him and crucify him, as if his non-violent stand for justice and his non-violent, radical love of people was stronger than their violence, as though it was so powerful that it would draw all people to himself.

The resurrection of Jesus does not simply point to the deity of Christ. It points also to the victory of life that is lived intentionally with all people, affirming the worth and the gifts of all people. It points to the power of the non-violent stand for justice and the vision of a new community that is inclusive of all.

The crucifix was for Gandhi, and surely is for all who take Christ seriously, the symbol of the grinding power of brute force that all followers of Christ must surely resist with all their God-given strength. And it is that awesome reminder of the life-giving power of a life of non-violent love that is willing to risk everything for the sake of that vision of the new community, based not on brute force but on God's forgiveness and the gifts of all. Not on the systematic arrest, torture, and elimination of the undesirable, but on the release of the captives and recovery of sight for the blind. Not on fearful acquiescence to the powers-that-be to do their thing, but on the bold confidence that God is bringing in God's Kingdom of justice and love, and nothing can ultimately stop it.

The crucifix is not only that awesome assurance that my sins are forgiven and I am right with God. It is that awesome assurance that the journey of non-violent resistance against evil and injustice is not a lost cause, but the very journey the crucified and resurrected Christ took, and the very journey which he beckons us to take today.

CHAPTER 17

HEALING IN BODY, MIND, AND SPIRIT

When the sun was setting, the people brought to Jesus all who had various kinds of sickness, and laying his hands on each one, he healed them.

–Luke 4:40

It was a Sunday morning at Cross Church, Milwaukee, back in the early 1980s. The service had been announced ahead of time, as a "Healing Service." When people came forward for Communion, they could have the opportunity to go to the left side of the altar or to the right side, to kneel for a special anointing with oil, the laying on of hands, and then a prayer of healing for the body, the mind, and/or the spirit.

We had studied Scripture and talked and prayed about adding this element to our Sunday morning worship. It was clear that the very early Church had done something like this. We read in the letter of James: "If any among you is ill, let the elders pray over him and anoint him with oil in the name of the Lord."

We didn't know whether some people would think we were trying to replace doctors and the whole medical system. We were concerned that some might expect miraculous cures, fail to receive such a cure, and then fault the Gospel and the Church for raising false expectations and making false promises. We were even concerned that some people would consider that the pastor and the participating Elders were arrogantly claiming special powers that ordinary Christians didn't possess.

And we wondered whether some might distance themselves from the congregation because they thought we were trivializing the message of the Gospel and God's forgiveness in Jesus Christ, and substituting a Sunday morning magic show.

All 12 Elders, along with a half dozen caregivers, had been prepared to play a role in the healing services. Three Elders, along with myself, were standing at the four prayer sites, two on either side of the altar. One or two caregivers or Elders stood at each prayer site to lay hands of support on the shoulders of persons who would kneel for anointing with prayer. The remaining Elders were distributing Communion at the two stations in front of the altar.

My real concern on that first Sunday morning we invited people to come forward for healing, was whether anyone would come forward. After all, it was a brand-new element in the service, and people don't easily do new things, even if there is the inner urge to do so.

But come they did. One by one. Each of us who were doing the laying on of hands whispered into the ear of the person seeking healing: "Tell me in a phrase or two, what your specific concern is."

The concerns of the persons who came forward were as diverse as the age and the gender and the race of the persons who came forward: "Problems with the two grandchildren I'm raising." "I'm going to the doctor Tuesday for her diagnosis of what may be cancer." "Problems with my co-workers on the job." "Constant pain in my lower back, especially when I get up in the morning." "A feeling of being overwhelmed at work, at home, and my volunteer work." "A problem of communication with my husband."

There was no question about the felt need for healing. And there was no question about whether people would come forward. Our fears about people's skepticism did not materialize. The feedback we received from those who came forward, as well as those who didn't, was all positive. The overall message communicated by the healing services, which were continued on a quarterly basis, and then on a monthly basis, was that the Gospel and the Church were all about healing. After all, that's what Jesus spent a good deal of his time doing as a sign of the coming of God's kingdom.

Of course, it became clear that some of the needs for physical healing called for medical attention. Often the individual needing such attention was not aware of resources that were available and could help. Or the person lacked the medical insurance to get the help or the necessary medicine.

A Parish Nurse

So it was an answer to prayer that we were contacted one day by the nearest hospital, Sinai Samaritan, and asked whether Cross Church might be interested in engaging a parish nurse.

As our Board of Elders and Social Ministry Committee considered the offer of a parish nurse, there were two questions on our mind: What would be the role of the parish nurse? And how would we fund such a position, since we were a resource-stretched urban congregation?

The sky seemed to be the limit when it came to the role of the parish nurse. Such nurses could conduct blood pressure tests, give flu shots, or answer specific questions people may have about their symptoms, after Sunday worship or at designated times during the week. They could disseminate basic information about health concerns in a variety of venues, such as the monthly newsletter, at meetings, or even in the Sunday worship time period. They could be available to do what registered nurses are permitted to do, on a one-to-one basis, by appointment, at a church office or on a home visit. In addition, they could lead group discussions, and they could pray with people with whom they were walking.

It was explained to us that parish nurses are not assigned by the hospital in a bureaucratic manner. At the very beginning of the process, nurses at the hospital were invited to put their names on the list of potential parish nurses, if they were interested in this kind of special relationship with a congregation and with a spiritual setting for the arts of healing. And when a congregation has decided that it is ready for a parish nurse, the congregation is given the opportunity to interview two or three nurses who had expressed an interest in serving at a given parish and/or had been recommended by the hospital as persons well-suited for a given congregational/community setting. The congregation then makes the final decision.

Leaders at Cross were quick to see the value of a parish nurse. Not only would such a person bring basic medical services to people who had no health insurance, but it would nudge the congregation and its leaders to live out more fully that part of the Gospel message that calls us to be a community of people that brings healing to each other and to the larger community.

So the bottom-line question became: Where do we get the funding? Sinai Samaritan Hospital answered that question with the assurance that they would fund the first year of the half-time parish nurse. We were amazed at their largesse. But as we probed a little bit, we discovered that the hospital saw this investment in their self-interest. Having a nurse at an urban congregation like Cross Church would actually save them money, they calculated. Having a mini-clinic outpost in a poverty community would hopefully deal with a lot of chronic conditions like high blood pressure, diabetic fluctuations, and cold and flu symptoms, before they escalated into more serious conditions. This would reduce the use of the emergency room at the hospital, reduce a major cost item in the hospital's budget, and improve the health index of the hospital's primary service area.

A committee from Cross interviewed three RN candidates recommended by Sinai Samaritan Hospital and unanimously chose Rick Cesar, an outgoing, committed emergency room nurse who expressed deep interest in being one of the pioneer parish nurses in Milwaukee. Even though he had strong Roman Catholic roots, he expressed real interest in serving at a Lutheran Church.

The passage of time soon bore witness to the wisdom of engaging Rick Cesar in 1993, in this new position on the staff, and this new direction of ministry at Cross. Rick Cesar quickly bonded with members of the congregation and with neighborhood folks who came for his services. He became a member of Cross and participated in the Sunday worship and in weekday parish activities. He even joined the Elders and the caregivers in making visits to senior citizens and to persons who found it difficult to leave their homes. It soon became clear that he was not only a top-notch nurse, but someone who was a lover of people, was motivated by the Gospel, and not afraid to witness to the Gospel.

Rick Cesar joined the Caregivers Committee at Cross and together, they creatively planned events and published articles in the monthly Cross newsletter that educated people on basic health information and "do's and don'ts" for parents, youth, senior citizens, and parish members of all varieties.

A special healing service for persons in their "autumn years" was initiated by the Caregivers and parish nurse. Persons with physical/mental disabilities were not only invited to this special service of healing, and offered transportation, but many were invited to help lead the worship. Depending on their gifts, they were invited to read Scripture, give a personal testimony, offer up a prayer, help usher, assist at Communion, or to be a support person at the anointing and laying on of hands with prayer.

The service gave the Elders and caregivers an excellent opportunity to interact with persons with special needs. It gave the congregation an opportunity to receive and nurture the gifts of persons who are quite often forgotten. And it gave the parish nurse and pastor a special opportunity to deepen relationships for further ministry.

One memorable moment in one of these special services was the personal testimony of a 19-year-old young woman, who was developmentally disabled, and who spoke with her own accent. She told her story of God's leading her to see how important she was as a witness to God's love and forgiveness. She gave her testimony with such excitement and joy that no one could question its authenticity. And her message was so articulate and so profound that everyone was enriched by her witness. We later prevailed on her to give a similar testimony at a Sunday morning worship, so that the whole congregation could be nurtured by her testimony and also come to see the gifts that every member of the congregation brings to the parish family.

Fortunately, for the sake of Cross Church, Rick Cesar saw the role of worship, with Scripture, testimony, prayer, and Communion, to be closely connected with the physical, mental, and spiritual healing of people. He not only affirmed it, he participated in the planning and the doing of it.

Cross Adult Center

About the same time that Rick Cesar came to Cross as parish nurse, Cross Church initiated the Cross Adult Center. This was a program designed and initiated by the Caregivers Committee at Cross, envisioned largely by Gloria Wright, a member of the Caregivers Committee.

The Caregivers Committee recognized that people in their "autumn years," or "seasoned" people, as Gloria Wright often described senior citizens, are often lonely and in need of stimulation, human fellowship, a balanced diet, and access to basic health care. The Caregivers recognized also that there were people with physical and/or mental disabilities who weren't "seasoned" in years, but who had the same needs as those in their autumn years. So the Caregivers purposely did not call the program the "Cross Senior Center." They called it the "Cross Adult Center," to include adults of any age who wanted positive interaction with others, who wanted a tasty hot meal, and who wanted access to health care services.

The Cross Adult Center gave Rick Cesar an opportunity to reach 30 to 40 adults from the congregation and from the community on a weekly basis, with basic health care services, such as blood pressure and cholesterol checkups, flu shots, and answers to questions people had about their various health symptoms.

One of the factors that impacts the health of persons of all ages and conditions living in the central part of a large metropolitan area, is fear–fear especially of crime and gangs. Aware of this, the Caregivers Committee and the Adult Center Board incorporated into the program of the Adult Center two regular experiences to help break down that fear.

Two to four inmates from the Chaney Center, the Sherrer Center, or the Women's Center, minimum security prisons within a mile of Cross Church, were regularly brought to the Adult Center to help with the cooking, the serving of the meal, and the cleanup. The volunteer service gave the men and women a chance to break out of their confinement and to get a real taste of positive community life. And the presence of these persons who were in the prison system, bringing food to the tables of the Adult Center participants, cleaning up an accidental spill, going to the kitchen to get some special seasoning requested by a participant, helped the Center participants, most of them "seasoned" women, to see these men and women no longer as threats, but as amazingly thoughtful, helpful volunteers who could be seen as their sons or daughters. The positive, weekly interaction between incarcerated persons and vulnerable members of the community definitely helped to dissipate fears and stereotypes on both sides and to contribute to healthier persons and healthier communities.

The Adult Center Board and the Caregivers Committee also saw the fears that senior citizens often have toward teenagers, especially young men, who are seen as potential purse snatchers or burglars. They also recognized that many young people stereotype persons in their "autumn years" as people who are either "out of it" or don't care to associate with teenagers.

Consequently, the Adult Center program was designed to regularly bring to the Center, teenagers from Shalom High School, an alternative school of about 100 students housed in a building next door to Cross Church. Usually, the students were paired up with one of the Adult Center participants to talk about a specific topic. At the beginning, the conversation was simply each person telling the story of his or her life. The young people were really impressed by the stories of these persons, old enough to be their grandparents. The stories of picking cotton in Arkansas or Mississippi, of walking five miles one way to a one-room school, or of getting baptized in the nearby river inhabited by water moccasins, resonated with these young persons, because they knew they could have been their own family stories, stories that most of them had never heard, because most of them came from families that didn't talk much about their family history. Amazingly, most of the students thoroughly enjoyed their conversations with these seasoned adults, and in some instances, special relationships were forged that spilled over into the days between the bi-weekly encounters at the Center. Clearly, the Center was addressing some intergenerational fears and stereotypes and was contributing to the health and well-being of the young and the "seasoned" folks.

Bread of Healing

Rick Cesar and the Social Ministry Committee came to see, soon after the Parish Nurse program was launched in 1993, that almost all the people who came weekly to the Bread of Healing program for a meal and emergency food, had serious health problems. There were high levels of diabetes, high blood pressure, heart problems, drug addiction, and mental health issues. Consequently, people who came for emergency food were invited to check in with Rick Cesar for any health needs they might have.

The word spread quickly that a registered nurse was available every Wednesday at the Bread of Healing program, and the result was a growing number of persons who came regularly for blood pressure checkups, flu shots, and medical advice that was nurse-appropriate. In conjunction with Project RETURN, the prison reentry ministry housed at Cross Church, AODA (alcohol and other drug abuse) support groups, one for men and one for women, were established and facilitated by trained counselors as part of the Bread of Healing program.

One day, Rick Cesar came to me and asked to speak privately with me about an important potential development in the Bread of Healing program. "I don't know what you or Cross Church would think about this," he said, "but we've been approached by the Wisconsin AIDS Resource Center, asking whether Cross would be willing to be a site for the expanding needle

Adults in their autumn years gather for a meal and a focus on a relevant topic affecting their lives, in the fellowship hall of Cross Church, for the weekly Cross Adult Center meal and program. A healthy, hot meal, lively conversation, cross-generational sharing, and blood pressure checks and consultations by the parish nurse, contribute to the physical and spiritual health of congregational and community participants.

exchange program. They're having difficulty finding a place in the African American community that will accept the program."

Not knowing a whole lot about the program, I asked, "Well, what are the reasons churches and clinics are refusing to house the program?"

"The main reason," Rick responded, "is because there are a lot of people, especially in religious groups, and even in drug treatment circles, who say that needle exchange simply encourages users to keep on using. But it's been shown that needle exchanging actually reduces the incidence of AIDS and diseases that can be transmitted by the use of contaminated needles."

"Well," I asked, "do needle exchanges actually make it easy for people to keep on using, and possibly to even increase the number of users?"

"As a matter of fact," Rick responded, "needle exchanges help wean people off of intravenous drug use. Coming out of the shadows of the drug-using community and talking with a medically-trained person who can help them into treatment, actually moves some people out of a death-dealing addiction into recovery."

I was convinced that it was a win-win situation. A needle exchange at Cross Church would reduce the incidence of diseases spread by the use of dirty needles, and it would hopefully get some drug users into treatment and recovery.

We didn't openly publicize the needle exchange at Cross, but the word soon got around via the intravenous drug users' grapevine. And the Bread of Healing program added one more dimension to its level of services offered to the community.

Bread of Healing Clinic

The services of Rick Cesar began to serve more and more people, including follow-up service for uninsured persons from the Aurora Sinai Hospital Emergency Room, where Rick was working half-time.

Dr. Tom Jackson, a leader at Cross Church and head of the Primary Care Department of Aurora Sinai Medical Center, together with Rick Cesar and Dr. Barbara Horner-Ibler, doing her residency at Aurora Sinai Medical Center, saw a growing number of persons with chronic illnesses who had no insurance and no ability to pay for their medicine.

In collaboration with Aurora Sinai Medical Center and the University of Wisconsin School of Medicine, Cross Church opened the Bread of Healing Clinic at Cross Church on January 1, 2000. The clinic has grown steadily so that by 2009, the clinic was seeing about 400 patients per month, with a staff consisting of a medical doctor, Dr. Barbara Horner-Ibler, a registered nurse, Rick Cesar, a pharmacist, a staff assistant, and several volunteer medical personnel.

There is no denying the fascinating growth over the years from healing services at Cross in the early 1980s, to an active Caregivers Committee in the mid-1980s, to a Bread of Healing program with meal/Bible study/emergency food in 1992, to a parish nurse in 1993, to an adult center in 1994, to a multi-service Bread of Healing Clinic in 2000.

Even as the United States moves closer and closer to offering healthcare services to all its citizens, regardless of their ability to purchase a healthcare insurance policy, it is people seeking to live out of the vision and the power of the Gospel who will always be working on two fronts, to serve people who fall through the cracks of existing medical services, and to try, at the same time, to eliminate the cracks. People of the Gospel will be working to transform health care policies in the U.S. to be sure that all people will be able to access quality, adequate healthcare. It is a matter of morality and justice that quality healthcare is a basic human right and should be available not only to those who can afford healthcare insurance, or who have no "pre-existing conditions," but to all people.

At the same time, it is people of the Gospel who believe that wellness is a matter that affects the body, the mind, and the spirit and it is a blessing from God. Therefore, healing services, caregivers groups, Bible studies, and parish nurses will always be important and vital in the life of the congregation, in the distribution of emergency food and in conducting a Bread of Healing Clinic. After all, Jesus went about healing people, teaching people, loving people, praying for people, as though body, mind, and spirit were intricately connected. And his followers have such a calling today.

An Accessible Church

In the late 1980s, Tom and Carolyn Jackson, after raising two of their biological children and one adopted child, made the daring decision to adopt two special-needs children from Nicaragua. One of the two children needed a wheelchair for mobility and presented real challenges to his parents in getting him up and down the many steps outside and inside Cross Church.

At first Tom Jackson carried Dimas, their five-year-old son from Nicaragua, up and down the steps, followed by another trip, or with some help from Carolyn, an usher, or a friend, to get the wheelchair to the desired location for Dimas.

That labor-intensive process of getting Dimas to church and to Sunday school continued for two or three years until Dimas grew heavier, and Dimas became self-conscious among his peers. To have his father carry him up and down the steps was embarrassing.

So Tom and Carolyn brought up the idea to the Church Council that Cross Church should consider becoming accessible to persons with disabilities, not only for Dimas, but for other members of Cross and for the sake of outreach and witness to non-members as well.

It was not difficult to convince the congregation that making the sanctuary, the fellowship hall, and the rest rooms accessible to persons with disabilities was an important part of our congregational witness to the Good News that God loves all people.

The bottom-line questions were: "How much would it cost?" And, "Does the congregation have the will and the ability to find the money to do it?"

Some research and some actual bids soon let us know that we needed a ramp to get wheelchairs into the sanctuary, and we would need an elevator to get the wheelchairs and persons with disabilities to the fellowship hall and to the restrooms below the sanctuary. We also discovered that the ramp would cost $5,000, and the elevator would cost $50,000.

The Church Council decided we could construct the ramp immediately. The elevator would take a little longer. Fortunately, there was a growing commitment to installing an elevator, especially when leaders realized that the ramp gave access only to the sanctuary, not to bathrooms or to the area for Sunday school classes and fellowship meals.

A proposal to a local Lutheran foundation garnered $25,000 and special gifts and fundraisers helped to raise the remainder of the cost. As a result, the elevator was installed in the fall of 1994. Suddenly we realized what we had been missing without wheelchair accessibility.

Not only did the ramp and the elevator serve Dimas' needs, but persons in wheelchairs and on walkers began appearing for services. We soon realized we had done the right thing, even if it was financially challenging for an urban congregation that partially depended on partner congregations and foundations to carry out its ministries.

When the disastrous fire struck Cross Church in 1995, just a few months after dedicating the elevator, at first we thought that our $50,000 investment in ministry to persons with disabilities was ill-timed. If only we had waited until after February 2, 1995, to install the elevator, we thought, we wouldn't have had to re-invest another $50,000 to replace the elevator.

A close inspection of the elevator, however, showed that the fire had leaped over the elevator and up to the roof and had left the elevator without any major damage. The fire, in fact, enabled us to all but finish the job of making the building totally wheelchair-accessible. Rebuilding the burned-out shell of a sanctuary enabled us to make all the bathrooms accessible, including one on the level of the sanctuary.

If anyone were to question the value of Cross investing in accessibility, that person would only need to reflect on two engaging stories.

One story gets played out every Tuesday from 10:00 a.m. to 2:00 p.m. That is the day of the Cross Adult Center ministry. At least five to ten persons, of the total of 35 to 40 who participate in the programs and the lunch, utilize the ramp, the elevator, and the accessible restrooms. In addition, the ramp and the elevator are used on a daily basis by persons coming to the Bread of Healing Clinic, Bible study, AODA (alcohol and other drug addiction) support groups, emergency food ministry, and job placement services.

Without a doubt, one of the most moving stories connected with Cross's accessibility ministry is the story of Kelly Schmidt. After the ramp and the elevator were installed, June Torrence, an active member of Cross who did home healthcare for various clients, told her client, Kelly Schmidt, about Cross Church. Kelly, who was 20-something and a wheelchair user, started attending worship. She found the lively music, the warm acceptance of Cross members, and the Gospel of Jesus' love for all, to be the bread that she needed for her soul. Even though it meant arranging for a special two-way transit pickup every time she came to Cross Church, she came to Pastor's class (12 sessions), joined the Cross Gospel Choir, and in 2007, celebrated her wedding vows with a man who also utilized the ramp and the elevator.

Cross Church has learned two important lessons on its journey of accessibility ministry. First, there were a lot of persons with disabilities in our congregation and community who were invisible or were minimized in our efforts at ministry and witness. Taking the leap of faith and investing in accessibility made these persons, some of them already members of Cross, much more visible. And interacting in worship and in the life of the congregation with these persons, helped us to see their many varied gifts, which contributed to the spiritual life and health of our congregation.

Persons with disabilities are much more than their disabilities. They are children of God with unique gifts, intended by God to nurture us all. Including persons with disabilities in Cross's outreach and congregational life definitely brought the healing power of the Gospel to people who are often avoided or forgotten by the Church. And it definitely nurtured the whole congregation in a deeper understanding of the Gospel and a more profound experience of the Body of Christ and the beloved community.

CHAPTER 18

SWIMMING UPSTREAM: THE COURAGE TO ACT

Be on your guard. Stand firm in the faith. Be men and women of courage. Be strong. Do everything in love.
–I Corinthians 16:13,14

February 2 is Groundhog Day for most people in the United States. But for members of Cross Lutheran Church, Milwaukee, it was the day in 1995 of the massive fire that destroyed the roof and the interior of the beautiful, sturdy, brick sanctuary that had served the central city congregation well, ever since its dedication in 1931. In the 1930s, Cross Church was made up of blue-collar, second-generation German immigrants, with about 1,500 members, including children.

At the time of the fire in 1995, however, the congregation numbered about 600 members, including children, about 80 percent African American and 20 percent Euro-American. Except for one faithful member from the old Germanic congregation, this was a new community of believers who had come together since the 1960s, in response to the congregation's outreach to the immediate African American neighborhood, to its emphasis on youth programming, to its flexible Sunday morning liturgies with a diversity of hymns and music, and to its involvement in local and global social justice issues.

The devastating fire on February 2, 1995, captured the attention of all the members of Cross, as well as the masses of people in metropolitan Milwaukee. The February 2nd afternoon edition of the *Milwaukee Journal* ran a front-page, four-column article, with a picture of the spectacular 4:30 a.m. fire filling almost the entire top half of the front page. The headline read: "Blaze Guts Center of North Side Strength." The article went on to give a report of the fire:

> A five-alarm fire raced through the 64-year-old Cross Evangelical Lutheran Church early Thursday, gutting the landmark building and destroying all but its brick foundation.
>
> Two firefighters were treated for smoke inhalation in the blaze, which was discovered about 4:40 a.m., authorities said.
>
> Flames shot through the roof of the church, 1821 N. 16th St., as Pastor Joseph Ellwanger and his wife, Joyce, listened to firefighters shatter the building's irreplacable stained glass windows.
>
> It took more than three hours to bring the fire under control. Those who came there to witness the tragedy—the pastor, his wife, and church members—clung to each other for support.
>
> "A church is the people, not a building," Joyce Ellwanger said. "We've faced a lot of challenges, and this is another one."
>
> No damage estimate was available. No injuries to church members were reported.
>
> Cross Evangelical, with its 600 members, has been a rock of support in this changing Northside community. The congregation was founded a century ago by Lutheran German immigrants, and is now 80 per cent African American.
>
> The church belongs to the Milwaukee Innercity Congregations Allied for Hope (MICAH) and is involved in a variety of programs, from ministering to former inmates to providing a food pantry.
>
> The church has also been on the cutting edge of liberal issues. Very early on, it was a church that made a concerted effort to welcome gays and lesbians and was involved in providing sanctuary for Central American refugees.

> There also have been a number of liberal human rights issues that the church has been involved in.
>
> The church is also home to an after-school tutoring program. Its neighbor is Shalom High School, an alternative school that uses church facilities and holds its graduation ceremony there every year.
>
> "The important thing is that we've got to figure out a way of continuing," Pastor Ellwanger said. "The physical damage to the building can be replaced."
>
> Late Thursday morning, Mayor John O. Norquist issued a prepared statement on the fire. "My prayers are with the Cross Lutheran Church congregation as they face the challenges this fire presents them," Norquist said.
>
> "Church members," he added, have made important contributions to the city for a long time. I am confident that they will continue to be an active and positive influence in Milwaukee for a long time to come."

The article goes on. Clearly the devastating fire of February 2, 1995, was a critical time in the life of Cross Church. With about 250 adult members, and many of them low-income persons, Cross Church had a huge decision to make. The faith and the courage of the members was evidenced the morning of the fire, as TV reporters interviewed Cross members standing in the street, watching the sanctuary burn. When asked whether they saw a future for Cross Church, members answered in their own way: "God has seen us through many times before. We can count on him to bring us through this time, too."

There were, to be sure, some members of Cross who questioned whether we should take the risks of taking on a mortgage of $750,000, just to carry on Gospel ministry in that neighborhood of concentrated poverty. There were a few, perhaps, who may have thought that this was the time to seriously consider retreating from some of the ministries and stands in which we had engaged that went against the grain of popular culture.

On February 2, 1995, an electrical fire destroyed the interior of Cross Church, leaving only the brick walls and the steel roof beams. The crisis pushed members of Cross to make difficult, risk-taking decisions and brought forth amazing signs of solidarity from the surrounding community and beyond.

But there were many signs along the way, in those days following the fire, that God was nudging us, pushing us, calling us, to have faith and courage to keep moving forward in the foolishness and the power of the Gospel.

There was the invitation to Cross Church, on the very day of the fire, from the Catholic Archdiocese, to utilize one of the three Catholic sanctuaries in the central city of Milwaukee that had been closed recently as a result of consolidating their urban parishes. And so three days after the fire, Cross members gathered at the former Holy Angels Catholic Church to praise God for amazing blessings being poured out in the midst of losses and ashes. For a whole year, Holy Angels' sanctuary and fellowship Hall, about two miles north of the burned-out sanctuary, was home base for Cross's witness and ministry—all for the mere payment of the utility bill.

There was, on the afternoon of the Sunday after the fire, during a break in a strategy meeting of urban Lutheran churches, a stunning encounter with Pastor Mary Martha Kannass and a lay leader from Hephatha Lutheran Church. "We prayed for you in our worship this morning," Pastor Kannass said in her unassuming tone of voice, "but we wanted to do more than pray for you. Here is this morning's offering." The fact that Hephatha Church, located in one of the most concentrated poverty pockets in the city, gave Cross Church "their all" still moves me to profound amazement and gratitude to this very day.

There was the astonishing surprise in the mail, a week after the fire, of a check for $10,000 from Rembert Weakland, Archbishop of the Milwaukee archdiocese.

There were generous gifts from Baptist, Jewish, Catholic, Presbyterian, and Lutheran congregations and from individuals from various points along the theological and denominational spectrum.

There was the amazing readiness of the world-renowned church artist and architect Richard R. Caemmerer, to serve as our re-building consultant and designer and fabricator of all of the stained glass windows that had to be replaced, as well as the chancel furniture. All of this demanding, time-consuming, matchless artistry for the outrageously low price of $500, plus actual cost of materials and shipping!

There was the breathtaking moment, two weeks after the fire, as Richard Caemmerer, on his first visit, stood with several Cross members, in the middle of the sanctuary, a scene reminiscent of bombed-out churches in Europe during World War II. As we looked up through the steel beams that had formed the superstructure for the old roof, we saw a bird's nest on the top beam. And peeping out over the edge of the nest was a tiny white bird that had to be a dove. What a sign from above–that there is life and beauty that can emerge from the ashes.

There was the news from the laboratory where we sent a specimen from one of the steel girders, to test whether or not the steel girders were strong enough to bear the weight of a new roof. If the girders were not strong enough, it would almost surely mean that we would have to tear down the walls that remained and build a totally new structure from the ground up. The word finally came back from the laboratory, with the news that the steel was actually stronger after the fire than before the fire. On the engineer's report was the scientific verdict: "The fire strengthened the steel."

As members of Cross came back after the fire, and as many members went the extra mile to help with the rebuilding, we discovered the spiritual truth, that "fire strengthens." God, in a very real way, was nudging, pushing, calling us to a deeper faith and courage.

And it does take courage to swim upstream—against the current of our own human doubts and cynicism, against the current of our culture's materialism and what's-in-it-for-me philosophy, and against the current of dogmatism and traditionalism of religious folks and society.

Swimming Against the Current

As I look back on 50-plus years of swimming upstream in our life together at St. Paul, Birmingham, Cross, Milwaukee, and Hephatha, Milwaukee, I see one episode after the other of swimming against the current:

- St. Paul leaders refusing to follow the advice of national church leaders to dissolve the congregation, and instead, finding another way to move forward with strength.
- Pastor and people at St. Paul participate in the civil rights movement and in non-violent demonstrations, in spite of church leaders and community leaders condemning the movement as anti-Gospel, too confrontational, and destructive of "our Southern way of life."
- Pastor and people at St. Paul participating in ecumenical worship in spite of the warnings from church authorities to desist.

- Pastor and people at Cross, Milwaukee, participating in community efforts to have stronger community representation in shaping Model Cities programs that affected low-income persons, in spite of strong criticism from long-standing members of Cross and from church officials, labeling such activity as "too political."
- Pastor and people at Cross electing women Elders to assist in worship leadership and spiritual care of members, and participating in joint worship with a neighboring Presbyterian Church, despite the district president's warning that I would be dropped from the clergy roll and the congregation from membership in the Lutheran Church–Missouri Synod, if we persisted in these practices.
- Cross Church declaring sanctuary and receiving into sanctuary an undocumented Guatemalan refugee, whose life was threatened if he remained in Guatemala, a decision made despite the possibility of legal action against the congregation from the Immigration and Naturalization Service of the United States, and despite the strong cultural norm at the time that viewed sanctuary congregations as being unpatriotic for questioning our country's foreign policy.
- Cross Church deciding to join the Association of Evangelical Lutheran Churches, as an act of solidarity with the professors and students of Concordia Seminary, St. Louis, who formed Seminary in Exile (Seminex), in their opposition to attempts by church leaders to censure Seminary leaders and professors for certain Biblical interpretations and admission of women students. Congregation and pastor did this, despite the fact that they did not know whether the young church body would be able to replace the subsidy that would be lost in leaving the Lutheran Church–Missouri Synod.
- Cross Church voting to become a Reconciling in Christ congregation (receiving gay and lesbian persons as members and affirming their God-given and constitutional rights), and celebrating same-gender unions in spite of the uncertainty of the response of the homophobic elements in the congregation, in the larger Church, and in the community.

Each of these actions was taken after much study of Scripture, wrestling with our conscience, and talking with sisters and brothers. There was not always a unanimous decision, but always an overwhelming majority. None of the decisions was easy. In fact, there were sometimes butterflies and anxieties, especially when it came to actions taken as part of the Civil Rights movement during the tenure of Birmingham Police Commissioner "Bull" Connor and Dallas County (Selma) Sheriff Jim Clark. Always there was some risk, risk of failure, of physical harm from the KKK, of resistance from congregational members, of disapproval and penalties from church or civic authorities, or loss of financial support from members of the congregation or from church officials.

Though we did not talk about courage much, these against-the-current decisions and actions required a fairly high degree of courage.

Pilgrimage to India

Strangely enough, it was in India in 2009 that I was pushed to think deeply about where we got the courage that is required of every person of faith to "stand up and be counted," to take risks for the sake of the Gospel.

Joyce and I went on a "Gandhi Peace Pilgrimage" in January of 2009, along with nine other persons, all of them Christians and all but one of them from Wisconsin.

Our band of peace pilgrims was meeting with an international group of 20 college students at the U.S. Embassy in New Delhi. We were sitting on one side of the beautifully finished table that was at least 20 feet long, and the students were sitting on the other side facing us.

Four persons from our group, including myself, made presentations about our perspectives on what makes for peace and how our understanding of Gandhi has helped us in becoming better peacemakers. I spoke of my involvement with Dr. King in the '60s, and how Dr. King had been influenced by Gandhi, especially in his understanding of non-violent resistance as a means of transforming society.

After we had finished speaking, it was time for the students to engage us in conversation. The first student to speak looked directly at me and asked: "Reverend Ellwanger, I know you marched with Dr. King. I've looked you up on the Internet, and I know some of the things you've done. I know, too, that those were violent times, when the KKK threatened people and killed people who stood up for equality of the races. Where did you get the courage to do the things you did?"

I was humbled and surprised by the question. Of all the more philosophical or academic questions he might have asked, he asked instead a question that might be asked by a person eager to be involved in action to bring about change, or by someone who is in the midst of a struggle requiring courage. It sounded like a very personal, existential question.

As we were leaving the embassy, the student who had asked the question came up to me and said in a very urgent tone of voice, "Be sure to pray for us." Detecting the urgency in his voice, I responded: "Tell me a little more about your concern for prayer."

"Well," he said, in a subdued but trembling voice, "I'm from Orissa and I'm a Christian. I'm sure you've heard about the troubles we're having there with Hindus threatening, attacking, and even killing Christians. It's a terrible time." I knew then that his question about the source of courage was indeed a very real question, emerging from people of faith putting their lives on the line for their faith in Jesus Christ.

If I had known how deeply rooted in real life his question was, I might have answered it with even more depth. As it was, I did answer the question as thoughtfully and as honestly as possible.

Discovering Courage to Act

"You ask a very probing question," I answered. "I must say that one of the sources of courage for me were the people around me. I saw people marching in the streets, at great risk to themselves. There was the immediate risk of dogs and billy clubs and tear gas and jail. And there was the risk of losing their jobs or being attacked by the KKK. When I saw people so committed to freedom and the cause of justice, it gave me courage to stand with them."

Then I added: "I have to tell you that I believe in a God who cares for his people. Trusting in a God who loves us and cares for us, helps us overcome our fears and gives us courage to act."

That answer was not a 250-page, carefully-honed answer to a profound, relevant question. But it was the beginning of an answer, and an answer that welled up from my soul and my experience, as did his question.

As we look around us, as followers of Christ in the first part of the 21st century, it might seem that courage is not quite as important as it was in the first three centuries of the Church's history, or in the period of the Reformation, or in the Civil Rights movement of the 1960s and 1970s. It might seem that a lively worship service is more important as a witness to the Gospel than summoning the courage to struggle against the demonic forces of our culture.

However, until our nation's swords are indeed beaten into plowshares, and until suburban Christians are not afraid to come into the heart of the city to walk in a deep and supportive manner with their sisters and brothers struggling to throw off the shackles of poverty, courage will not simply be a fruit of the Spirit needed by a few Christians, but a necessity for all Christians who want to make an authentic, credible witness to the crucified and risen Christ.

Martin Luther King, in his homily at the funeral of three of the four girls killed in the bombing of the 16th Street Baptist Church in Birmingham, at a very tense time in Birmingham, might have considered a level of quietism and even a withdrawal from challenging the injustices of Jim Crow segregation as the word of wisdom for the moment. Instead, King boldly challenged the tearful, angry overflow congregation of mourners: "These four girls call us to substitute courage for caution in our struggle for freedom and human rights."

It was Cesar Chavez, in the midst of the struggle for fair wages and dignity for farm workers in 1968 and after a 25-day fast who stated: "I am convinced that the truest act of courage is to sacrifice ourselves for others in a totally non-violent struggle for justice."

It was Jesus, according to Luke's account in the first chapter of Acts, who gave his disciples an awesome mission: "You shall be witnesses to me in Jerusalem, Judea, Samaria, and to the uttermost parts of the world." And in recognition of the massive demonic forces arrayed against them, Jesus added a promise: "You will receive power from on high." It was the promise of strength and courage, not simply to say the right words, but to have the power and the courage to do what needed to be done, to risk for the sake of the Gospel.

We can recognize courage when we see it. We are deeply moved by the courage of anyone who takes risks for others, for what is right, for the sake of truth, for the sake of the Gospel. We can see throughout history that when followers of Christ and congregations take a courageous stand of unconditional love, for human dignity, for reconciliation, for the common good of all, for peace, for justice, that is when people take notice and are willing to consider, and even to believe, the message of the Gospel.

Sources of Courage

So the question of the student from Orissa, India, is an important question: "Where do you get that courage?"

For me, the example of Carolyn Freeman has been instructive over the years. She was 15 years old and living in Birmingham in 1961, when she joined me and another 15-year-old girl from St. Paul congregation, Betty Wells, in integrating a Sunday evening youth fellowship at a white Lutheran congregation in Tuscaloosa, Alabama. After a positive experience of fellowship among black and white youth, a first-time experience for all the youth involved, Carolyn had gotten a glimpse of the beloved community and had moved out of her comfort zone to experience it.

We were all surprised three days later to learn that the young intern pastor who had invited our youth to join his youth for a Sunday evening of historic racially-integrated fellowship had been beaten by the KKK and left to walk back to Tuscaloosa on the railroad tracks after midnight. Equally surprising was the KKK's warning to me by phone three days later, that "you and the two girls are next."

When I told Carolyn Freeman of the Klan's threat to the three of us, I asked her: "Are you afraid, Carolyn?"

Carolyn's immediate response is unforgettable: "No, I'm not so much afraid as I am ashamed."

Taken aback by Carolyn's mysterious answer, I asked her, "What do you mean that you're ashamed?"

Without any sign of fear or uncertainty, Carolyn responded: "I'm ashamed that others have suffered so much for the freedom of our people and all people, and I have suffered so little."

I have reflected often about Carolyn's unmistakable courage in the face of real threats and the KKK's attempt to plant a disabling fear in her soul. What was the source of such surprising courage?

She had a sense of purpose that was deep, much bigger than herself, and linked to God's will for her, for other people, and for all people. She was convinced that God wanted freedom for her and for all people. And she was convinced that she had a responsibility to help usher in that freedom. If she had thought that that Sunday night of freedom from the strictures of racial segregation had been just one night's experience for Betty and her to enjoy, she would have been fearful when she heard of the Klan's threats. But she had a much bigger vision of the meaning of that night and of her part in the coming of freedom beyond that night.

Furthermore, she had a sense of connection with a huge company of saints who had gone before her and who surrounded her at that moment, all of whom had contributed so much to the coming of God's freedom that she felt humbled and ashamed that she had not been more involved in the huge struggle for freedom. The normal fear that any human would feel when threatened by a vicious, hateful gang of men like the Ku Klux Klan, was swallowed up by that vivid sense of the presence of brave men and women who had put their lives on the line, and had often lost their lives, for the cause of freedom for every human being.

On an even deeper level, Carolyn's courage in the face of threats emerged from a profound determination to end the suffocating racial segregation and the blatant cruelty of cross-burnings, beatings, and lynchings. For Carolyn, freedom was not a philosophical or academic purpose for which she was striving. She felt the absence of freedom deep in her soul. This freedom was not just a slogan; it was something for which she yearned. Consequently, she could muster the courage to face the threats of the Klan to help bring an end to the oppression that weighed on her and her people for some 350 years and that was very real for her.

And still another source of Carolyn's courage was the fact that she was very hopeful that freedom was indeed coming. The Supreme Court had unanimously ruled in 1954 that racially segregated schools were unconstitutional. After a year-long boycott of buses in Montgomery, that same court had ruled in 1956 that segregated seating on the buses was illegal. She felt the emerging signs of freedom deep in her mind and spirit. Hope that God is bringing about freedom and justice breeds courage.

Above all, Carolyn had an amazing faith in God's love for her in Jesus Christ. She had been baptized just a few months before the freeing experience in Tuscaloosa and the subsequent threat of the Klan. As a child of God, she knew she was in God's hands and that she had power beyond her own strength.

Carolyn gives us guidance for finding courage in the 21st century:

- Believe that your life has purpose, a purpose much bigger than yourself, a purpose tied in with the very purposes of God.
- Remember the cloud of witnesses that went before you and that surround you even now, witnesses who have put their lives on the line for the very purposes of God for which you strive.
- Identify closely with people for whom spiritual and physical oppression is very real, so that you feel more deeply the importance of standing against the demonic, oppressive forces of our culture.

- See the many places in the world where God is bringing in the kingdom of freedom and justice and love and forgiveness and peace and reconciliation, and be filled with hope that God is transforming people and the Church and the world.
- If you are a baptized child of God, you have been called by God for God's transforming purpose. You have the power of God's Holy Spirit within you. And God will never let you down, or let you go. You are his forever.

So be full of courage. Put your life on the line for God's great purposes. God is indeed involved in transforming individuals, the Church, and the world. And you are called to be part of it all.

ACKNOWLEDGEMENTS

In looking back over more than seven decades of an enriching experience of the struggle for an authentic witness to the Gospel, for a just and lasting peace, and for the formation of the beloved community, I must acknowledge first the mysterious, forgiving, enriching hand of God and presence of Christ. I am truly grateful for the journey from storefront church in St. Louis to rural church in Waymansville, Indiana, to segregated church and society in Selma to African American church and community in Birmingham (with the added plus of enriching ecumenism and faith-led justice work usually called "civil rights movement") and finally to two urban, racially-integrated churches in Milwaukee.

It has been a journey that I can only attribute to God's leading and to the guidance of the Holy Spirit. I must acknowledge the special gift of my parents, Walter and Jessie Hanger Ellwanger, for nurturing my faith and teaching me the value of walking with those at the edges. It was, after all, my pastor-father who accepted calls to the storefront church in St. Louis and to a supervisory role of caring for African American congregations in and around Selma, Alabama. And it was both my father and mother who demonstrated in their day-to-day living that such out-of-the-box Christian discipleship was not a burden, but real fulfillment.

I certainly must acknowledge the contribution of all the members of the two congregations I was privileged to pastor, St. Paul, Birmingham, and Cross, Milwaukee, and the members of Hephatha, Milwaukee, the congregation I have been privileged to participate in since my retirement from parish ministry. The ebb and the flow of mutual enrichment, of joys and challenges in relationships and mission, in these three congregations has been the stuff of reality that has translated the struggle for a genuine witness to the Gospel and for justice and peace and the beloved community, from the theoretical and the abstract to the authentic and the real. They have been the flesh-and-blood context in which the word of God has come alive, and the transformation has taken place. I have told the stories in this volume of several of these sisters and brothers with me on this journey. Unfortunately space did not allow for the telling of hundreds of other stories that also gave me strength for the struggle.

I would be remiss if I did not acknowledge scores of colleagues and organizers who have served as mentors and partners in this journey of growth and transformation.

- In Birmingham, there were two African American pastors who especially challenged and nurtured me: Will Herzfeld, Lutheran pastor in Tuscaloosa, Alabama, and C. Herbert Oliver, Presbyterian pastor in Birmingham, both of whom showed me what it means to risk for the sake of the Gospel.
- In Milwaukee, there have been too many to name them all, but a few I must:
- Ernest Glenn, African American Presbyterian pastor of a congregation four blocks from Cross Church, and Brother Booker Ashe, Director of the House of Peace Catholic service agency just two blocks from Cross Church. The three of us, along with our congregations, served a common community at N. 17th St. and Walnut for over 25 years. Together, we worked at forging ecumenism at the personal, congregational, and missional level.
- Many pastors of the Evangelical Lutheran Church in America "North Side Strategy" group that met weekly for spiritual nurture and support. Pastors who were on the urban ministry journey with me for more than a dozen years, some for more than 25 years, included Dennis Jacobsen, Mick Roschke, Mary Martha Kannass, and Rick Deines. We taught each other what it meant to be open to each other, to walk with those at the edges, to respond to the Holy Spirit's nudges, to be "in the city for good," and to be prophetic as well as pastoral.
- Seven African American pastors from the National Baptist tradition: James Leary, Joe Games, Robert Harris, Archie Ivy, Joe Jackson, Louis Sibley, and Willie Brisco. Not only do they have in common with me the special demands and learnings that come with the two-year stint of presidency of MICAH, the congregation-based organizing group in Milwaukee, but they have helped forge among some of us clergy in MICAH an uncommon level of trust, and commitment to a common mission of service and doing justice that does not always exist among clergy of the same denomination.

- Ana Garcia Ashley, fiery, committed, capable Director of the Gamaliel Foundation, who traces her heritage back to the Dominican Republic, and who guided me through my two-year stint as president of MICAH, in a way that nurtured and honed the organizing skills I had picked up in Birmingham. Above all, it was Ana who issued an invitation, or should I say "a call," upon my retirement from parish ministry, to work as organizer with WISDOM, the Wisconsin congregation-based organizing affiliate of the Gamaliel organizing network.
- David Liners, lead organizer of WISDOM, who walked with me during the 11 years I served as organizer, 2002 to 2012. He has demonstrated in his own unique manner, how organizing can be very serious business, follow the basic principles of tried-and-true organizing, speak the truth to power, and at the same time be relaxing and even having "fun."

I need to acknowledge that my journey of more than seven decades and my experience of the struggle, has been shaped by countless persons along the way, too numerous to be listed: grade school and high school teachers, college and seminary professors, classmates and roommates, co-workers on such jobs as paperboy, pea pack and bean pack with Del Monte in northern Illinois, and threshing crews in southern Indiana, peace and justice advocates, politicians and public officials, family members and friends. Acknowledging the multitude of persons who have impacted me along my journey, is not to minimize the powerful impact of those named above and in this book, but to humbly acknowledge the many threads God has woven into my tapestry.

Special thanks to Ron Klug, who has walked with me through the process of producing this volume. Having spent his entire professional life at various levels of writing, editing, and publishing with Concordia Publishing House, Harper San Francisco, and Augsburg Fortress, he has given suggestions and advice tempered by years of experience. We met in 1967, when he was a student at University of Wisconsin Milwaukee and I was just starting my pastorate at Cross Church. A deep determination to be part of a Gospel community that was seeking to be relevant in the turbulent 1960s, was the gravitational pull that brought us together, and has kept the relationship alive ever since.

QUESTIONS FOR REFLECTION AND DISCUSSION

Chapter 1: Accompaniment as a Lifestyle

- What do you understand by the term "accompaniment ministry"?
- What has been your experience of accompaniment ministry?
- What did Ellwanger learn from his trip to El Salvador?
- What do you think of the way Margaret Souter chose to spend the remaining years of her life?
- In a similar situation, what would you do?
- What people in your community are in need of "accompaniment"?
- What would it mean for your congregation to have an accompaniment ministry?
- How might your congregation get started in such a ministry?
- What did you find most interesting and helpful in this chapter?

Chapter 2: God's Preferential Option for the Poor

- What have been your most meaningful contacts with poor people?
- What do you think of the term "God's preferential option for the poor"?
- Who are the poor in your community?
- How does your congregation reach out to the poor in your community?
- Have you had any experience with a food pantry or other service for the hungry?
- What has been your experience with urban/suburban church partnerships?
- What is your congregation doing now to share in God's concern for the poor?
- What additional needs are there? How could you begin to help meet them?
- What does your congregation and you personally do to help the poor beyond your community?
- What did you find most interesting and helpful in this chapter?

Chapter 3: Nurturing and Growing the Congregation

- What do you think of Ellwanger's statement that what makes for a thriving congregation anywhere is that the ministry must be "gospel-centered and must be geared to the spiritual hunger and needs of people"?
- How did the "old guard" of Cross Church and Pastor Ellwanger differ in their vision for the congregation?
- What were some significant changes that happened in the life of the congregation?
- How did the "Pastor's Class" contribute to the growing of the congregation?
- What part did Bible class play?
- What are the main ways your congregation is nurtured and grows?
- What did you find most interesting and helpful in this chapter?

Chapter 4: A New Song

- What has been your experience of worshipping in an African-American, Hispanic, or other non-European setting?
- What is the musical style of your congregation? Is it a good match for the people of your congregation and community?
- What were the steps by which the style of worship and music changed at Cross Church?
- How does your congregation handle the diversity of musical tastes in the congregation?
- Do you agree with Ellwanger's support of a diversity of music in every service? Why or why not?
- What forms of music do you prefer in church worship? How willing are you to have other forms included?
- What are some other ways to provide diversity in worship and music?
- What did you find most interesting or helpful in this chapter?

Chapter 5: Reaching and Empowering Youth

- How does your congregation involve youth in ministry?
- How are youth represented in the leadership of your congregation?
- What does your congregation do for youth?
- What could you learn from the experience of Cross Church?
- What did you find most interesting or helpful in this chapter?

Chapter 6 Raising up Leaders

- How do you understand the term "leadership"?
- How did "Roxanne" become a leader?
- How does your congregation raise up leaders and empower them?
- In what sense are you a leader?
- Who encouraged you to become a leader?
- What encouragement do you need most to expand your leadership?
- How are Lois Glover and Craig Dent examples of leadership? What can you learn from them?
- Who are the leaders in your congregation? How did they become leaders?
- What did you find most interesting or helpful in this chapter?

Chapter 7: Overcoming Sexism: The Ongoing Saga

- What is the official position regarding the role of women in your denomination or fellowship?
- How does that work out in practice?
- What, if any, are the barriers to women being full participants in the life of your congregation?
- How might these barriers be overcome?
- What is the bigger problem n your congregation---the need for female leaders or the need for male leaders?
- What were the steps by which women came to full leadership in Cross Church?
- Are there more women than men in your congregation? If so, why do you think this is so? Do you see this as a problem?
- Do you know any women like Lula Williams, Marilyn Crump Miller or Virginia Walker-Riley? If so, tell about them.
- What did you find most interesting or helpful in this chapter?

Chapter 8: Race Matters: Combating Racism and Celebrating Diversity

- How do you respond to the incident of the ambulance in Birmingham in 1962?
- Has there been an incident in your life that revealed the extent of racism in our country?

- How has racism changed in the U.S. since the 1960s?
- What evidence of racism do you see in your everyday life?
- What is the difference between personal racism and systemic racism?
- What is your response to the march in Selma? Imagine you were along. How would you have felt?
- What happened in the Bloody Sunday march?
- To what extent were you aware (or unaware) of the Civil Rights Movement of the 1960s?
- What is the racial composition of your community?
- What is your congregation doing to deal with the issues of racism?
- What else could it do?
- What did you find most interesting or helpful in this chapter?

Chapter 9: Gay/Lesbian Ministry

- What were the attitudes toward gay and lesbian people that you experienced as a child or teenager?
- How has your attitude changed since then?
- How was Pastor Ellwanger's attitude changed by his encounter with the district attorney in Birmingham?
- How did Cross Church engage members in addressing the questions of homosexuals in the church?
- How did Cross Church handle the controversy over the blessing of commitments made by gay people? What do you think of this action?
- What were the results of this way of proceeding?
- What is your congregation's stance toward gay and lesbian people?
- How can members of a congregation differ on controversial issues and remain together?
- What did you find most interesting or helpful in this chapter?

Chapter 10: Gifts from Abroad: Refugees in our Midst

- What were the steps by which Cross Church became involved in ministry to refugees?
- What were the results for Cross Church in offering sanctuary to "Jorge"?

- What has been your experience with refugees?
- Who are the refugees in your community?
- How has your congregation been involved with them?
- What more could be done? What are some first steps that could be taken?
- What did you find most interesting or helpful in this chapter?

Chapter 11: Treatment Works

- What changes occurred at Cross Church as a result of becoming more aware of the needs of chemically dependent people?
- According to Sam Marjonov, what are the components of an effective treatment program?
- What are the three levels by which Hephatha Church tackles the issue of substance abuse?
- How did the churches in MICAH try to assist in solving the problems of drug abuse?
- What are the arguments for treatment as a way to deal with drug addiction?
- What does your congregation do to help people in your community deal with alcohol and drug addiction?
- What other kinds of help are available?
- What else is still needed?
- What did you find most interesting or helpful in this chapter?

Chapter 12: Walking with Those Incarcerated

- How would you answer Ellwanger's question: "Why do many congregations fail to include prisoners and people coming out of prison as part of their vision of ministry?
- How was Pastor Ellwanger "nudged by the Spirit" into ministry to prisoners and those returning from prison?
- What were some of the successes of Project RETURN?
- What are the jails or prisons nearest to your congregation?
- How does your congregation minister to those in prison? Those returning from prison?
- According to Ellwanger, what are ways in which the prison system needs reform? To what extent do you agree with his assessment?

- What is restorative justice? What do you think of the idea?
- What is the relationship of restorative justice to treatment alternatives for offenders?
- What did you find most interesting or helpful in this chapter?

Chapter 13: Congregational Partnerships: Bridging City and Suburb

- What kinds of city and suburban or rural church partnerships are described in this chapter?
- Which of these seem most valuable to you?
- Has your congregation had experiences of partnership with another congregation? What were the results?
- What further possibilities do you see for your congregation to partner with other congregations?
- What barriers would have to be overcome?
- What did you find most interesting and helpful in this chapter?

Chapter 14: Beyond Denomination: Ecumenical Work and Worship

- What is your attitude toward cooperation with churches of other denominations?
- What is the dominant attitude of your congregation toward such cooperation?
- What were some experiences in Ellwanger's journey toward more ecumenical cooperation?
- What is the experience of your congregation in having joint worship services with other congregations?
- How is your congregation engaged in service projects with other congregations?
- What further opportunities are there for interdenominational cooperation in your community?
- What barriers are there to such cooperation? How might they be overcome?
- What did you find most interesting or helpful in this chapter?

Chapter 15: Doing Justice in the Public Square: Congregation-Based Organizing

- What do you understand by "congregation-based organizing"?
- What did Ellwanger learn from his first experiences of congregation-based organizing in Birmingham and Selma?
- Why is remembering the civil rights movement of the 1960s important?
- What are some accomplishments of MICAH in Milwaukee?
- How can congregations work for justice when members are not in agreement about the issue?
- How do you respond to the idea that churches should not be involved in "politics"?
- What did you find most interesting or helpful in this chapter?

Chapter 16: Non-Violence in a Culture of Guns, Gangs, and Militarism

- What do you think of the prayer vigils at the site of homicides? Would you want to participate in such a prayer service? Why or why not?
- "If we pray for peace in the stillness of a beautiful sanctuary, we had better work for peace in the midst of a violent world." Do you agree? Why or why not?
- What does it mean for you to be a peacemaker?
- How can children learn to be peacemakers?
- What is your congregation doing to nurture peacemakers?
- What more could your congregation do?
- What do you understand by the term "militarism"?
- What is the relationship between militarism and the problems of our cities and rural areas?
- What is the difference between militarism and a nation's right to defend itself?
- What do you think of non-violent direct action, such as protests and marches, which may result in violent responses?
- Could you sign the pledge of non-violence used in Birmingham in 1963?
- What did you find most interesting or helpful in this chapter?

Chapter 17: Healing in Body, Mind, and Spirit

- Have you every participated in a service of healing? If so, share your experience.
- Do you know of a congregation that has a parish nurse? What does the parish nurse do?
- What was the mission of the Cross Adult Center?
- How did the Bread of Healing Clinic begin?
- How does your congregation meet people's needs for healing in body, mind and spirit?
- How accessible is your church building to people with disabilities?
- What did you find most interesting or helpful in this chapter?

Chapter 18: Swimming Upstream: The Courage to Act

- Which of the items on the "swimming against" list strikes you as most challenging?
- What risks has your congregation taken?
- Are there any ways it has "swum against the current??
- How did Ellwanger answer the question, "Where did you get the courage to do the things you did?"
- Where is courage needed in your life? In the life of your congregation?
- What would help you find the courage you need?
- What did you find most interesting or helpful in this chapter?

INDEX

Page references in italics indicate illustrations.

— A —

— B —

— D —

— E —

— F —

— G —

— H —

— I —

— J —

— O —

— P —

— Q —

— R —

— S —

— T —

— U —

— V —

— W —

— Y —

— Z —

ABOUT THE AUTHOR

As a preacher's son, Joseph Ellwanger grew up in three diverse settings: In St. Louis, where his father, Walter Ellwanger, was pastor at a storefront church. In Waymansville, Indiana, where his father served a small rural congregation. And in Selma, Alabama, where his father was supervising pastor over 33 African American Lutheran congregations in Alabama and upper Florida and president of the Alabama Lutheran Academy and College (currently called Concordia College Alabama) in Selma.

After graduating from Concordia Seminary in 1958, Ellwanger's first taste of pastoral ministry was at St. Paul Lutheran, Birmingham, Alabama, a small African American congregation in the southwest part of the city known as Titusville. He found himself in the "eye of the hurricane," as two of the key actions of the civil rights struggle focused on Birmingham in 1963 and on Selma in 1965. Led by the Spirit, he felt compelled to participate in the campaigns of the Southern Christian Leadership Conference, led by Dr. Martin Luther King, Jr. in Birmingham, 1963, and in Selma, 1965.

On Saturday, March 6, 1965, Ellwanger led 72 members of the Concerned White Citizens of Alabama, in a march to the Dallas County courthouse in Selma, to demonstrate solidarity with the voting rights demonstrations that had been carried out by the Southern Christian Leadership Conference day after day since the first of January, 1965. He participated in the "Turnaround Tuesday" march over the Edmund Pettus Bridge, on March 9, to publicly demonstrate support of the 500 courageous demonstrators who had been beaten back on Bloody Sunday, March 7, when they attempted to cross the Pettus Bridge and to begin the planned march from Selma to Montgomery. After a meeting on March 12 with President Lyndon Johnson, along with an interfaith group of 15 other clergy, in which they urged quick passage of a strong voting rights act, Ellwanger and his wife Joyce, joined the climactic final leg of the Selma-to-Montgomery march in Montgomery on March 25, 1965.

After nine years as pastor of St. Paul Church, Ellwanger accepted a call to Cross Lutheran, in the central city of Milwaukee, leaving his congregation in Birmingham, as he said, "with a huge lump in my throat." During his 34-year pastorate at Cross Church, he led the congregation through several periods of challenge and change, including the development of a racially integrated congregation, the launching of a prison ministry, the declaration as a Sanctuary congregation, the acceptance of gay and lesbian members, the development of a clinic for persons with no medical insurance, the rebuilding of the sanctuary after a devastating fire in 1995, and major contributions to the launching of an interfaith congregation-based justice organizing coalition called MICAH (Milwaukee Inner-city Congregations Allied for Hope).

Ellwanger is the author of *Let My People Go* (Medford, OR: Medford Press, 1971), a history of African Americans in the United States, written for junior and senior high age groups, and he is co-editor of *Urban Hymnal Supplement* (Milwaukee, WI: Cross Lutheran Church, 1980).

It is the author's hope that the stories and insights from 55 years of urban ministry and peace and justice actions recorded in this volume, will do more than describe the struggle of taking risks for the sake of the Gospel, for deepening community, and for the doing of justice. The stories are recorded so that the reader may experience real strength for engaging in that struggle.

CPSIA information can be obtained
at www.ICGtesting.com
Printed in the USA
FSOW04n1659250315
5916FS